Health Care for the Urban Poor

Health Care for the Urban Poor

Directions for Policy

Edith M. Davis
Michael L. Millman

and Associates:

Patricia Maloney Alt
Albert A. Bocklet
Ann Lennarson Greer
David E. Hayes-Bautista
Ann Akridge Jones
George Dorian Wendel

Foreword by Eli Ginzberg

LandMark Studies
ROWMAN & ALLANHELD
Totowa, New Jersey

ROWMAN & ALLANHELD
(formerly Allanheld, Osmun & Co. Publishers, Inc.)

First published in the United States 1983 by
(A Division of Littlefield, Adams & Company)
81 Adams Drive, Totowa, New Jersey 07512

Library of Congress Cataloging in Publication Data

Davis, Edith M.
    Health care for the urban poor.

    (Conservation of human resources series ; 21)
    Includes bibliographical references and index.
    1. Poor—Medical care—United States.   2. Medical
policy—United States.   3. Health surveys—United
States.   I. Millman, Michael L.   II. Title.   III. Series.
[DNLM: 1. Delivery of health care—United States.
2. Ambulatory care.   3. Poverty—United States.
4. Urban population—United States.   5. Health policy
—United States.   W 250 D261h]
RA418.5.P6D37   1983   362.1'0425   82–8868
ISBN 0-86598-088-8   AACR2

83 84 85 / 10 9 8 7 6 5 4 3 2 1

Printed in the United States of America

Contents

Tables, Figures and Maps

Foreword

Most forewords have a ceremonial rather than a functional purpose. An established writer commends the work of a younger colleague; a sponsoring agency explains its interest in an investigation's results which are being reported to the public; the significance of a new work is interpreted within the context of a series of related studies and publications.

This foreword is functional, not honorific. It is intended to convey to the reader an account of the genesis of the book that follows and its principal objectives, information that is essential for an understanding of its unique approach and its findings.

Health Care for the Urban Poor: Directions for Policy was designed, as its subtitle suggests, to present a critical review and assessment of the status of health care for the poor in large U.S. cities at the close of the 1970s and to identify major issues that are emerging to test the system of care for the indigent in the next decade. Its focus is local government, particularly municipalities, as the level of government directly responsible for assuring that services are provided to the poor, a focus which has become more vital in the context of shifting federal policy and dollar flows.

From this purview, it examines the changing dimensions and settings of major efforts to provide health care to the poor that were implemented during the decade and a half from the launching of the Johnson administration's Great Society in 1965 to the retrenchment and retreat of the federal government from the arena of social welfare pledged by President Reagan in 1980. Throughout the intervening years, the federal government persisted in its commitment of substantial funding to facilitate the access of low-income individuals and families to an improved level—qualitative and quantitative—of health care. Termination of this commitment and the redefinition of inter-governmental authority and responsibility lend urgency to a study of the local role in the financing and delivery of health services.

The work antedates the administration of President Reagan. It was undertaken in 1978, concurrent with the initiation by the Robert Wood Johnson Foundation (RWJF) and its cosponsors, the U.S. Conference of Mayors and the American Medical Association (AMA), of the Municipal Health Services Program (MHSP), a demonstration that provided incentives for municipal governments to take the initiative in improving health care for their underserved residents. Reflecting historic acumen and prescience, the Foundation identified the growing indigent population of the nation's inner cities as a persistent challenge to the health care system, despite more than a decade of liberally funded entitlement and service delivery efforts by the federal government. It further recognized the critical role of local government not only in the implementation of solutions—if solutions were to be found—but more fundamentally in the definition of problems and priorities, the design or redesign of systems, and the planning of actions that could translate programs into service delivery.

The Municipal Health Services Program offered substantial grants to five of the fifty largest cities in the United States for the support of proposals that seemed likely to have an appreciable impact upon the delivery of ambulatory care to the poor and to be sustainable by the locality at the termination of a five-year period of support. The following excerpts from the Foundation's guidelines for proposal development set forth the goals and assumptions of the program:

- Consolidating and building upon existing services offered by public health departments, hospitals and local health agencies.
- [To] be planned and carried out as a cooperative undertaking involving the leadership of the local government, the municipal hospital, and the public health department.
- This blending of resources is intended to bring together in single neighborhood locations the services of public health programs (e.g., clinics for maternal and child health, community mental health, drug and alcohol abuse, V.D. and T.B. services) with traditional outpatient general medical services previously available through the municipal hospital.
- With Foundation support to meet the planning and start-up costs of neighborhood sites . . . it is anticipated that local governments can afford to bring improved general medical care to a substantial number of their citizens and maintain those services after Foundation support has ended.

Thirty-six cities responded with proposals, and awards were made to the following: Baltimore, Cincinnati, Milwaukee, St. Louis, and

San Jose. In making its selections, the Foundation gave heavy weight to the merits of the individual proposal, the feasibility of implementation, and the involvement of the local leadership, particularly the political leadership, in the program, from initial planning to completion.

A few observations about the award-winning cities. In no case was one of the nation's largest urban concentrations selected, a reasonable geographic distribution was achieved, and no state received more than one award. There is considerable variation in the size, type, and proportion of minority populations in each city; the economy of the cities ranges from cumulative decline to rapid expansion; and the cities differ in governmental structure, as well as in their relations with overlying county and state governments. While no set of five cities could encompass the full range of diversity among the nation's fifty largest urban centers, it is fair to state that those chosen had the potential for providing results that would be broadly applicable to problems encountered in most, if not all, large cities.

Conservation of Human Resources, Columbia University, was designated to monitor the progress of the demonstration in each of the five cities as a means of testing both the underlying assumption of the superiority of neighborhood-based ambulatory care over hospital outpatient departments and emergency rooms in terms of both costs and acceptability, and the capacity of local government to design and implement basic changes in the traditional health care system. For this purpose, it was necessary to inform ourselves of the status of health services for the poor in these cities at the close of the 1970s and, in particular, of the outcome of earlier efforts to improve the delivery system. Case studies of the five cities thus provided the framework for an examination of the critical issues that confront most urban centers. *Health Care for the Urban Poor*, which is a report of our findings, approaches these issues thematically, and the analysis is supported by data derived from the nation's fifty largest cities. The resulting study may be said to have a dual focus. In a narrower sense it serves as a benchmark against which to assess the capacity of each of the five participants in the MHSP to implement a self-designed program for reform within the confines of its particular delivery system. In a broader sense it defines the problems, the resources, the options, and the dilemmas facing all large cities as they struggle with their mandate of guaranteeing health services to the poor—the unfinished business of Medicare and Medicaid.

To set the problem in perspective, the volume opens with an historical review and assessment of the major federal health policy initiatives which had substantial impact on the delivery of ambulatory care from 1965 to the present: categorical health programs, Medicaid, and the development of community health centers. Chapter One, "From Johnson to Carter: Ambulatory Care for the Urban Poor," points out that while Medicaid in particular improved access dramatically for the urban poor, persistent underutilization and poor health indices continued to characterize many low-income segments of the population who were ineligible for federal assistance. Although vastly expanded during this period, categorical health programs were flawed both by their administrative difficulty and by the limited scope of care—primarily maternal and child health services—they provided. Community health centers, while never a major factor in terms of size and volume, provided ambulatory services of good quality and often were the sole source of care for their patients. Nevertheless, high unit costs, the managerial instability frequently associated with community-based sponsorship, and the absence of linkages with back-up hospitals for inpatient and specialty care have often compromised both fiscal viability and continuity of care.

Although the late 1960s saw a major new flow of funds into health care services for the poor, particularly through Medicaid entitlement but also through financing for a new community-based delivery system, the vast network of community health centers that was anticipated never occurred once the Democratic party lost the presidency in 1968. Much of the 1970s up to the start of the MHSP was an attempt to stretch the available dollars across continued high expectations and extended facilities.

Chapter Two, "The City's Role in Health," describes the structure and financing of care for the poor, and the socioeconomic and political environment in which it is provided. It sets out the framework of intergovernmental relations—federal, state and local—that carry their divided responsibility for providing basic services to those urban-based groups that cannot afford to pay directly for their care and are not covered by a third party.

The five demonstration cities, Baltimore, Cincinnati, Milwaukee, St. Louis, and San Jose, revealed considerable variation in the way in which health care for inner-city populations was delivered and the methods of paying for it. But variation aside, common factors at work also exercised major influence, such as the much enlarged role of the federal government. Following the enactment of Medicaid and the implementation of Office of Economic Opportunity initiatives to develop community health centers, local structure and financing underwent important transformations. For the first time, a high proportion, but by no means all, of the poor were enrolled in a federal-state entitlement program that assured to the providers reimbursement for services rendered. Further, the federal government, with money as bait, pressed strongly for the establishment and expansion of ambulatory care facilities in or close to neighborhoods where the poor were concentrated.

This last point calls attention to a common demographic factor: the late 1960s and the 1970s saw a continuation of the large-scale post-World War II relocation of population, with middle-class whites mov-

ing to the suburbs and new in-migrants, black and Hispanic, drawn
to the inner cities to live and if possible to find work.

There is still another facet of shared experience. Each of the five
cities contained at least one public hospital that provided a considerable, if varying, proportion of the total health care for the inner-
city poor.

A closer look at these cities revealed substantial differences in the
structure of local government; in the relations between local government, the county, and the state; and in the scale, scope, and sophistication of the public health departments at all three levels of
government—in particular, the extent to which they had moved from
a traditional preventive services focus to the provision of therapeutic
care. The five cities also differed in their tax base, their level of expenditures for health services, and their sensitivity to the needs of
low-income residents.

Chapter Three, "Access to Ambulatory Care for the Urban Poor,"
explores the concept of access and its measurement, and then pro-
ceeds to assess each city against a set of indicators that include resource availability, utilization of services, and barriers to access. The
mix of institutions engaged in the provision of care is described, and
problems of financial access are examined in detail. One of the un-
anticipated findings relates to the diminishing number of practitioners
in the inner city at the time of the Great Society reforms. As older
physicians retired or died they were not replaced. Contrary to conventional wisdom—that the poor had no choice but to resort to hospitals and clinics for ambulatory services—our studies reveal that
many inner-city residents continued to seek and receive care from
private practitioners, undeterred by distance and inconvenience.

Medical schools located in or close to low-income neighborhoods
have always provided a considerable amount of free or low-cost ambulatory care, among other reasons because referrals from emergency
rooms and outpatient departments enable them to fill their teaching
beds with appropriate patients. Other voluntary hospitals which un-
dertook teaching programs did much the same, but with per diem
costs rising rapidly, they were becoming increasingly selective by the
time Medicaid was passed. Hence, in all but one of the five cities
philanthropic institutions were not the principal source of either inpatient or outpatient treatment for the poor in the mid-1960s when
Medicaid was passed, although the extent of their contribution varied.
Rather, the main support system was the public hospital, operated
by the city in Baltimore and St. Louis, by the county in Milwaukee
and San Jose, and in Cincinnati by the state of Ohio to which it had
been transferred from the city.

The cities differed both in the success of their community health
centers that were initiated with federal funds, and in the governance
of the centers—whether they remained independent or were integrated, as in Cincinnati, within a larger municipal system. In addition

to community health centers, a variety of alternative ambulatory care centers were in or adjacent to low-income neighborhoods, providing more restricted types of services to smaller numbers of poor patients.

The fourth chapter, "Current Issues in Providing Urban Ambulatory Care," examines local perceptions of the generic problems common to many metropolitan areas, problems which relate primarily to the status of the public hospital and the provision of neighborhood-based care. It takes a close look at the future of both of these delivery systems, and at the potential for their coordination to provide a better level of health care services to the poor and the near-poor than could be expected if each were to continue independently, as in the past. The chapter calls attention to a high level of political, professional, and community concern in all five cities about the future of the public hospital, although these concerns vary substantively. Political struggles were precipitated by a range of issues: from a steep decline in patient use, to the high costs engendered by the public hospital as a result of its affiliation with a medical school, and its emphasis on specialized services and high technology over the provision of primary care for the neighborhood poor. Additional issues involved managerial difficulties, particularly in the areas of staffing and reimbursement. Different health care clienteles and competing provider and consumer groups each raised problems and advocated solutions dictated by self-interest.

Another issue of broad concern was the extent to which the poor and the near-poor should continue to seek ambulatory care from the public hospital, in view of the high costs of outpatient departments and the suboptimal conditions under which services were provided, reflected in long waiting times, lack of physician continuity, and the distance many patients had to travel to reach the hospital.

These considerations led many communities in the latter part of the 1970s to explore, even in the face of a cutback in direct federal funding, the possibilities of strengthening and expanding their community health centers and linking them more effectively with the public hospital for back-up and referral services. The critical aim was to provide the poor with primary care services that at once were comprehensive, offered continuity, and were of good quality. An inherent requirement was that the emerging system should engage the community in both its planning and governance.

Chapter Five, "Strategies for Improving Municipal Health Services in a Changing Environment," considers the issues currently confronting localities that have been precipitated by rapidly changing federal policy. Starting with the waning years of the Carter administration and accelerating with the onset of the Reagan administration, the shifts in philosophy and behavior of the federal government toward health care financing in general and assistance to low-income populations in particular have meant a reversal, from several decades of expansion to containment. The Omnibus Budget Reconciliation Act

of 1981 provided for cutbacks in Medicaid funds, for prospective budgeting for Medicare, and for reductions in the funding of community
health centers and the National Health Service Corps. In addition to
these potentially large declines in the direct flow of funds from the
federal level, other cornerstones of Reagan policy have serious implications for the efforts of cities to meet their health care mandate.
These include the shift of authority for social welfare programs to the
state, the replacement of planning and regulation with increased reliance upon market forces, and the assumption of considerable responsibility for the poor by the private sector.

Shifts in overall philosophy and social welfare policy at the federal
level, however, are not the only challenges to the health mandate of
urban government. The state of the economy is a major determinant
both of the demand for public services and of the tax resources available to meet the demand. Large cities have been affected differentially
by the recession, and much will depend upon prospective economic
conditions and employment rates. Not too far removed is the resistance of the middle class to increasing taxation, which has manifested
itself in local tax revolts and reduced revenues for government expenditure. What has been observed thus far has been the tightening
of local budgets for the support of current levels of service, even less
revenue for upgrading or expansion, and increasing demand.

The chapter reviews early state and local responses to the "new
federalism" and describes the various adaptive mechanisms that are
being devised. Local government strategies to cope with the altered
financing environment rely heavily upon managerial improvements
and increased efficiency, but their potential to avert retrenchment is
uncertain. And given their own shrinking revenues, it is unlikely that
philanthropic organizations can fill the gap in public resources. Other
environmental factors could, conceivably, compensate to some degree
for budgetary strictures. These include structural changes within the
health system: a rapidly growing supply of physicians; the prolifer-
ation of alternative, cost-reducing delivery modalities; and an ever-
changing medical technology.

In this volatile and uncertain political, social, and economic environment, the Municipal Health Services Program is being implemented. The program has a singular objective: for the poor and the
near-poor, to provide or improve access to ambulatory care at a neighborhood facility under conditions that would permit financial viability;
that is, a facility that would require no additional municipal subsidy
and whose operating costs would be considerably less than those of
a hospital outpatient department or emergency room for comparable
services.

A major facet of the evaluation of the MHSP by the Conservation
project is its focus upon the process of implementation within the
distinct economic and political milieu of the individual cities. Parallel
with the conventional assessment of outcome in terms of the primary

goals and objectives of the program, the evaluation examines the political, organizational, and institutional forces whose actions and interaction are major determinants of outcome. A monitoring, rather than a retrospective, methodology has been adopted for this process analysis that relies upon resident Field Associates for the tasks of continuing observation, data gathering, and preliminary analysis and interpretation in each city. Each Field Associate is a university-based expert in policy research. Their joint effort represents a multidisciplinary approach to the evaluation of the MHSP, drawing upon the insights of several fields: sociology, public health, political science, urban affairs, health administration, and public administration.

In addition to the present baseline volume, Conservation of Human Resources will prepare for publication a final report on the MHSP following termination of the project in 1983–1984. It must be obvious that this evaluation will reflect in microcosm the dilemmas and the constraints of local health policy-makers nationwide, as well as the perspicacity of their choices, and their skillfulness in modifying existing institutions and operations and in negotiating the political realignments that are required for survival during this first half of the 1980s.

Attention should be drawn to another major aspect of MHSP that will be of interest to urban health authorities everywhere. Prior to inauguration of the program, its scope was broadened through the development by the Johnson Foundation of a collaborative effort with the Office of Research and Demonstration (ORD) of the Health Care Financing Administration (HCFA). Through the authorization of Medicare and Medicaid waivers at each of the MHSP sites, the participating cities were permitted to extend the range of ambulatory services and to liberalize reimbursement for the target population. The HCFA demonstration included provision for a study of changes in access, utilization, and costs referable to the MHSP by the Center for Health Administration Studies (CHAS), University of Chicago, under the direction of Drs. Ronald Andersen and Gretchen Fleming. Like CHR, CHAS has designed its evaluation to start with a baseline study. Its data sources include an extensive telephone survey of the target population in each of the cities in order to compare users and nonusers of MHSP facilities at the first and fourth years of the program. The CHAS study adds an important dimension to the MHSP evaluation, and its findings will be a significant contribution to municipalities in their struggle to establish health care priorities for the poor.

One final word about the present work. Its singular contribution is its focus upon service delivery at the local level—the ultimate determinant of the efficacy of policies designed and adopted by the federal and state governments. This approach is particularly timely in 1982. While this book does not analyze specific Reagan administration proposals, it responds to the generic health policy directions that have been enunciated. Its timeliness is thus combined with long-term pertinence.

As director of the Conservation project, I want to add a few words about the members of the health care staff who have assumed primary responsibility for the work up to this point and who will see it through to a successful end. Direct supervision rests with Miriam Ostow and Charles Brecher, while Edith M. Davis maintains day-to-day oversight of the project, including continuing communication with the Field Associates. Edith Davis is the principal author of the present book, which is the elaboration of a first draft prepared by Michael Millman, who preceded her as project director of the evaluation from its initiation in 1978 until his resignation to join the Department of Health and Human Services in the fall of 1980. Maury Forman contributed background research and collected statistical data for the project.

Our Field Associates are Patricia Maloney Alt, Baltimore; Albert A. Bocklet, Cincinnati; Ann Lennarson Greer, Milwaukee; George Dorian Wendel, St. Louis; and David E. Hayes-Bautista, San Jose. Ann Akridge Jones preceded Patricia Alt from 1978 to July 1980. The simplest way for me to acknowledge the critical importance of their contribution is to call the reader's attention to the fact that they are listed as full-fledged coauthors of the present work. They are the linchpins on which the success of the final evaluation rests.

Eli Ginzberg, Director
Conservation of Human Resources
May 1982

Research Staff

Conservation of Human Resources, *Columbia University*:

        Eli Ginzberg, Director
        Charles Brecher
        Miriam Ostow
        Edith M. Davis
        Michael L. Millman
        Maury Forman

Field Associates:

Baltimore:
        Ann Akridge Jones (to July 1980), *The Johns Hopkins University*
        Patricia Maloney Alt (from July 1980), *University of Baltimore*
Cincinnati:
        Albert A. Bocklet, *Xavier University*
Milwaukee:
        Ann Lennarson Greer, *University of Wisconsin-Milwaukee*
St. Louis:
        George Dorian Wendel, *Saint Louis University*
San Jose:
        David E. Hayes-Bautista, *University of California-Berkeley*

Acknowledgments

The authors wish to acknowledge the assistance which has been provided by several groups of colleagues in carrying out this evaluation of the Municipal Health Services Program (MHSP).

Drs. Ronald Andersen and Gretchen Fleming of the Center for Health Administration Studies at the University of Chicago shared the results of their parallel evaluation of the impact of the MHSP on access and costs. Their project officer at HCFA, Dr. Tony Hausner, coordinated research activities and made available data on the Medicare and Medicaid waivers.

In each of the cities, members of the mayor's staff, the health services administrators and numerous other public officials have shared time and data with our Field Associates to enable the purposes of the evaluation.

The research assistants who have worked with the Field Associates in each city have made valuable contributions to this volume.

The administrators of the MHSP, Dr. Carl Schramm, Andrew Green, and Gary Christopherson, provided us with program management reports and information on administrative decision-making.

Finally, Shoshana Vasheetz and Heidi Jones of the CHR staff devoted countless hours of patient endeavor to preparation of the manuscript for publication. Leslie Ahmed coordinated administrative support for the project, which often required night and weekend work.

To all of them our heartfelt thanks.

CHAPTER ONE

From Johnson to Carter: Ambulatory Care for the Urban Poor

In order to set the Robert Wood Johnson Foundation's Municipal Health Services Program (MHSP) in its appropriate historical, political, and social context, this volume begins with a discussion of the major federal public health policy initiatives of the decade beginning in 1964–1965. The Great Society years of the Johnson administration were responsible for the introduction of several new, substantive, and far-reaching programs designed to intervene in the health care system's financing and service delivery patterns on behalf of the citizenry, particularly the poor. These programs worked substantially to the benefit of the urban poor and marked a significant new encouragement of and subsidy for the provision of ambulatory care services. This chapter presents a conceptual framework for an analysis of the major elements of public policy in the arena of health services for the poor during the Johnson, Nixon, Ford, and Carter administrations, and examines the specific impact of these policies in large U.S. cities, with special attention to the five cities funded under the Municipal Health Services Program.

It may be useful at the outset to discuss briefly the background of the prominent pieces of health legislation that were passed by Congress in the mid-1960s and to describe the environment that permitted the endorsement by legislators of numerous substantial efforts at social intervention. The first two years of Lyndon Johnson's presidency, 1964 and 1965, ushered in the Medicare and Medicaid legislation; soon, community health center legislation as well as a greatly expanded array of categorical health programs were enacted, all to the benefit of the nation's poor. Although for decades groups had pressed for such programs as federal aid to general education and support for medical costs of the elderly and the poor, Johnson's consummate political skill and favorable relationships with congressmen boded well for an executive legislative agenda, particularly after the 1964 election gave him a large margin of victory, which it was possible to interpret as a mandate for social change.

The economic conditions of the mid-1960s contrast sharply with those at the beginning of the 1980s. The economy was growing steadily, unemployment was low at around 4.5 percent, and inflation had hardly been perceived as a problem. The economy was expected to continue its incremental growth, although some sectors perhaps more slowly than others. Policy-makers also expected that the trend of increasing tax revenues due to economic expansion would continue, permitting the financing of both military and domestic spending. Two major interventions occurred, however: the onset of rampant inflation and the contributory oil crisis with its dramatic price increases. The growth rate of the economy slowed; and as the decade of the 1980s began, inflation ran in double digits annually, unemployment reached 8.9 percent, and personal income and tax revenues were no longer growing at the rates of the 1960s. The climate of the 1980s will be explored more fully, as will federal, state, and local policy responses, in Chapter Five.

To go back, however, to the mid-1960s; it did not take long for the environment to exert pressures for change in the new programs of the Johnson administration. Before the Great Society had much of an opportunity to realize its agenda for reordering social structure and benefits to the advantage of the poor and disenfranchised, an array of events and forces exerted countervailing influences. In some cases, compromises involved in getting the legislation through Congress weakened the intent or content of the original drafts. The inherent expectation of some of the new programs was that existing power groups would willingly (or grudgingly) make way for newly enfranchised minorities as legitimate contenders for jobs, public dollars, and political power in the local governmental arena, which is a very difficult political reality to achieve. The political and economic effects of the war in Vietnam almost surely had an impact on the implementation of domestic social programs, and the Vietnam conflict led to the fall of Johnson's administration. The incoming Republicans were sharply critical of the concepts and the results of the Great Society programs, and some of the harshest criticism fell on the Medicaid program as being costly and abuse-ridden. Costs of the Medicare and Medicaid programs and of community health centers had, for whatever reason, been grossly underestimated by those who prepared the legislation, and in the first years of the programs had risen quickly. This phenomenon led to government attempts to reduce the financial impact of the programs by cutbacks in eligibility, scope of coverage, and rates of payment for entitlement programs and a halt in funding new health centers, despite the fact that the health programs had perhaps more direct impact, measured by use of services and improved health status, on the poor population than most Great Society social programs.

How were the major health care programs for the poor structured, how did the dollars flow from federal sources to point of service delivery, and what in fact was the impact on the poor of the influx of resources for their health benefits? Historically, both the financing and the delivery of health care for the poor were primarily a local responsibility. Cities and counties operated infirmaries, hospitals, and public health services with local tax revenues. After 1965, the federal and state governments significantly expanded their participation in the financing and/or delivery of services. Table 1.1 shows the trends in national personal health care expenditures by payment source, and the particularly rapid growth of federal participation is evident. Theoretically, there were two major approaches to this federal and state involvement. These can be characterized as the individual-based (or insurance or entitlement) approach and the institution-based (or provider or grant program/direct service) approach. Specific programs can be placed along a continuum, from the individual insurance pole exemplified by Medicare, to the direct institutional service pole illustrated by the Veterans Administration hospital system. While the ends of the continuum are theoretically distinct, in practice the two different strategies interacted a good deal. Some programs exhibited certain characteristics of both strategies, and often programs representing one coexisted with programs representing the other, each responding to gaps or deficits in the other. There has also been a definitely political aspect to the course of the programs as each developed its own constituencies, often leading to both inter- and intra-program competition for funding, for staff, and for precedence, as will be illustrated in specific cases below.

Within each strategy, different programs are characterized by alternative administrative and political structures and mechanisms. The flow of dollars from federal source to point of service delivery takes many different channels. The federal flow is also joined by matching or partial matching moneys from state governments and local governments in both Medicaid, an individual-based program, and in many categorical programs, which are provider-based.

Medicaid serves as an example of the administrative and political mechanisms characteristic of the individual-based, insurance approach. The Medicaid program is an entitlement program administered by the states, which purchase services on behalf of beneficiaries who meet income and categorical criteria. These criteria are set at minimum levels by the federal government but may be modified extensively by individual states, as may the range of services to which beneficiaries are entitled under the program. A key characteristic of

TABLE 1.1

NATIONAL PERSONAL HEALTH CARE EXPENDITURES, BY PAYMENT SOURCE, SELECTED YEARS, 1929-1980 (in dollars)

Year	Total Expenditures All Sources	Direct Payments	All Third Parties					
			Total third parties	Private		Public		
			Total	Insurance	Other	Subtotal	Federal	State and local
			amount (in millions)					
1929	3,202	2,829	373	-	84	289	87	202
1940	3,548	2,886	662	-	94	570	145	425
1950	10,885	7,133	3,752	992	320	2,440	1,136	1,304
1960	23,680	12,990	10,690	4,996	537	5,157	2,199	2,958
1965	36,000	18,584	17,416	8,729	788	7,899	3,785	4,114
1966	39,853	19,746	20,107	9,142	813	10,153	5,291	4,862
1967	44,990	19,355	25,535	9,545	815	15,175	9,571	5,603
1968	50,766	29,766	30,000	11,344	862	17,794	11,452	6,342
1969	57,276	23,159	34,117	13,069	901	20,147	13,212	6,934
1970	65,372	26,128	39,244	15,744	1,040	22,460	14,561	7,899
1971	71,979	27,479	44,500	17,714	1,205	25,582	16,804	8,778
1972	80,177	30,674	49,502	19,433	1,266	28,804	18,968	9,836
1973	88,688	33,410	55,278	21,911	1,291	32,076	21,125	10,951
1974	101,107	35,233	65,774	25,751	1,468	38,555	25,866	12,689
1975	116,522	37,725	78,797	31,077	1,539	46,182	31,531	14,650
1976	131,276	41,554	89,722	36,528	1,743	51,450	36,281	15,170
1977	147,968	48,855	99,113	38,819	2,157	58,138	41,083	17,055
1978	166,627	53,057	113,570	44,969	2,196	66,405	46,718	19,687
1979	189,100	62,000	127,100	50,200	2,600	74,400	53,100	21,300
1980	217,900	70,600	147,300	58,100	2,900	86,400	62,500	23,900

SOURCE: Robert M. Gibson, "National Health Expenditures, 1979," Health Care Financing Review, Summer 1980 (Health Care Financing Administration, U.S. Department of Health and Human Services); and Robert M. Gibson and Daniel R. Waldo, "National Health Expenditures 1980," Health Care Financing Review, September 1981 (Health Care Financing Administration, U.S. Department of Health and Human Services).

the Medicaid program is that it functions as an insurance program: in theory, beneficiaries enter the health care market as consumers who may choose any provider they wish to deliver services. In actuality, because Medicaid generally pays providers less than the full cost of producing services, many providers decline to participate in the Medicaid program, which limits the beneficiaries' choice of provider. The level of federal participation in financing of Medicaid services, derived from a formula based on a state's per capita income, ranged in 1979 from 50 to 78 percent.[1] Thus, the state/local contribution ranged from 22 to 50 percent. Inclusion of particular services as covered under Medicaid has spawned interest groups and spurred development of provider capacity in such services as nursing homes in many states. Providers have formed powerful lobbying groups to affect the levels of allowable charges and the specifics of state-determined reimbursement formulas. The administrative structure of Medicaid entitlement, based as it is on eligibility determination for prospective beneficiaries, has fostered the development of an expanded welfare bureaucracy to carry out mandated certification, reimbursement monitoring, quality of care evaluation, and fraud and abuse investigation. Each of these endeavors is subject to periodic political interest, investigation, and exploitation. The costs of Medicaid, as an entitlement program, are relatively open-ended because they are dependent on the health care-seeking behavior of beneficiaries in a predominantly fee-for-service market, and on cost-based payments to institutional providers for these services. The flow of dollars under Medicaid is essentially federal to state (with additions) to locality (in some cases with additions), sometimes through fiscal intermediary to provider, paid on the basis of billings submitted by each provider for services to entitled beneficiaries.

The flow of resources is somewhat different under a provider-based program, principally because the administrative mechanisms are different. There is great variation among programs as well. Federal resources are used in the direct production of services in the case of the National Health Service Corps program. Physicians and other staff are paid federal salaries as U.S. Public Health Service (PHS) employees but are assigned to locally operated institutions (some public, most private) to deliver care to the poor. These federal salary costs are then partially paid back to the federal government out of patient care revenues (some of which are partially federally financed through Medicaid and Medicare), generated by billing by the local institution or the physicians themselves (if enough revenues are generated to cover these costs). Thus, even a direct federal service program has complex administrative mechanisms that tie in other levels of financing, administration, and politics.

In many categorical programs that are targeted for the poor, the resource flow consists of a large transfer of funds from the federal level to the state government, which then parcels out resources to selected local providers—public, private, or a combination of the two. Maternal and child health (MCH) and family planning moneys follow this route's variants. The role of the local (city and/or county) health department varies from place to place and program to program. Sometimes the health department receives funds and contracts out to private institutions for services; sometimes only the health department provides services; and sometimes it shares funding and responsibility for service delivery with other institutions, as is often the case in family planning programs.

In some categorical programs, federal dollars go directly to a locality, which may then either operate services directly or contract for them. Federal grant dollars may also go directly to individual provider institutions for service delivery to the poor, as is the case with neighborhood health center and hospital-affiliated primary care center programs.

What is most striking about this discussion of resources for the health care of the poor is the multiplicity of avenues the dollars may follow. Each program has an independent array of criteria for participation by providers and recipients; each has its own bureaucratic structure, political constituency, historical context, and set of reporting requirements. At the local level resources must be turned into services, and thus at the local level all the inconsistencies among programs must somehow be smoothed into a functional health service delivery system. Although federal moneys play a significant role in assisting localities to fulfill their missions in providing health and hospital care to their citizens, local officials must continually struggle to consolidate the federal funds that flow from different legislative authorities into local programs designed to meet locally defined needs. Federal action has typically been characterized by a piecemeal, categorical approach to the critical issue of which groups in the society ought to receive what kinds of services. Further fragmentation can be attributed to vacillating attitudes concerning which is the most appropriate party—state or local health departments, hospitals, nonprofit community groups, the patient—to translate federal money into services that will actually reach the targeted population with a minimum of waste. A heated debate also continues as to whether the public sector or the private sector is the more appropriate arena for providing health services to the poor. Given that public financing of care is bound to continue in large volume, the issue becomes one of how services can be most effectively and efficiently produced, and of what changes are politically feasible in a given locality.

The layers of federal programs accumulating over the years have left a legacy upon which new efforts must build. That legacy is evident in many ways: continuing streams of intergovernmental revenue with parallel sets of personnel, facilities, agencies, and procedures. Important but less tangible parts of the legacy are the patterns of political alliances over the years; the political scars that remain from one conflict or another; the community interest groups which become developed, organized, and sophisticated at competing for resources; and the health arena participants' institutional memories of past failures and successes, which can be applied to new endeavors.

In the context of this background, the remainder of this chapter will examine the impact of the three major variants of federal efforts to improve health care for the poor since 1965: categorical health programs (primarily MCH), Medicaid, and the neighborhood health center movement. The effects and status of each of these three major policy initiatives nationwide and in each of the five cities participating in the Municipal Health Services Program will be assessed. These differing strategies for providing care for the disadvantaged will be discussed as important elements of the context in which new local health strategies must operate.

Categorical Programs

MATERNAL AND CHILD HEALTH PROGRAMS

The maternal and child health programs of the 1970s had their origins as early as 1912 in the establishment of the Children's Bureau, an investigative agency created because of pressures from social reformers concerned with the issues of child labor and its abuses. Reports of the agency on the possibilities of ameliorating maternal and infant mortality through social intervention created more pressure for reform and led to legislation in the 1920s and 1930s that authorized grants to states to enable them to provide medical services to mothers and children. The Social Security Act of 1935 established federal-state cooperation in providing MCH, crippled children's, and child welfare services, most of which were preventive services. The major goal of MCH programs has been the reduction of maternal and infant mortality. Over the next forty years, a series of amendments added categories of eligibility, expanded bit by bit the types of illness singled out for special attention, and shifted emphasis among diagnostic and preventive services, among specialty treatment categories (dental care, family planning, mental retardation, metabolic diseases, etc.), and between rural and urban areas. Thus, the focus of the MCH program has been modified over the years to reflect the special interests of one administration or another, such as Kennedy's concern with mental retardation or Johnson's with antipoverty mechanisms, and the changing epidemiology of prenatal, infant, and children's illnesses.

Maternal and child health programs in 1976 represented almost 20 percent of the $840 million the federal government disbursed to state health departments for public health activities. Davis and Schoen have enumerated the major distinguishing features of the MCH programs under the Social Security Act as follows:

First, they aim funds at mothers and children, especially crippled children. Second, they give funds to those supplying medical services rather than to the recipients. Third, funds are allocated through a formula that gives special priority to rural areas and areas in severe economic distress. Fourth, while concentrating services in needy areas, they make care available free of charge regardless of income, thus the programs are not strictly poverty programs. Fifth, states and local areas must match federal funds. Finally, they are federal-state programs in which states have substantial flexibility to allocate funds and design projects.[2]

The preponderance of the state position in administering MCH programs was solidified during the late 1960s and early 1970s by amendments that consolidated, into a single federal program-funding authorization, all previously separate maternal and child health programs, crippled children's programs, Maternal and Infant Care (MIC) project grants, Children and Youth (C&Y) project grants, and all MCH research and training moneys. The states were given almost total authority by 1974 for determining how to use MCH moneys, all of which went to the states as formula grants.

The MCH programs appear to have had an impact financially and in health outcomes. As Davis and Schoen point out, MCH programs accounted for more than one-third of all federal expenditures for community health services. They also note that total federal, state, and local MCH expenditures reached $443 million in 1973. In part because of the variety of services provided under the MCH umbrella and in part because of gaps in the statistical information collected by the programs, it is difficult to determine the total number of persons who benefit from MCH programs and who these service recipients are. According to Davis and Schoen estimates, in 1972 the major categories of MCH programs served the following numbers of persons: Maternal and Infant Care projects, 141,000; maternal health services in health departments, 700,000; family planning services, 3,200,000; Children and Youth projects, 500,000; and crippled children's services (1973), 513,000. Although comprehensive evaluation of the efficacy of the MCH programs has never been undertaken, some limited studies have indicated, as Davis and Schoen point out, that certain MCH programs (especially more comprehensive project grants) have reduced both maternal and infant mortality in their service populations, compared to similar groups not receiving services.

Davis and Schoen are critical of the MCH program for the lack of cohesive policy leadership from the former Department of Health, Education, and Welfare (HEW), which has allowed states to design their own programs with little evaluation or guidance. Federal funds, they charge, are not contingent upon demonstrated efficacy, efficiency, or equity, and few attempts are made to coordinate MCH activities with other federal programs such as Medicaid.

As noted above, the MCH programs have been criticized for several deficiencies, including the lack of coordination of similar programs serving generally similar populations; the fragmented, noncomprehensive nature of the programs; the constraints placed on financially pressed localities which seek flexibility in use of resources to achieve efficient service production; the duplicative and confusing nature of administrative, accounting, and reporting structures; and the fostering of independent bureaucratic interest groups that may impede implementation of integrated primary care services.

Of key importance in many cities is the effect of ongoing local power relationships that shape the environment for program implementation. A frequent scenario has the state health department caught in a bind between sets of program-specific federal guidelines, on the one hand, and local health departments with strong initiatives to consolidate categorical funds and activities into comprehensive primary care programs, on the other. Materials illustrating the current status of MCH programs in each of the five cities in this study provide an opportunity to extract some lessons relevant to these criticisms, particularly the inter-agency stress generated by conflicting objectives.

Milwaukee. In 1978 a controversy arose over the continued funding by the Wisconsin State Health Department of the Milwaukee Health Department's Maternal and Infant Care project. At the heart of the controversy were the different perspectives maintained by state and city health officials. The state wanted a small downtown clinic for the MIC and Children and Youth programs, which could possibly be expanded at some later date. With a small clinic the state could more easily meet the federal pressure for accountability of funds and the classification of services delivered to a defined population.

Communication had become strained between state and city officials when the city's MIC project was suddenly defunded in September 1978. The city received formal notice only shortly before termination, forcing staff to send patients elsewhere for services.

Subsequently, the city submitted a proposal in response to the state's request to receive bids for a combined MIC and C&Y Project under one administration. As part of the proposal, the city health department formed a consortium of the Medical College of Wisconsin, the Milwaukee County Medical Complex, Mount Sinai Hospital, and Milwaukee Children's Hospital. The proposal was rejected by the state in February 1979 on the grounds of "substantial technical deficiencies," covering such areas as the size of the proposed geographic base, assurances about comprehensiveness and continuity of services, registration procedures, and eligibility.

Since the Milwaukee consortium wanted to add these two categorical programs to the already ongoing services partially funded by the city health department and the Robert Wood Johnson Foundation grant, the proposal was not favorably reviewed. "It was a mistake," according to one state Title V planning analyst. "It was an attempt to share the wealth. It was an attempt to merge Title V programs into the Robert Wood Johnson project. . . . The consortium tended to scare off other hospitals from submitting their own grant proposals." State officials believed these politics prevented other parties from competing fairly. They perceive the Milwaukee Health Department as having its own vision of how things should be run in Milwaukee, a vision not consistent with the state outlook.

The city health commissioner argues that federal and state MIC guidelines are very rigid and that he and others find them barriers to providing care. A former city C&Y director reiterated this stance by stating that the state's guidelines are primitive and inflexible. "We can't have the State dictate whom we can take care of," he says. "When Title V disappears there will still be high-risk moms."

Cincinnati. A similar set of structures and conflicts is evident in Cincinnati, which held a $1.2 million MIC grant in 1978. The organizational structure for the MIC program is both confusing and controversial. More than half the MIC program funds are expended internally within the health department, while the remainder is subcontracted to the University of Cincinnati Medical Center, General Hospital Division. The Cincinnati Health Department does not have tertiary care capability, and more important, its staff did not (before 1980) enjoy admitting privileges at General Hospital. Therefore, continuity of care for the target population is accomplished through contractual arrangements with General Hospital.

The Ohio State Department of Health maintains that MIC expenditures must be clearly identifiable in terms of MIC personnel, both administrative and professional, as well as services. The city's point of view is that it would be inefficient to graft onto the normal operations of the department a separate and identifiable MIC component. The health department would prefer to enhance its existing maternal and infant care activities with MIC dollars.

This controversy has continued for a number of years. During 1979 a meeting initiated by the health department was held with participation of Ohio department of health representatives and HEW representatives from Region 5 and from Washington. The city department of health strongly advocated its position of supporting its normal operations with MIC funding, rather than administering a totally separate MIC component, but no final resolution was achieved.

The organization of the MIC program is confusing, primarily because of the health department's effort to maintain its prerogatives while at the same time satisfying state requirements, at least on the surface. A designated MIC organization does exist within the health department, but at practically all levels of this internal organization, individuals are performing MIC as well as other related health department functions.

St. Louis. In contrast to the two cities discussed above, St. Louis has been able to absorb successfully the MIC program into its public health structure. Contributing factors to success are difficult to single out. One might suggest the following, however: the particular distribution and concentration of the poverty population in relation to program requirements, an accounting system for tracking intergovernmental funds, the structure and policies of the state health department, and relationships with the local HEW regional office.

By stipulation of the MIC grant, the project must concentrate on the population served at two northside clinics, Courtney and Wohl (North Kingshighway), and the city's Continuing Education School for Pregnant Students. These clinics serve an almost exclusively black, low-income population. The low-income white southside population is not served by this project.

In the late 1970s the city health division received $404,000 annually in MIC funds, with the State of Missouri Division of Health and Bureau of Maternal and Child Health Services acting as the pass-through agency. An additional $30,000 derived from third-party billing under Medicaid and self-pay patient billing was used pursuant to federal legislation to expand the program. The city provides matching funds for the MIC project by assigning indirect costs and services (a percentage of gross payrolls) and "in-kind" free delivery services at City Hospital for MIC patients who choose the public hospitals (roughly one-half do so). There are no C&Y projects.

St. Louis provides an example of an issue that has arisen in other states as a barrier to some innovations in primary care. While the St. Louis MIC program has been praised by the Missouri State Division of Health because of its multidisciplinary and comprehensive approach (i.e., its use of nurse-practitioners, nutritionists, and counselors) and its recruitment, outreach, and follow-up approach with young, high-risk patients, the program may encounter future problems because of changing state policies regarding nurse-practitioner reimbursement. A restrictive interpretation of the Nurse Practice Act has meant that nurse-practitioners' services are not covered for Medicaid reimbursement. Nurse-practitioners provide the majority of the services, and the city is "having a hell of a time collecting money from the State," said the city's fiscal officers for MIC and family planning. This unresolved issue could have implications for many health department activities and emphasizes the significance of the broad local policy picture and its effects on program implementation.

San Jose. There are no C&Y or MIC programs in Santa Clara County, a result of explicit county policy. According to the original guidelines for such projects, participation in the program was determined by certifying entire areas. San Jose experienced explosive growth during the sixties, with leap-frog patterns of development. This resulted in very poor areas suddenly being juxtaposed with wealthy ones. Under the program guidelines, wealthy and poverty-level families in an area would be equally eligible for services, which the health department considered inappropriate.

Baltimore. The distinguishing feature of Baltimore's MIC and C&Y programs is the fact that categorical program participation is not limited to public sector providers. Baltimore has sizeable programs, including, as of 1978, a $1.2 million MIC program with 10 percent to 20 percent direct revenues, and a $6.28 million C&Y grant. While most MIC services are provided in city health department clinics, the C&Y services are provided by more than seven different subcontractors, including voluntary hospitals and prepaid health plans. Direct reimbursement to these contractors for services delivered is supplemented by approximately $4 million in health department grants to cover the balance of costs in the program.

SUPPLEMENTAL FOOD PROGRAM FOR WOMEN, INFANTS, AND CHILDREN (WIC)

The special Supplemental Food Program for Women, Infants, and Children, known as WIC, was created by the Child Nutrition Act of 1966. Unique among categorical health programs, WIC and a handful of other nutrition programs are administered by the Food and Nutrition Service of the Department of Agriculture, rather than by the Department of Health and Human Services (HHS). Thus, an entirely separate federal bureaucratic reporting system must be dealt with by state and local health agencies who administer WIC locally.

The objectives of the WIC program are to provide nutritious foods to beneficiaries identified as nutritional risks and to research the benefits of such nutritional supplements. The program is targeted to beneficiaries who are poor, by means of eligibility determination based on local health agency criteria for eligibility for free or discounted health care.

Project grants are made to state health departments to make nutritious foods available to infants, children, and pregnant or lactating women, through local public or nonprofit private health agencies. Funds are used to purchase supplemental foods for participants or to redeem vouchers issued for that purpose. Local agencies must provide free or discounted care to participants, must serve populations at nutritional risk, and must be able to perform required reporting. Beneficiaries qualify if they live in a designated project area, are eligible for reduced-cost services, and are certified by a professional as needing supplemental nutrition. Areas are approved for the program on the basis of need. No matching funds are required. Total grant expenditures amounted to $247.3 million in fiscal year (FY) 1976. In FY 1975, fifty-two state and territorial agencies served a peak caseload of 497,000 participants.[3]

The WIC dollar flow is particularly complex, with a great variety of participants at the local level. From their federal source in the Department of Agriculture, funds pass through the state health department, a local contractor agency, generally multiple agencies who subcontract to screen potential recipients and provide nutrition education, and contracting grocers who accept voucher coupons in exchange for food.

As with many such categorical programs, local complaints abound regarding state and federal attempts to impose, and often alter, information requirements and eligibility standards. Efforts to ensure accountability and hold down the budget frequently lead to confusion in program operations.

The fact that WIC programs are under the auspices of the U.S. Department of Agriculture presents some special problems. "It does not have any communication with HEW," says one state official. He explains that WIC and Medicaid's Early and Periodic Screening, Diagnosis, and Treatment (EPSDT) program, for eligible persons under 21, have similar high-risk health screening but each has its own process. Also, some of the same information is required of persons eligible for Medicaid. "In some cases we have a high proportion of family group members eligible for all three programs or at least two of the three. The state is trying to get one data service for all of these," he adds. The problem he outlines is that of duplication of data services. For example, the Agriculture Department is installing a state-wide electronic data system for the WIC program, but the health department already has a subcontract with the Hypertension Program to process similar information. As the state administrator complains, "This is a gigantic waste of money. People in Washington deal with their programs as if they were the only ones, as if they were in a vacuum with no other program in mind."

The multiple sets of eligibility, operating, and reporting requirements affect poor patients as well as program administrators. The patient must sort through mystifying materials on the availability of services; must produce reams of personal identification, income, expense, residence, and demographic information; and must often spend inordinate amounts of time appearing for the many independently scheduled categorical services for which he or she may be eligible.

FAMILY PLANNING

Family planning services are authorized under several different pieces of legislation, each of which operates in a slightly different manner. Provision of family planning services is not directly limited to the poor due to the nature of these services, which are often not available in discreet fashion to such seekers as the young, and which may not be uniformly offered by the private sector.

One of the largest sources of funds for family planning services is Title X of the Public Health Service Act, known as the Family Planning Act. It makes available to public and private nonprofit agencies project grants to provide educational, medical, and social services to enable individuals to determine the number and spacing of their children.

Project grants flow directly from the federal government's Department of Health and Human Services to the recipient agency. No specific matching requirement is mandated other than that federal funds may not equal the total project budget.

Family planning moneys are also provided through the MCH program, Title V of the Social Security Act. As described in the previous section, this money flows to state health departments, with half of it going into formula grants and the other half into project grants. It is estimated that in FY 1975 about 1,220,000 women received family planning services under Title V. More funds are available as special project grants to states under Title XX of the Social Security Act, the Social Services and Public Assistance programs which became effective in 1975. Federal funds support 75 percent of the costs of grants under Title XX. Welfare-eligibles may participate in these services, usually provided by local government as social services. Family planning is also a mandated service for persons eligible for assistance under Title XIX of the Social Security Act, the Medical Assistance Program, Medicaid. These are considered medical services and are provided under individual entitlement to purchase of services, rather than under provider grants.

The confusion of grants and delivery modes in family planning can be seen by contrasting two cities, St. Louis and San Jose. In the city of St. Louis, for example, the federally funded Title X Family Planning Program is provided by a range of public and private nonprofit agencies, including Planned Parenthood, the Urban League, and free-standing clinics under various auspices. The city health department receives the largest Title X contract in the state as a provider agency.

All Title X Family Planning Act funds come from the regional office of HHS to the St. Louis Family Planning Council, a federally funded administrative umbrella agency that distributes the money through contracts with thirteen provider agencies in the metropolitan St. Louis area. The Family Planning Council also distributes some Title V and Title XIX funds from the state division of health to the contractor agencies. Although Planned Parenthood receives one of the smallest family planning grants, it serves larger numbers than any individual public agency. The Title X grant to the city health division in 1978 totaled $389,001, augmented by $40,000 from Medicaid.

Family planning services are conducted at six city sites—at the four (in 1978) municipal public health centers and two city hospital clinics. In public clinics, family planning is regarded as the low-income patient's entrance into the health delivery system. Like the MIC project, with whose offices it has merged, the family planning project follows a multidisciplinary approach, providing more costly ancillary services, patient counseling, and follow-up visits than some other private agencies.

Santa Clara County and San Jose, California, receive family planning funds through Title X, which is centralized and orderly, and through Title XX, which is decentralized and more complex. Title X funds come directly from HHS to the county, which acts as the federally mandated single agency. All family planning services are covered, including infertility but excluding abortion. Those persons below 150 percent of the poverty level, adjusted for a family of four, are eligible for services. Subcontracts have been given to two community facilities, Alviso and Our Health Center, the latter a clinic operated by Planned Parenthood of Santa Clara County. Nearly $7.5 million was granted in FY 1977 to public and private agencies in California.

The Office of Family Planning of the California Department of Health administers state general funds for family planning as well as federal Title XX funds. The state policy with respect to family planning funds is to encourage decentralization and participation of many providers at the local level. State family planning moneys, which represent the majority of funds, have more liberal eligibility standards than do federal Title XX funds. Based on *individual* income adjusted for family size, rather than *family* income, state funds allow teenagers to receive services regardless of family income. Federal Title XX funds reimburse for services provided to those whose *family* income is below 223 percent of poverty level, adjusted for family size. The combined total of Title XX and state general fund moneys for family planning in California for FY 1977 was $17.2 million.

Family planning services are also available under Medi-Cal, California's version of the Medicaid program. Eligibility requirements for Medi-Cal are more stringent than for Title X, Title XX or state family planning services. The match for family planning under Medi-Cal is 90 percent federal funds and 10 percent state funds, compared to 50 percent federal funds and 50 percent state funds for other Medi-Cal services.

While the general goals of federal, state and local agencies may be essentially similar—to improve the delivery of health care to poor mothers and children—perceptions of how best to accomplish these ends differ. From their perspective, HHS officials see federal dollars disappearing into the hinterlands, with only the echoes of program statistics and agency plans to indicate that somewhere services are being delivered to some people. Evaluation studies may suggest ways to adjust program guidelines to get better returns for the federal dollar, but often the results are highly variable according to local circumstances.

The perspective of states varies according to the role each has elected to adopt relative to its local health departments: centralized authority over the management of public health activities, decentralized authority in an advisory capacity, or some mixture of the two. For most states the major difficulty is selecting and achieving their own programmatic goals amid numerous conflicting pressures. On one side is the federal government with its demands for accountability, while on the other side local health departments argue for greater discretion in the use of funds. States are faced with the dilemma of being charged either with poor oversight and management, or with taking too much administrative overhead from grants in order to maintain monitoring personnel. Further, urban areas must be balanced against rural areas having different needs and capacities to operate programs. The pros and cons of private versus public providers frequently must be weighed. And finally, in view of the expanded regulatory powers states are being forced to adopt, they are increasingly confronted with decisions involving the use of funds from one set of programs as leverage to achieve other objectives.

Local health agencies, although long caught in the categorical mode, would prefer to design total primary care systems using common personnel and facilities to treat the same patients, rather than to fragment services into discrete single-purpose programs. Local agencies depend upon bundles of funds that must be incorporated into a departmental structure. The flexibility needed to compete for and use outside funds effectively to provide services for the poor is often hampered by local strictures imposed by Civil Service Commissions, Offices of Management and Budget, and a host of bureaucratic and political interests, as well as by excessive federal paperwork requirements. The variability among funding and eligibility criteria has meant that categorical services have only partially been able to meet the health needs of the poor.

Medicaid

"Medicare appeared in the guise of an insurance company," write Robert and Rosemary Stevens, "and Medicaid as an extension of welfare programs in the states."[4] On the continuum described earlier in this chapter, however, Medicaid, as an individual entitlement program, rests closer to the insurance pole than to the provider-grant program pole.

The Medicaid program, Title XIX of the Social Security Act as amended, is a direct offspring of several earlier pieces of social services legislation. The original Social Security Act of 1935 provided for public assistance to persons who could not work. Over the years, cash assistance was also provided to several categories of eligible needy, with the costs of medical expenses considered in determination of the level of support required. In 1950, the Social Security Amendments set up a federal matching fund for direct payment to medical care providers for services to persons on the public assistance rolls. The Kerr-Mills Act of 1960, another amendment to the Social Security Act, defined a specific set of services to be provided to beneficiaries, included the medically needy elderly who were not on public assistance, raised the level of federal participation, and established the concept of a governmental obligation to pay an open-ended amount for services for entitled beneficiaries in programs administered independently by the states. The history of these welfare-oriented medical assistance programs directly shaped the Medicaid program.

As Karen Davis and Cathy Schoen point out:

> Medicaid replaced the Kerr-Mills Act, expanded the scope of eligibility and benefits, and attempted to impose more uniformity on state programs. However, it followed many of the general principles of earlier welfare-linked programs of medical assistance for the poor. It preserved a joint federal-state responsibility, with federal matching funds and broad, federally established requirements. State governments were given administrative responsibility and discretion to set eligibility standards and benefit coverage.
>
> Medicaid expanded and improved the existing program of medical care for the poor and the aged. It increased federal sharing (which in 1976 ranged from 50 to 78 percent of the total depending on a state's per capita income), required states to cover everyone eligible for cash assistance (the aged, the disabled, and families with dependent children), and permitted states to extend coverage to all the medically needy. It delineated a mandatory set of medical services that each state was to provide and an optional set of services for which federal sharing was available. It initially required all states to have comprehensive health benefits by 1975. The additional annual cost of the program was estimated to be $250 million above the $1.3 billion already being spent under the existing program in 1965.[5]

Although it is usually discussed in conjunction with the Medicare program, for the purpose of this chapter we have juxtaposed Medicaid with the categorical programs, treating it as an additional strategy in the provision of ambulatory health services to the disadvantaged of urban areas. Medicaid and the categoricals share several similarities:

- They are both financed with combined federal-state funds and administered by the states.
- There is a wide diversity in the size, scope, eligibility, and distribution of benefits across states.
- The principal beneficiaries for both programs are poor mothers and children (although the benefits are broader and adult males are covered under Medicaid).
- Both are subject to similar administrative problems, such as changes in eligibility and benefits, and information-processing difficulties.

Notwithstanding the considerable contribution of Medicaid toward changing the utilization patterns of the poor, early expectations about the impact upon the health care delivery structure now appear to have been exceedingly naive. The following conclusions were extracted from a 1967 report by the Committee on Public Health of the New York Academy of Medicine:

> It should be emphasized that with the enactment of Medicare and Medicaid, there no longer is any social or medical reason for the continuance of the

Municipal Hospital System of New York City. Since it may be presumed that there will be no more medical indigency, the reason for the existence of the Municipal Hospital System will be removed. . . . All patients will be alike in one respect: they will be paying patients. All will therefore be private patients. Ability to pay for health care will no longer be a basis for classifying patients or for providing different accommodations.[6]

Although this euphoria would not last long, local health and hospital agencies interpreted the anticipated effects variously. Some were concerned about the viability of their current mission. Others, however, saw the increased revenue as an opportunity to improve their institutions and compete more vigorously with the voluntary sector. Community groups embarking on the neighborhood health center experiment also saw the potential for additional revenue sources that would not be subject to the scrutiny and uncertainty of annual grant-giving.

But Medicaid fell far short of these early expectations. Soaring costs led to a variety of piecemeal economy efforts at the national and state levels. These changes complicated already unwieldy administrative structures, further emphasizing the differences among state programs.

The Medicaid program did have a major impact on accessibility of health services for the poor, especially the urban poor. In 1976, total Medicaid expenditures reached $13.98 billion to serve 23.9 million recipients;[7] by 1979, the expenditures were at $21.7 billion, while recipients numbered 22.9 million.[8] Much evidence suggests that Medicaid recipients have had access to health services in volumes that approach the use of services by middle-income Americans, while low-income persons not eligible for Medicaid still use services at much lower rates.[9]

The Medicaid program has come under as harsh and persistent criticism as any social intervention of the War on Poverty, largely because the costs of Medicaid so far exceeded the projections of those who framed the legislation. Davis and Schoen astutely describe the three sources of the increase in Medicaid costs: the increase in the number of recipients covered under the Aid to Families with Dependent Children (AFDC) program (which rose from 60 percent to 90 percent of those potentially eligible by state definition in the early 1970s and doubled between 1968 and 1972); the rise in medical prices, particularly after 1974; and the high cost of nursing home care for the impoverished aged and disabled, which represents nearly 40 percent of annual Medicaid expenditures. The perception of the public and of policy-makers has been that Medicaid's costs were increasing at uncontrolled rates, and successive amendments and regulatory and administrative changes were introduced to try to contain costs. Given the decentralized, state-by-state administration of Medicaid, these piecemeal changes have further complicated the eligibility, benefits, and reimbursement scenarios at the local level.

Several other major criticisms of Medicaid are closely related to the cost problems and inconsistent administration described above. A substantial equity issue is involved in the widely variable eligibility levels and benefit packages offered from state to state. The rural poor have, on the whole, been less likely to benefit from Medicaid than have the urban poor. Many of the poor nationwide (especially intact families, childless couples, and single persons) are excluded because only categorically eligible poor (mainly AFDC) can receive Medicaid benefits in most areas. States and localities with greater resources and smaller poverty populations may be able to provide a wider range of benefits, or may reimburse providers at higher levels.

Another related problem has been the unwillingness of private physicians and health care institutions to participate in the ambulatory care portion of the Medicaid program. The foremost reason for non-participation has been the generally low level of physician fees and of hospital visit reimbursement rates under Medicaid, which has caused many providers to refuse to treat Medicaid patients. The reimbursement issue may have obscured a further question of discrimination against minorities, many of whom are Medicaid recipients. The issue of discrimination is particularly evident in the area of nursing home services, especially in the South and West.

Thus, the Medicaid program has not assured equal access to mainstream medicine for America's poor, regardless of place of residence or color of skin. On the contrary, in some cases it may have helped to disrupt traditional sources of care for the poor by exercising an adverse effect on utilization by certain of the poor of public hospitals and public health department services. Medicaid certainly did not provide to the neighborhood health centers (to be discussed later) the financial cushion they hoped for and depended upon, because it did not generally recognize them as institutional providers like hospital outpatient departments (OPD). Rather, Medicaid paid for an extensive mix of services as though they resembled a typical private office visit. As a further disincentive to innovative methods of providing primary care, Medicaid generally failed to reimburse for services provided by middle-level practitioners, further hampering efforts of clinics to provide economically viable services. A final critical point that should be noted is the fact that under Medicaid, as under other health insurance programs, ambulatory care is the least adequately reimbursed service, in contrast to acute hospital care and long-term care, which are generally reimbursed on a cost basis.

These problems inherent in the structure of the Medicaid program are exemplified by the experience of localities which have attempted to improve access to health care for the urban poor. California is unusual in that there are a large number of well-established, freestanding primary care clinics providing ambulatory care services, in comparison with other states. While benefit levels under California's Medicaid program (Medi-Cal) are comparatively comprehensive, reimbursement levels for providers are low, which presents special problems for community clinics. The low reimbursement rate for office visits has been a disincentive, with the result that in recent years only a small number of physicians (many black) are willing to accept Medi-Cal patients. The rising costs of practice in California, especially malpractice premiums, have served further to squeeze office-based physicians from the market.

California's primary care clinics have existed in a no man's land somewhere between the private physician's office and the hospital outpatient department. The clinics have received the same reimbursement rate as an office-based physician, rather than the cost-based rate of a public or voluntary hospital OPD. The genesis of their differential treatment lies in part in the unclear legal status of community clinics and the tradition of a "free clinic" physician extending his provider billing number to the entire organization in order for the clinic to bill third-party payors for services, which were then reimbursed at the physician office visit rate. As clinics grew in number, size, and sophistication, this arrangement became less tolerable on practical as well as ideological grounds. A statewide organization of clinics succeeded in having legislation passed that defines them as distinct legal entities, apart from the physician's office. This was followed by agitation by the California Council of Primary Care Clinics to raise the reimbursement rate to a par with hospitals. As of 1979, the clinics had not managed to improve their lot vis-a-vis the physician and, indeed, they received a smaller rate hike than private physicians.

Aside from issues of reimbursement, eligibility determination has also posed a problem. As is frequently the case, determination of eligibility for services is the responsibility of the welfare or social services department, not the county health agencies. California's county plan for colocation of human services was designed to overcome some of the barriers to more effective linkage between eligibility and service delivery. With the advent of the Proposition 13 tax limitation law, however, concern arose over the county's ability to cope with these problems in the face of decreased numbers of eligibility workers.

California state health officials, oriented toward experimentation and prompted by the passage of Proposition 13, contemplated, from 1979 through 1981, a number of proposals for reorganizing state health care financing to curb rising costs and more closely control services to Medi-Cal recipients. The intent of one group of reorganization proposals was to channel Medi-Cal funds as much as possible into county hospital-based, prepaid health plans by tightening controls over fee-for-service Medi-Cal payments. This could involve such measures as decertifying hospitals and other types of providers for Medi-Cal, contracting only with those that agree to payment on a prospective basis. Alternative proposals would have directed patients predominantly into private sector institutions.

In Missouri, where benefit packages and eligibility criteria are more restrictive than in California, the same problems of inadequate levels of ambulatory care reimbursement, discrimination against freestanding in favor of hospital-based services, and onerous bureaucratic eligibility criteria noted in California also exist. A large and critical problem is a new unwillingness on the part of the state to reimburse for middle-level practitioner services.

Historically, ambulatory care in all settings in Missouri has been inadequately reimbursed under Medicaid. Hospital-related institutions, including OPDs and emergency rooms (ER), and physicians received Medicaid vendor numbers; but freestanding clinics, public and private alike, were denied vendor numbers until January 1980, when the state of Missouri contracted with a private intermediary to manage Medicaid reimbursement claims. Because of this difference in treatment, the history of Missouri Medicaid reimbursement for freestanding clinics and OPDs has been different. Until recently OPDs were reimbursed on a visit basis, according to a Medicaid rate schedule which paid a flat $8.00 (later raised to $9.00) per visit, no matter whether a major or minor medical procedure was involved. In July 1979, as a result of political lobbying efforts including the hospital division in St. Louis, the state legislature changed the OPD reimbursement rate to "80 percent of reasonable cost" in order to reflect more realistically actual medical costs incurred. This new rate applied to public and private hospital OPDs.

Freestanding clinics sponsored by HEW, because they had no vendor numbers, billed the state Medicaid reimbursement office under the category of "professional services," using the vendor numbers of their physician medical directors, who in turn signed their reimbursement checks over to the bank account maintained by the clinic.

Municipal public health clinics have a different history. The city of St. Louis has had a long tradition of free health care in the city-run clinics, supported by a combination of general revenue funds and moneys from state and federal categorical grants. There simply was no motivation for third-party billing under Medicaid or Medicare on the part of the city health division. Since 1978, the health division has been billing the state for Medicaid reimbursement for professional services, using Medicaid vendor numbers of the health centers' salaried doctors and depositing the revenue into the health division account.

Several major ongoing conflicts in the administration of Medicaid exist which affect the viability of community health services. The first conflict relates to the very low levels of Medicaid reimbursement which characterize Missouri, no matter what the medical setting. Clinics may have a "dim future," according to the city's Ambulatory Care fiscal officer, if Medicaid reimbursement rates remain low while the volume of patients increases. Currently, the health centers are also using the state reimbursement schedule for Medicaid to set the billing rates for self-pay patients.

A more serious conflict has emerged between St. Louis Ambulatory Care and the state Department of Social Services over billing for middle-level practitioner services and the state's interpretation of what constitutes "on-site" physician supervision for nurse-practitioners. The nurse-practitioner controversy began in the fall of 1979 with a request from the director of the Missouri Department of Social Services for clarification from the state attorney general as to whether Medicaid reimbursement was allowable in payment for services rendered by nurse-practitioners and physician assistants in rural health clinics. Essentially, the director was concerned whether the functions of nurse-practitioners, as described in a new federal statute (Publ. L. 95-210) were consistent with Missouri state law. On January 2, 1980, the state's attorney general handed down an official legal opinion:

NURSES: RURAL HEALTH CLINICS: Registered professional nurses under Chapter 335, RSMo, do not have the authority to engage in primary health care that includes diagnosis and treatment of human illness, injury or infirmity and administration of medications under general rather than direct physician guidance and supervision. Therefore, registered professional nurses cannot perform all the duties and functions of "nurse practitioners" provided for in the Rural Health Clinic Services Act, Pub. L. 95-210.[10]

Local experts have debated whether nurse-practitioners are bound by the decision. Nevertheless, there is concern that nurse-practitioners across the state will be reluctant to place themselves in legal jeopardy. The outcome of this controversy will have a major impact on community clinics and public health agencies, given their reliance upon nurse-practitioners.

Before 1981 there were few significant Missouri Medicaid cutbacks in eligibility, copayments, service limits, or reimbursement levels. But the state had an inadequate Medicaid rate and a history of Medicaid eligibility restricted largely to AFDC families—a program with its own restricted welfare eligibility determination. In addition, many spokesmen believe that Medicaid reimbursement budgets are kept low through a structural safeguard of poor administration in the Division of Family Services. The program has been accused of limiting eligibility through high rates of errors in processing (nationally one of the highest) and failure to follow its own eligibility criteria. The new state attempt to restrict the Medicaid reimbursement funds to physician or direct physician-supervised services could be regarded as a potentially significant cutback in the Medicaid program. Spokesmen in the St. Louis Division of Health and Hospitals describe the state Division of Family Services reimbursement office as well aware that a significant level of medical services at the OPDs and freestanding clinics have been performed for many years by middle-level practitioners and nurses.

To sum up the Medicaid experience of California and Missouri in light of the other study cities, one can say that despite differences in the benefit packages, eligibility criteria, and reimbursement formulas of these states' programs, there are common elements relevant to any endeavor to improve inner-city health services. In reimbursement, Medicaid programs favor hospital-based care over freestanding clinics and office-based physician services. Paperwork and delays in reimbursement further squeeze out many of those private physicians who are still willing to see Medicaid patients.

The initial period of Medicaid implementation was marked by radical adjustments in program content and administration, leading to disillusionment over the early expectation of "mainstreaming" the poor. There are still significant problems in most places related to eligibility, claims processing, and the shortfall between the costs incurred by the clinics which provide services to Medicaid recipients and the reimbursement they receive for the services.

In the generous and not-so-generous states alike there have been and will continue to be attempts to ferret out ways of reducing Medicaid costs. States with broad coverage have more latitude to cut less visible and less traditional benefits. States with poorer coverage are apt to seek administrative means of tightening patient certification and claims-processing procedures to slow cost rises.

Within this cost-containment milieu, independent and local government health centers have argued for greater reimbursement parity with hospital outpatient departments. In some cases they have been successful, but there is concern by state budget-makers that widespread adoption of this practice would lead to higher overall Medicaid costs. The counter-argument posited is that comprehensive care delivered at neighborhood sites would ultimately prove less expensive than hospital-based care.

EARLY AND PERIODIC SCREENING, DIAGNOSIS, AND
TREATMENT (EPSDT)

The Early and Periodic Screening, Diagnosis, and Treatment (EPSDT) program was created by the Social Security Amendments of 1967. Its objective was to assure that Medicaid-eligible children were assessed for potential health problems at an early stage and repeatedly through childhood so that illnesses or deficiencies that could lead to adult disabilities were diagnosed and corrected during childhood.

The EPSDT program can be perceived in some ways as a categorical program grafted onto Medicaid. This amalgam has been a constant reminder of the failures of both approaches. The categorical child health programs have not satisfactorily met the needs of their target population, and the mere availability of Medicaid financing has not ensured effective case-finding and follow-up treatment.

The basic distinguishing characteristic of EPSDT is that states were required actively to identify and treat health problems in children eligible under Medicaid. This novel active approach is contrasted to the usual Medicaid entitlement mechanism whereby those eligible must take it upon themselves to discover their entitlement and seek services. States vary in the types of services available and the designated providers. The EPSDT program has been under constant criticism because of the reluctance of states, fearful of the cost implications, to carry out full implementation. This has been compounded by the federal government's sluggishness in enforcing the law's provisions.

To offer concrete examples of EPSDT operation at the local level, two programs will be compared. They differ in degree of health department participation and in philosophy about provision of screening services.

Milwaukee began offering EPSDT services in 1974 through the county health department. Excessively high costs per screen ($180) due to low productivity led to transfer of the program to the city health department, which integrated EPSDT screening with other child health services and reduced costs to $24.92 per screen in 1977. From a target group of 65,000 children, 3,620 were screened in 1977 through school health and well-baby clinics on referral by the health department. Most outreach services were provided with Comprehensive Employment and Training Act (CETA) personnel.

A unique aspect of the EPSDT program in Wisconsin is a built-in incentive program in which the state gives a larger cost refund if the child screened is found eligible for treatment. For example, if a child is referred for a vision test and is found to need glasses, the agency that performed the EPSDT screening would receive $10, compared to $6 if the child had not needed glasses. Similarly, an incentive program has been proposed to improve the lagging outreach component.

The EPSDT program exists in a modified form in California, where it is called Child Health and Disability Prevention (CHDP). State policy has been to encourage the participation of private providers, with the county functioning as a coordinating and recruiting agent. There was difficulty in recruiting private providers, however, because the regulations governing the program were too stringent for many and had to be changed to make the program more inviting. Approximately 120 private providers were operating in Santa Clara County in 1977. The health department certifies the providers, so that they are eligible to receive funds. The county health department receives all administrative funds for the CHDP program. Its responsibilities include education, outreach, and follow-up. The administrative contract does not provide funds for screening; therefore, for screens, the health department is paid like any private provider, directly from the state. This policy is consistent with the health department's philosophy that the best care for CHDP eligible children is comprehensive care, unavailable in its programs. No data are available as to the degree of compliance of San Jose/Santa Clara County with EPSDT mandates. This is not unusual, however, because compliance and enforcement have been notably lax nationwide.

The EPSDT program languished throughout the 1970s, following a brief spurt of activity after implementing regulations were issued in

1973. Legislation to replace EPSDT, such as the proposed Child Health Assurance Program, has, however, also languished in Congress. Prospects for either rejuvenation or replacement of EPSDT are mixed, at best, and perhaps elimination is more likely. Certainly, the EPSDT experience has been unsuccessful.

Community Health Centers

A third major federal strategy for improving the delivery of health services to the urban poor has been the community health center program. While the delivery of primary care services by groups of health professionals in facilities close to the neighborhoods of defined service populations was not a new idea, the community or neighborhood health center initiatives of the War on Poverty era took on a distinct identity due to a number of characteristics, which will be discussed below. We can place community health centers in our schema of alternative federal strategies by noting that this program is firmly in the institutional/provider range of the continuum. Under early rules, although the centers' services were certainly targeted to the poor, means tests for eligibility were not used and anyone could walk in and register to receive services, for which there often was no billing. Health centers were originally financed largely by federal grants, and only as time passed, as bureaucratic control shifted, and as priorities were reordered, was an emphasis placed on centers becoming self-sufficient through collecting revenue for patient services. The emphasis on Medicaid revenues represented a melding-in of the insurance approach.

The federally funded community health centers of the sixties and seventies had their origins in programs that were not strictly health programs at all. The antipoverty efforts of the Johnson administration were centered in the newly created Office of Economic Opportunity (OEO), which took responsibility for a broad range of programs whose activities ordinarily would have been located in the functionally oriented traditional bureaucracy for housing, health, jobs, etc. Sponsored by OEO, the new health centers had more on their agendas than just the delivery of comprehensive primary care services.

The OEO–sponsored community health centers were designed in part to assume the traditional role of family doctors and other health workers in areas where few of these personnel practiced. The community health centers generally provided a full range of primary care services and acted as the patient's advocate through the rest of the health system. They could in a sense be seen as filling resource gaps left by the categorical programs and Medicaid's financing approach for certain of the poor. But community health centers operated with multiple goals, many of these not directly related to health service delivery. Health was defined very broadly, as including physical, mental, social, economic, environmental, and political aspects. Thus, improved housing, better sewer and water systems, employment, job training, community economic development, counseling, advocacy with other social services and, perhaps most important, personal and minority group power building were all major goals of neighborhood health programs. The most influential phrase in the OEO rubric was "maximum feasible participation" of the poor and minority groups being served. Community control over service delivery was the rule of the day. Federal regulations required that community health centers be controlled by a consumer-majority, community governing board with broad policy-making powers, a requirement that still stands today.

The multiple objectives, activities, and constituencies within neighborhood health centers often led to organizational instability and sometimes to collapse. Yet as Davis and Schoen point out, "Most of the neighborhood health centers did survive, flourish, and become stable sources of accessible health services."[11] The scope of the program never reached what was originally anticipated. After OEO began the community health center program, an HEW report in 1967 presented a plan for meeting the health care needs of the nation's poor through the establishment of 1,000 health centers to serve 25 million persons at a cost of $3.35 billion by 1973. By 1976, however, there were only approximately 125 centers serving 1.5 million persons with a budget of $197 million.[12]

As the Johnson administration gave way to Republican presidencies, the OEO programs were dismantled. Under Nixon, the OEO health centers were transferred to HEW's Public Health Service to be merged with its community health center program. The PHS health centers were more exclusively focused on health services, and soon this orientation predominated in the former OEO sites as they were subjected to funding constraints and productivity requirements. During the seventies, PHS clinics came under federal pressures to resemble well-managed private group practices, but these centers are still subject to the policies of community governing boards—51 percent of which must be consumers—and rely on a wide range of categorical funding, all of which helps to maintain some of the original OEO character.

The neighborhood health center was intended to provide high quality health care for the poor, especially for ethnic minority poor, in a facility that was physically accessible—hence, in their neighborhood. Location of centers in minority neighborhoods, the targeting of services to these groups, initial federal regulations, and the proviso of community control led to the use of center services predominantly by poor minority groups. Some critics have thus charged that the program perpetuated a dual system of second-class care for the poor. The program did, however, apparently appeal to and fill service and power needs of poor minority groups in many areas.

Some observers contend that the community clinic movement, including federally funded and, even more so, the single-interest-group nonfederally funded clinics, has provided an alternative model of health care for disenfranchised peripheral social groups who have rejected and/or been rejected by the traditional health care establishment. Such groups as blacks, Asians, Chicanos, feminists, gays, the elderly, and alternative life-style advocates have all developed community clinics to serve the particular health needs of their own clientele in Santa Clara and Alameda counties, in California.[13] Health tends to be defined very broadly by these groups, and power to control one's environment, especially in terms of medical intervention, is a major agenda item. Although survival was tenuous for many of the nonfederal clinics, those which have endured tend to have very loyal and ideologically resolute constituencies. They must be considered a part of the health care system, filling as they do the particular needs of their supporting groups for services and for identity and power.

As of the mid-1970s, neighborhood health centers represented a strategy that had provided considerable amounts of incremental health services in poor communities. The HEW monitors required a much greater degree of performance reporting for community health centers than was required under categorical programs, including utilization, productivity, and financial management data. The centers that have survived have produced substantial documentation of provision of a wide range of primary and special services to a low-income population, a majority of which is from minority groups. Assessments of quality of care in the centers indicate that it is as good as or better than care available from such sources as health department clinics, hospital clinics associated with medical schools, Children and Youth projects, and private group practices.[14] No definitive conclusions can be drawn about the centers' impact upon health status of the populations served; yet in some communities served by the program, substantial drops have been noted in both maternal and infant mortality, concomitant with identifiable increases in utilization of prenatal and infant care services.[15]

Neighborhood health centers have come under criticism for being unduly expensive per unit of service produced, compared to private physician services. It must be recognized that the centers provide a varied and complex mix of services, however, and generally a large volume of care as well that requires an investment in management and reporting overhead. Centers have generally had difficulties in coping with the reimbursement environment since the early days when they were prohibited from serving insured or paying patients. Suddenly required to become self-sufficient through billing and collecting for services, the centers in many states found themselves caught in a fiscal identity crisis between the positions of private physician and hospital outpatient service. For Medicaid purposes, most states refused to recognize health centers as institutional providers like hospital OPDs, and there was no other legal entity under which centers could be encompassed. Thus, most centers had to rely on billing at private physician rates, using one or more of their medical staff for billing purposes. The private physician rates were generally too low to support even solo-practice physicians, much less the costs of a health center. Even in cases where institutional rates were set, these failed to cover costs. In addition, the centers provided services to those patients who fell between the cracks of both private and public reimbursement coverage, and often provided services that were outside the scope of benefits paid for by Medicaid, Medicare, and private carriers. A widespread problem was the failure of many states to reimburse for services provided by middle-level practitioners, a group that had been widely recruited and sponsored by health centers as cost-efficient providers of primary care. Related financial problems in many centers resulted from overheavy staffing patterns in relation to utilization. This problem was exacerbated by the lack of reimbursement coverage for many of the types of services provided, such as nutrition counseling, and social and environmental services. Thus the financial picture for established community health centers continued to deteriorate as federal regulations pushed harder for self-sufficiency, and services continued to be cut down to the basics of medical care. As services were cut, utilization often dropped further. Often the utilization trends were also adversely affected by the demographics of underserved communities, where population tended to be dropping consistently.

The community health center program experienced other problems. Among them was a general lack of integration with other health care providers in the community, particularly with local hospitals. It was often difficult for physician staff to obtain admitting privileges at local hospitals, which compromised the continuity of care for patients. Recruitment and retention of personnel, particularly professional personnel, was a consistent challenge for the health centers. Physician turnover has been very high, especially among young physicians. Some of the recruitment and staff retention problems may be related to management difficulties, resulting from uncertainties of funding from year to year, heavy involvement in personnel issues by community boards, and inability to offer competitive salary levels based on adequate budgetary control. The community health center program suffered from poor program coordination and planning at both the local and the federal level, leading to competition among centers and among other programs for limited funding to accomplish overlapping objectives. Much evidence for this point was presented in the earlier discussion of categorical programs.

In the remainder of this section, the experiences of the five study cities with neighborhood health centers will be reviewed. The experiences were dissimilar in many respects, but are illustrative of many of the accomplishments and problems described above. The dissimilarities are instructive for what they reveal about how local circumstances affect responses to federal stimuli, and how the legacies from past programmatic efforts reinforce the local interest groups' perceptions and reactions, which will affect future stimuli.

ST. LOUIS

An interesting bench mark for ambulatory care in St. Louis is provided by a study of the area's health needs, carried out between 1955 and 1957 by the American Public Health Association (APHA) at the request of the mayor. The APHA report, although published in 1957, presented the basic outlines of the medical care facilities in the city and county, which were by and large those in existence some seven years later at the outset of the Great Society. Initiated in response to a bond issue that called for a health needs assessment prior to health facility construction, the study examined population estimates and health status in relation to need for hospital beds and ambulatory care. Although it overestimated the 1970 population by nearly 50 percent, the study determined that only one new district public health center should be built. This facility was located adjacent to the newly opened and then much praised Pruitt-Igoe Public Housing Complex. It is ironic that by 1965 Pruitt-Igoe, designed for 3,300 families, was nationally known as a public housing disaster and was already being abandoned; by 1973, the project was completely empty, and it was demolished in 1975. The Jefferson-Cass Municipal Health Center, opened in 1960, was closed in 1976, and its functions were absorbed by the nearby and newly opened Courtney Comprehensive Health Clinic operated by the city as a Model Cities program.

From 1957 through 1966, the only freestanding ambulatory health centers were the church-related Grace Hill Health Center and the four municipal clinics. As the antipoverty and neighborhood-oriented activities of the OEO expanded locally in the middle 1960s, neighborhood health clinics or health centers began to emerge. Indeed, during the high point of the growth of OEO neighborhood organizations in St. Louis, it became a mark of stature of the neighborhood organization to be able to gain and maintain a neighborhood health clinic. At the time, there was little question in the minds of city health officials that the residents of poverty neighborhoods were not receiving adequate medical care from either private or public sources. From 1966 through 1970 seven nonmunicipal health centers were inaugurated with local political support in poverty neighborhoods in St. Louis. Five of the seven (Greeley, Yeatman, Montgomery-Hyde Park, St. Louis Comprehensive, and Pruitt-Igoe) were brought into existence at least in part through the stimulus and organizational abilities of staff of OEO–funded neighborhood organizations commonly referred to as community-based organizations (CBO). Yet only the Yeatman and St. Louis Comprehensive centers were launched with substantial coordinated planning efforts going beyond the capabilities of CBO staff, including federal technical assistance of several kinds and significant federal funding from the very beginning. A sixth center, Sheridan, was established under the auspices of Jeff-Vander-Lou, an unusual group within the Yeatman District which has been very successful in developing new and rehabilitated housing. A seventh, the Carondelet Family Care Center, was organized in 1969 by students from St. Louis University working in conjunction with a neighborhood group in the Carondelet District of South St. Louis. Being totally outside the OEO and Model City target neighborhoods, Carondelet was the only neighborhood health center to arise in the 1960s (and survive to the late 1970s) without federal assistance.

The history of the health centers begun in the late 1960s was affected by the struggle between OEO and the Department of Housing and Urban Development (HUD), after the Model City program was superimposed on existing OEO districts in 1968. St. Louis CBOs, most of which were brought into being by OEO, became increasingly adept at maneuvering among OEO, HEW, HUD, and City Hall. The competition was intense among Model City/OEO CBOs, each striving to get "one of each" federal benefit available for its neighborhood. But not all CBOs could win in every competition, and decisions about which neighborhood got which facility were complex. Those health centers inaugurated largely by staff of CBOs usually began modestly, utilizing at the outset only volunteer and part-time medical personnel. Four of these, Greeley, Sheridan, Montgomery-Hyde Park, and Pruitt-Igoe, received no significant federal financial assistance and, as a result, were terminated by 1975. The older Grace Hill eventually obtained considerable federal funding (from HEW) and thus has survived to the present. Both Yeatman with its satellite and St. Louis Comprehensive Health Center were products of more elaborate planning processes involving inputs from several federal funding sources; HEW's early and substantial funding support in their evolution virtually guaranteed their survival to the present. The two remaining nonmunicipal health centers inaugurated since 1970, Cochran Gardens and People's Clinic, received no significant direct federal funding as of 1978. Thus, St. Louis provides examples of several of the types of community health centers described above.

MILWAUKEE

In Milwaukee, a number of local community-based efforts to provide health services to medically indigent populations were initiated in the late 1960s. The most ambitious project, the Cream City Neighborhood Health Center, is no longer in existence. The OEO contributed a large proportion of this clinic's total funding. Two smaller clinics, begun with OEO as well as other support, still survive. They are the 16th

Street Community Health Center and the South Side Community Health Clinic. A third community-based effort, the Guadalupe Children's Medical and Dental Clinic, was begun and continues to operate without any federal support.

The Cream City Neighborhood Health Center was located in the inner-city north and sought to serve the mostly black residents of the Harambee area. In spite of substantial community support and $1.5 million in OEO grants, the program ceased operations in 1971. The history of the conflicts which led to termination of the Cream City program are illustrative of situations across the country.

The initial planning for Cream City dates back to 1965. Discussion about the feasibility of establishing a neighborhood health center in the inner-city north was originally begun by local health professionals and representatives of local health care institutions. The committee formed by representatives of these organizations invited the Cream City Medical Society, an organization of local black physicians, dentists, and pharmacists, to participate. This latter group eventually took the lead in the attempt to establish a neighborhood health center. Support from the Social Development Commission (the county anti-poverty agency), the Regional Medical Program, and the Milwaukee Foundation, a local charitable institution, was used to hire a planning staff and set up an office.

The director of the Bureau of Milwaukee Area Services of the state Department of Local Affairs and Development was enlisted to assist and expedite the planning of the center. The "expediter," who met with the national director of OEO about Cream City, believes OEO's enthusiasm and interest were spurred by the hope that the Cream City effort would furnish them with information useful in developing guidelines for the establishment of health maintenance organizations (HMO), which were beginning to generate much interest at the federal level. According to the expediter, the committee in Milwaukee was "immediately conscious of a negative impact from the federal government. (They) interfered. They had ideas on how to do this. They came every month—they were the main cause of its [Cream City's] failure."

The ensuing two years encompassed a continuing struggle among three groups, each with conflicting notions about what Cream City should be. There was the local community, representatives of which had been brought in to compose eventually two-thirds of the thirty-person Cream City board, and who were interested in health education and screening. There was the group of physicians who broke away from the Cream City Medical Society to form their own free-standing corporation—Medical/Dental Limited—and who were interested in contracting with Cream City to provide primary care. And there was OEO, which exerted pressure to hire physicians who would be on salary and work exclusively for Cream City.

The conflicts of interest of the participants—sponsors, providers, and the community—culminated in a struggle over four main policy issues. The first area of conflict was the arrangements for the delivery of primary care by physicians. The black physician group was intent upon remaining a private, fee-for-service group practice, while OEO, with its interest in HMOs, wanted full-time, salaried employment and resisted using public funds to subsidize a private enterprise. The second major policy conflict arose over OEO's insistence that Cream City contract for community board training with an outside professional. Community members, who felt that they knew all about boards, were incensed that the $30,000 for this training would come from their second year, clinic operating funds. The third area of conflict involved all three groups in a disagreement about the role of training of community health workers for employment in preventive and educational services. The expediter and the community saw this training and employment as the most innovative part of the program. The physicians, however, had reservations about the activities of the community health workers, and OEO apparently also had reservations, for funding for this activity was eliminated in the second year.

Finally, differences on the issues discussed above sharply divided the providers and consumers in their choice of director for Cream City. Each faction preferred an administrator who was in philosophical agreement with them. In 1971, with these issues still outstanding, the Cream City Neighborhood Health Center ceased operations. The inability of the three major interest groups to reach a compromise is cited as leading to the failure of the center.

CINCINNATI

The city of Cincinnati offers some interesting lessons by virtue of the characteristics of its publicly sponsored ambulatory care services. One distinctive feature is the flow of federal community health center funds to the local health department as the grantee, an arrangement initiated by HEW's Region 5 and the Cincinnati Health Department in 1975. The other unusual feature is that the Cincinnati Health Department contracts with some local neighborhood health committees for community provision of primary care clinic services, a practice begun in 1973. In 1978, the health department funded six contract centers and nine health department centers within a coordinated, citywide Primary Health Care System. The history of the development of these arrangements is instructive.

During the early 1960s, a strong health commissioner initiated a substantial volunteer program, began organizing and staffing new community clinics based on the European health facility model, and initiated mass immunization programs. As later federal health programs expanded, the activities which had begun in Cincinnati with a volunteer movement matured and became firmly established under Great Society programs, with infusions of federal categorical and block grant dollars. The commissioner's constant push for greater funding and more direct personal health services, however, eventually led to discord with a conservative city council and his resignation in 1967. By the end of the decade the department's programs and leadership were in disarray, as parallel forces among department employees and community groups exerted pressures for change. The dissatisfactions of employees led to the formation in 1969 of a Workers' Council. Over the same period, residents of the various medically underserved neighborhoods of the city began to complain about the low quality and, in most cases, limited availability of clinical services in their areas. The Workers' Council and community groups melded into a strong, community-based, health advocacy organization called the People's Health Movement, which lobbied to achieve a city charter amendment, a referendum enlarging the Board of Health and ensuring a consumer majority, and reconstitution of the entire board. Meanwhile, some of the city's 44 neighborhoods had organized "health committees" to advocate consumer control of new or expanded health services for their communities by having the health department contract with them to purchase nonphysician support services for city or neighborhood-owned health clinics. In January 1973, the city fathers acceded to the demands, and the unusual precedent of the contract centers was established.

The HEW grants to the health department had a distant history in another example of community activism. Originally, the Cincinnati General Hospital and Medical Center applied to OEO for an ambulatory patient care grant to serve the West End and Lincoln Heights communities. At a joint meeting of the West End community representatives and sponsors of the Medical Center's project, it became clear that unless the community had control of the board, the terms of the grant could not be fulfilled. The requirement for community control of a medical center board led the Medical Center to withdraw immediately its application. The communities formed their own ambulatory patient care board, applied for HEW funds, and in 1972 received grants to establish comprehensive services. Overspending and poor fiscal management seemed to characterize the community-sponsored program from the beginning. Therefore, in 1975 HEW decided to transfer funding to the Cincinnati Health Department to be allocated throughout the Primary Health Care System of Cincinnati (which included all health department clinics and contract centers).

Several arguments have been advanced in favor of Cincinnati's Primary Health Care System. The need for each clinic to develop a total range of specialty and supporting services was eliminated by sharing such services at selected clinics with the capability to handle them effectively. Other advantages of this system included the efficiency and cost controls achieved through central administrative services for records and reports, data processing, billing, and purchasing; and uniformity of standards achieved through systemwide evaluation of performance. Finally, a major advantage was the opportunity to negotiate at a department level with the University Medical Center, area hospitals, private agencies, and other city departments to integrate services more effectively.

The primary care system or network approach appears to have worked well in Cincinnati and has been viewed favorably by HEW. The model is useful for planning other ways in which to consolidate primary care funding and route it through a public agency.

BALTIMORE

Baltimore represents a fairly typical city experience with OEO and subsequent HEW neighborhood health centers. The OEO moneys provided for Baltimore neighborhood health center programs in the 1960s went to the visible poverty areas in the west and northwest sections of the city. The programs developed were in response to community pressure exercised in conjunction with overall demands for expanded civil rights for blacks. The oldest OEO clinic was established cooperatively with Provident Hospital (located in West Baltimore) and is now under the auspices of a community health care corporation, Constant Care. As HEW took over responsibility for neighborhood health centers, its geographic focus remained in the west and northwest areas. By 1978, HEW sponsored six grantees in Baltimore: Constant Care, the Mercy-Southern Health Care Center, the North Central Health Corporation, the Park Heights Community Health Center, the West Baltimore Community Health Corporation, and the East Baltimore Medical Plan. A seventh grantee, the Chesapeake Health Plan, was approved, but as of late 1978 had not been funded. The Chesapeake Health Plan is a prepaid medical plan provided by Chesapeake Physicians Professional Association, which serves residents primarily in the eastern sections of Baltimore.

Federal funds provided approximately one-half of the operating expenses of these six community health centers, as well as some 38 National Health Service Corps physicians. All of the centers have cooperative arrangements with area hospitals but function as independent community entities.

A 1979 HHS project in Baltimore was a primary care consortium, composed of representatives from the six federally funded community health centers, as well as from the health department, Central Maryland Health Systems Agency, and Children and Youth programs throughout the city. The purpose of the consortium was to develop a general approach to two specific problem areas which face community health centers: health education and quality assurance. Although the specific goals were fairly limited, the consortium represented a first step in approaching the volatile issues of cooperation among providers and of regionalization of services. The Baltimore environment is much more competitive than that of Cincinnati, at least in the arena of primary care. The relationships of the variety of back-up hospitals associated with the health centers are tinged with the search for inpatients to fill their beds, and this concern filters down to the level of the centers. Relationships of community hospitals to ambulatory care projects will be a point of interest in development of new models of care.

SAN JOSE

San Jose presents an environment where community health centers have been growing, thriving, and going through developmental changes in possibly greater numbers than in any other MHSP city. The centers in Santa Clara County are also strongly grounded in community interest group history and control. These programs tend to be organically developed by community groups which seek funding for services after they are already firmly established, in contrast to cities where funding groups sometimes grope to put together a community board in order to legitimize funding for a project. Although there are many alternative histories of health center program development in San Jose, the story of one program that was encouraged by a number of federal initiatives over the years is informative.

Like other area community clinics, the Alviso Family Health Foundation began as a small volunteer-services facility in a rural, medically underserved Chicano community. A health committee appointed by the community succeeded in obtaining a small planning grant from OEO with the help of Stanford and San Jose State universities. With these funds they were able to rent a building and set up a storefront free clinic with volunteer medical personnel and interested community members. The small rural clinic attempted to retain its community control philosophy, but as services expanded, it slowly became more organized, with less community control and input. .

The clinic grew further after designation as an HEW–subsidized clinic. A more permanent facility with an expanded scope of services, Alviso became more structured, with mandates and conditions to use its resources to serve a wider population base. Originally the patient population at the Alviso clinic was 90 percent Chicano; by 1978 this group represented less than 50 percent of patients. Among the ethnic groups found in Alviso's patient population are Chicanos, blacks, Vietnamese, Cambodians, Laotians, American Indians, Chinese, Japanese, and others. Patients from many economic levels and payment sources come from Sunnyvale, Mountain View, San Jose, and Alviso to use the facility. It is still funded by HHS, but reliance upon this source declined from 80 percent of its revenues to about 30 percent by 1978.

Under the Reagan governorship, Alviso in 1972–1973 was the first service provider in California to enter into a prepaid health plan arrangement with the state, and had enrolled 3,000 prepaid patients by

1979. According to clinic administrators, not much thought was given to the consequences of the plan, which was conceived mainly as a new source of revenue. The plan locked Alviso into contracts for back-up services with Stanford Medical Center and Valley Medical Center, expensive teaching institutions compared to local community hospitals. Alviso's use of a local community hospital for some of its back-up services has been the source of conflict in the past between Valley Medical Center and Alviso.

Alviso clinic administrators reported an active patient load of 21,000 with an average of 7,000 to 8,000 visits per month in 1977. The 1977 clinic budget exceeded $4.5 million. Alviso, in order to expand its geographic base and attract more enrollees to its prepaid health plan, has initiated establishment of two satellite clinics, one in eastside San Jose and a second in central and south-central San Jose—the Franklin-McKinley Clinic. This site, which has its own community advisory committee, was slated for a great deal of expansion from its original primary care services. Franklin-McKinley is the recipient of federal Urban Health Initiative (UHI) funds and is operated by Alviso under a contract with Santa Clara County. Public services to be colocated by the county at the clinic include social services, outpatient alcoholism services, community mental health, and vocational services. The UHI objectives of integrating multiple funding sources and programs fit nicely with Alviso's needs. As a spin-off with its origins in an OEO–sponsored project, the satellite clinic represents an interesting agglomeration of several strategies: prepaid health care, the integration of federal programs, county-delivered public health services, colocation of social services, and community activism.

Summary

We have reviewed three types of strategies for improving the lot of the urban poor in the health arena. Initiated by the federal government but in actuality joint ventures with states, counties, cities, and community groups, these strategies have attempted to address problems of financing, limited resource capacity, access to services, and the differential health status of groups within the population. As the illustrations and our discussion have shown, each strategy, while leading to improvements in access to health services for the nation's poor, has been subject to shortcomings in management structure, to costs which exceed resources, or to inequitable distribution of benefits. Many of the urban and rural poor are still without access to adequate services and still exhibit low health status by such measures as infant mortality, incidence of certain communicable and chronic diseases, and life expectancy.

Categorical program funding has left many of the near-poor—those not eligible for welfare support—substantially without primary health services, and has presented local health officials a panoply of conflicting regulations and restrictions to be dealt with. The patient is faced with a bewildering list of criteria for participation and a complex array of providers to locate in order to obtain various services. Integration of resources and services, while often sought by local officials, is generally opposed by special interest groups as well as by a diverse bureaucracy required to maintain single-program accountability. Thus, the obstacles to achieving comprehensive services under categorical funding remain unchanged.

Short of a major overhaul of the Medicaid system cities have no choice but to design their ambulatory care strategies in the context of the current and increasing constraints in the program. This means that the differentials in eligibility and benefits among states are likely to persist or even widen. At the same time, inflation will lessen everyone's purchasing power. A significant proportion of the uninsured near-poor will remain ineligible for Medicaid. Private providers cannot be counted upon to participate in greater numbers (unless expected increases in physician manpower supply seriously alter current behavior patterns). Local health officials advocating improved ambulatory care reimbursement rates or a reallocation of current Medicaid funds will be expected to demonstrate, if not cost savings to the total system, at least some form of cost benefit. Some less ambitious efforts, such as administrative actions, may provide marginal improvements in the revenue picture.

Third, as we have seen in the review of federally sponsored community health centers, the OEO experience and its aftermath led to the establishment in many areas of a new alternative model for primary care service delivery. Experience with community health centers varied widely across cities. In Milwaukee and St. Louis, the period was marked by false starts and disorganization, with a number of health center failures. In Baltimore and San Jose, despite some funding and program uncertainties over the years, a joint federal-local effort emerged to establish a number of relatively stable health centers, generally affiliated with voluntary hospitals in Baltimore, and generally community-oriented and -managed in San Jose. In Cincinnati, a unique partnership developed that linked federal and local government as well as public and private sector providers by funneling all federal community health center dollars through the local health department to private centers via contracts. In some cities, community health centers have acquired active constituencies and vocal support at the local level, and have organized federations with other centers to lobby for funding at the state and federal levels. The community health centers that were able to achieve relative stability became established members of the local health care system and the major source of care for certain segments of the poor and minority community.

While there are many different ways to measure the success or failure of the community health center movement, whatever their opinions, local governments are obliged to come to terms with the centers as political forces in the community. This may mean integration within a citywide health network, peaceful coexistence, or outright competition for patients and funding.

While the disadvantaged in all our nation's cities have many common problems in terms of the availability, quality, and comprehensiveness of care, these similarities should not obscure the fact that no form of social intervention that is national in scope is likely to be implemented in the same way and with equivalent results in every locality. As the illustrations offered in this chapter indicate, a host of variables must be considered in each community, and it is not easy to predict how they will interact. This does not mean that local, state, or federal governments should avoid reforms of existing programs or experiments with new systems, but merely that a strong appreciation for and a detailed knowledge of the diversity among communities is a necessary precondition for devising effective solutions. Indeed, there are lessons of national importance to be learned from local governments which take the initiative to identify gaps in health services and build upon existing resources. Inevitably, this involves integrating current federal programs into the planning process.

What are the legacies of the past federal strategies for improving ambulatory health care for the urban poor? Although sufficient financing has not been available for adequate implementation of the community health center model, agreement is fairly general that comprehensive primary care at the neighborhood level is desirable to meet the health care needs of the urban poor. It is also generally accepted that the neighborhood primary care resources should be closely linked to the major existing sources of specialty and inpatient care, the local hospitals. Such linkage is becoming more and more attractive to the hospitals, as well, as they compete for patients. It is also clear that given existing interest groups, power bases, and resource shortages, improvement strategies must make major efforts at integration of existing programs rather than the creation of new structures. Thus, it will be essential to tap into the support constituencies of existing sources of strength at the local level, including such political leadership as the mayor and the health officials as well as the local health institutions. In order to assure that resources are allocated to best fill community needs and in order to assure political viability of new programs, needs assessments that include the input of community group constituencies will be valuable exercises. All these lessons have direct implications for the conceptualization and structure of such new strategies for the urban poor as the Municipal Health Services Program, which will be demonstrated in succeeding chapters.

References

1. Robert M. Gibson, "National Health Expenditures, 1979," *Health Care Financing Review* 2, no. 1 (Summer 1980): 7.

2. Karen Davis and Cathy Schoen, *Health and the War on Poverty: A Ten-Year Appraisal* (Washington, D.C.: The Brookings Institution, 1978).

3. Office of Management and Budget, *Catalog of Federal Domestic Assistance* (Washington, D.C.: Government Printing Office, 1976).

4. Robert Stevens and Rosemary Stevens, *Welfare Medicine in America: A Case Study of Medicaid* (New York: The Free Press, 1974), p. 53.

5. Davis and Schoen, *Health and the War on Poverty*, p. 51.

6. Committee on Public Health, "Health Services in New York City," *Bulletin of the New York Academy of Medicine* 43, no. 9 (September 1967): 844.

7. Davis and Schoen, *Health and the War on Poverty*, p. 56.

8. Gibson, "National Health Expenditures," p. 7.

9. Davis and Schoen, *Health and the War on Poverty*, pp. 62–67.

10. State of Missouri, Office of the Attorney General, Statement January 2, 1980.

11. Davis and Schoen, *Health and the War on Poverty*, p. 170.

12. Ibid., pp. 160, 170–71.

13. David Hayes-Bautista, "Deviant Delivery Systems," paper presented to Western Health Consortium, San Francisco, California, February 12, 1976.

14. M. A. Morehead, R. S. Donaldson and M. R. Seravalli, "Comparisons Between OEO Neighborhood Health Centers and Other Health Care Providers of Ratings of the Quality of Health Care," *American Journal of Public Health* 61 (July 1971): 1294–1306.

15. Davis and Schoen, *Health and the War on Poverty*, pp. 184–85.

CHAPTER TWO

The City's Role in Health: Structure and Financing of Care for the Poor

Traditionally, the responsibility for provision of health care for the poor has fallen upon units of local government. We have discussed the role of policy initiatives and dollar flows that originated at federal and state government levels. The actual delivery of services occurs at the local level, however, and the legal responsibility for caring for the poor rests with city and county governments.

In view of the critical role of local government in financing and delivering much of the health care for the poor, we will now closely examine responsibility for health care services delivery within the context of local government. How are functions distributed among city and county public health and hospital departments? How do these agencies relate to one another and to the central authority of elected and appointed officials? How do the federal and state governments make their presence felt at the local level?

The fifty largest cities, those which were eligible to apply for funding through the Municipal Health Services Program (MHSP), provide the basis for our examination of structure and financing. In 1975, these fifty cities ranged in size from New York, with an estimated population of 7,481,613, to Charlotte, North Carolina, at 281,417. Of the five cities selected to participate in the MHSP, four were among the top 25, while Cincinnati ranked 31st with 412,564 people. Baltimore, in seventh place, was the largest, with a population of 851,698, more than double that of Cincinnati. Milwaukee ranked 14th at 665,796; San Jose, 21st at 555,707; and St. Louis, 24th at 524,964 (see Table 2.1).

TABLE 2.1

SELECTED DEMOGRAPHIC AND SOCIOECONOMIC INDICATORS FOR THE FIFTY LARGEST
U.S. CITIES

Cities ranked by size	Estimated population 1975	Urban conditions index (rank)	Percent population change 1960-1975	Percent poverty 1970	Percent pre-1940 housing 1970
1. New York	7,471,613	222 (17)	- 3.9	14.7	62.1
2. Chicago	3,099,391	255 (12)	- 12.7	14.3	66.5
3. Los Angeles	2,727,399	85 (32)	- 2.5	11.2	31.6
4. Philadelphia	1,815,808	271 (10)	- 9.3	15.1	69.5
5. Detroit	1,335,085	266 (11)	- 20.1	14.7	61.8
6. Houston	1,326,809	40 (43)	41.4	13.9	17.3
7. Baltimore	851,698	279 (9)	- 9.3	18.0	60.0
8. Dallas	812,797	48 (40)	19.6	13.3	18.1
9. San Diego	773,996	42 (42)	35.0	11.0	21.7
10. San Antonio	773,248	99 (29)	31.6	21.5	25.8
11. Indianapolis	714,878	59 (37)	50.1	9.5	39.7
12. Washington, DC	711,518	193 (18)	- 6.9	16.3	47.0
13. Honolulu	705,381	15 (49)	139.8	8.9	20.0
14. Milwaukee	665,796	161 (20)	- 10.2	11.2	55.0
15. Phoenix	664,721	21 (48)	51.4	11.6	11.2
16. San Francisco	664,520	237 (14)	- 10.2	13.6	66.9
17. Memphis	661,319	86 (31)	32.9	20.4	23.0
18. Cleveland	638,793	400 (3)	- 27.1	17.0	73.3
19. Boston	636,725	303 (7)	- 8.7	15.3	77.3
20. New Orleans	559,770	340 (6)	- 10.8	26.2	49.4
21. San Jose	555,707	11 (50)	172.1	8.6	13.9
22. Columbus, OH	535,610	106 (28)	13.6	13.2	39.0
23. Jacksonville, FL	535,030	31 (46)	166.1	16.8	20.9
24. St. Louis	524,964	487 (1)	- 30.0	19.7	73.9
25. Seattle	487,091	128 (25)	- 12.6	10.0	47.6
26. Denver	484,531	131 (24)	- 1.9	13.4	41.0
27. Kansas City, MO	472,529	151 (22)	- 0.6	12.5	51.3
28. Pittsburgh	458,651	344 (5)	- 24.1	15.0	74.4
29. Atlanta	436,057	157 (21)	- 10.5	19.8	30.3
30. Nashville-Davidson	423,426	31 (45)	147.8	13.1	24.8
31. Cincinnati	412,564	289 (8)	- 17.9	17.1	59.3
32. Buffalo	407,160	388 (4)	- 23.6	14.8	85.7
33. El Paso	385,691	78 (36)	39.4	20.4	22.7
34. Minneapolis	378,112	234 (15)	- 21.7	11.5	68.1
35. Omaha	371,455	91 (30)	23.2	10.4	46.1
36. Toledo	367,650	123 (26)	15.6	10.7	56.8
37. Oklahoma City	365,916	84 (34)	12.8	13.9	29.1
38. Miami	365,082	114 (27)	25.2	20.3	29.9
39. Fort Worth	358,364	83 (35)	0.6	13.3	26.7
40. Portland, OR	356,732	176 (19)	- 4.3	12.6	57.2
41. Newark	339,568	422 (2)	- 16.2	22.1	68.4
42. Louisville	335,954	246 (13)	- 14.0	17.0	53.2
43. Long Beach	335,602	85 (33)	- 2.5	11.2	31.6
44. Tulsa	331,726	57 (38)	26.8	11.9	25.9
45. Oakland	330,651	225 (16)	- 10.0	16.2	53.3
46. Austin	301,147	40 (44)	61.4	15.9	17.0
47. Tucson	296,457	30 (47)	39.3	13.6	13.1
48. Baton Rouge	294,394	56 (39)	92.5	18.6	20.7
49. Norfolk	286,694	132 (23)	- 6.0	17.3	30.5
50. Charlotte	281,417	48 (41)	39.6	14.8	19.3

SOURCE: For population estimates, Bureau of the Census, City Government
Finances in 1975-76, GF 76, No. 4 (U.S. Department of Commerce),
Table 1. For urban conditions index and components, Paul Dommel et
al., Decentralizing Community Development (Washington, D.C., U.S.
Department of Housing and Urban Development, 1978), App.2.

The first section of this chapter will discuss the variations in municipal health care roles among large U.S. cities as of the mid-1970s. The variety of legal and structural arrangements between city and county will be examined. An assessment will be made of local government responsibilities in terms of the range of financial commitments to health care made by cities and counties, and in terms of the delivery system: health department services and public hospital services. The public sector delivery systems in Baltimore, Cincinnati, St. Louis, Milwaukee, and San Jose will be described briefly here, and in detail in Chapter Three.

The second section of the chapter will deal with the array of forces underlying the structure of the public health services in each of these five cities and shaping the demands upon the system as well as the resources available to it. A primary group of such forces includes demographic and socioeconomic trends in the locality, with reference to their implications for urban decline versus urban growth. A closely related set of considerations includes the status of minority ethnic group tension and local health politics. The third group of underlying forces is related to the overall structure of local government; included are the relationships among major actors, the relative strengths of mayor and city council, the characteristics of the local budgetary process as it relates to health services funding, and the effects, if any, of civil service or union constraints on management and production of local health services.

By examining the structure, financing, and delivery systems for public health care for the urban poor, and by exploring the cities' underlying socioeconomic trends, political environments, and governmental structures, we will begin to clarify the dynamic relationships which influence decisions about the allocation of resources within the local health arena as well as between health and other local government functions. We will then be able to comprehend better the status of publicly sponsored ambulatory care for the urban poor in each of the five cities.

Variations in Municipal Health Care Roles

Under the American federal system of government, most units of local government are creatures of the states. States are empowered to issue charters, to define the jurisdictions, and to delineate the powers and responsibilities of local governments. Thus, the states are the key determinants of the legal structure of localities. Particularly important, states control powers of annexation and taxation for local governmental entities, including not only counties and municipalities, but also towns, townships, and the great variety of special districts. Local government responsibility for service delivery and local capacity to generate revenue to finance those services thus depend upon crucial decisions made beyond the local level.

There is tremendous variability in the structure of local government and in the financing of local services. In many localities, there are multiple governmental entities with overlapping jurisdictions, sometimes with duplicative functions. Responsibility for provision of a particular service may vary from state to state, county to county, or city to city. Hospital services may be provided by a municipality, county, township, hospital district, or other entity, any of which may have taxing powers. Among the array of services commonly provided by local government, welfare and education show the greatest variation in terms of the locus of financial responsibility.[1] Health services also are characterized by a great variety of arrangements for financing and delivery.

This section of the chapter will address first the structure of local government responsibility for health services. It then will detail the financial commitment to health services by municipalities and by all local government units within the counties which contain central cities.

STRUCTURE OF LOCAL GOVERNMENT RESPONSIBILITY FOR HEALTH

Most of the nation's fifty largest cities are located in areas where county governments also exist. The municipality is generally contained within the boundaries and jurisdiction of the county. In some cases, the municipality is independent of the county. This is true of St. Louis, Philadelphia, San Francisco, and Baltimore, for example. New York City subsumes five counties, whose governmental activities have atrophied and been replaced by municipal functions. The geographic boundary relationship of municipality to county has great significance for the structure and financing of health services. This is due to the fact that in the case of most large cities, central cities have lost upper- and middle-income residents to suburban county areas, creating a great imbalance in tax base between city and county, to the disadvantage of the city. The demands placed upon the city health services delivery system by the remaining concentration of low-income citizens exacerbate the imbalance. St. Louis has suffered particularly harshly as an independent city because city residents are ineligible for public health department or public hospital services provided by the adjacent county and because no county tax revenues are available to subsidize costly central city services.

In many areas, even where municipalities are part of the surrounding county, both city and county operate a public health department. Among the fifty cities which in 1975 had the largest estimated populations in the United States, thirty-three operated municipal public health departments (see Table 2.2) in 1978. Forty-four cities are part of surrounding county jurisdictions; in only two instances was there no county public health department. Thirteen of the fifty largest cities had public health departments that were operated as combined en-

TABLE 2.2

AUSPICES OF OPERATION OF PUBLIC HOSPITAL AND HEALTH DEPARTMENT SERVICES
FOR FIFTY LARGEST CITIES, 1978

Cities ranked by size	Health Department		Hospital(s)[a]				
	City	County	City	City/County	County	Hospital authority	State
1. New York (city subsumes 5 counties)	Yes	-	17	-	-	-	-
2. Chicago	Yes	Yes	-	-	1	-	1
3. Los Angeles	No	Yes	-	-	2 (1 univ.)	-	1
4. Philadelphia (independent city)	Yes (combined)	Yes	-	-	-	-	-
5. Detroit	Yes	Yes	1	-	-	-	-
6. Houston	Yes	Yes	1	-	-	2	-
7. Baltimore (independent city)	Yes	-	1	-	-	2	2 (1 univ.)
8. Dallas	Yes	Yes	-	-	-	2	-
9. San Diego	No	Yes	-	-	-	-	1 (univ.)
10. San Antonio	Yes (combined)	Yes	-	-	-	2	-
11. Indianapolis	No	Yes	-	-	1	-	1 (univ.)
12. Washington, DC (independent city)	Yes	-	1	-	-	-	1 (univ.)
13. Honolulu	Yes	No	-	-	-	-	-
14. Milwaukee	Yes	Yes	-	-	2	-	-
15. Phoenix	No	Yes	-	-	1	-	-
16. San Francisco (coterminous w/county)	Yes (combined)	Yes	-	2	-	-	-
17. Memphis	No	Yes	-	-	1	3	-
18. Cleveland	Yes	Yes	-	-	2	-	1 (univ.)
19. Boston	Yes	No	3	-	-	-	-
20. New Orleans	No	Yes	-	-	-	-	1 (univ.)
21. San Jose	No	Yes	-	-	1	-	-
22. Columbus, OH	Yes	Yes	-	-	-	-	1 (univ.)
23. Jacksonville, FL	No	Yes	-	-	-	1 (univ.)	-
24. St. Louis (independent city)	Yes	-	4	-	-	-	-
25. Seattle	Yes (combined)	Yes	-	-	1 (univ.)	-	1 (univ.)

City	(66% Yes)	(84% Yes)	8 Cities 29 Hospitals	6 Cities 8 Hospitals	17 Cities 21 Hospitals	10 Cities 20 Hospitals	18 Cities 20 Hospitals
26. Denver (coterminous w/county)	Yes	Yes (combined)	–	–	–	–	1 (univ.)
27. Kansas City, MO	Yes	Yes	–	–	1	–	–
28. Pittsburgh	No	Yes	–	–	1	–	1
29. Atlanta	No	Yes	–	–	–	3	–
30. Nashville-Davidson	Yes	Yes (combined)	2	–	–	–	–
31. Cincinnati	Yes	Yes	1[b]	1	1	–	1 (univ.)
32. Buffalo	No	Yes	–	1	1	–	–
33. El Paso	Yes	Yes (combined)	–	–	1	1	–
34. Minneapolis	Yes	Yes	–	–	1	–	1 (univ.)
35. Omaha	Yes	Yes (combined)	–	–	1	–	1 (univ.)
36. Toledo	No	Yes	–	–	–	–	1 (univ.)
37. Oklahoma City	Yes	Yes (combined)	–	–	–	1	2 (univ.)
38. Miami	Yes	No	–	–	–	1	–
39. Fort Worth	Yes	Yes (combined)	–	–	–	1	–
40. Portland, OR	No	No	–	–	–	2	1 (univ.)
41. Newark	Yes	Yes	–	–	–	–	1 (univ.)
42. Louisville	Yes	Yes (combined)	–	1	1	–	1 (univ.)
43. Long Beach	Yes	Yes	–	–	1	–	–
44. Tulsa	No	Yes (combined)	–	–	1	–	–
45. Oakland	Yes	No	–	–	2	–	–
46. Austin	Yes	Yes	1	–	1	–	–
47. Tucson	No	No	–	–	1	–	–
48. Baton Rouge	Yes	Yes (combined)	–	–	1	–	1 (univ.)
49. Norfolk (independent city)	–	Yes	1	–	–	–	1
50. Charlotte	No	Yes	–	–	–	3	–
TOTAL	66% Yes	84% Yes	8 Cities 29 Hospitals	6 Cities 8 Hospitals	17 Cities 21 Hospitals	10 Cities 20 Hospitals	18 Cities 20 Hospitals

[a] Hospitals include all public general acute, rehabilitative and chronic facilities, and exclude tuberculosis, mental, and jail facilities.

[b] University of Cincinnati Medical Center includes the Cincinnati General Hospital, a city/county facility, and Christian R. Holmes Hospital, a state facility.

SOURCE: U.S. Conference of City Health Officials and U.S. Conference of Mayors, Directory of Local Health Officials (Washington, D.C., 1978). American Hospital Association, Guide to the Health Care Field (Chicago, 1979).

tities with the county health department. In twelve other cases, both the municipality and the county operated public health departments in 1978. Depending upon the locality, there may be some division of responsibilities between city and county health departments, especially in the realm of personal health service delivery. Both city and county health departments generally provide traditional public health services such as water, milk, and restaurant inspection; vital statistics registry; communicable disease registry; and vector control. Nevertheless, often only one of the two agencies is the recipient of categorical grant funds for such specific preventive services as a Maternal and Infant Care (MIC) program, a high blood pressure control program, a specific family planning program such as Title XX or Title X, or a Women, Infants and Children (WIC) nutrition program. Depending upon local history and upon policies of the state department of health, which distributes most categorical funds, either the city or the county health department may be the one that emphasizes personal preventive health services.

The responsibility for provision of health services for the poor is translated in most localities into the operation of public general hospital facilities. The auspices of operation of the public hospital may be any one or a combination of levels of local government, including city, county, city/county, or hospital authority. Additionally, in many large cities, state governments operate public general hospitals, often affiliated with university medical schools which are major providers of care to the urban poor. Table 2.2 shows the number of public hospitals operated in 1978 by various levels of government in each of the fifty largest cities. Excluded from the tally are psychiatric, tuberculosis, research-specific, and jail or school annex facilities; included are chronic and rehabilitative institutions.

By 1978, only eight of these cities operated public hospitals. New York was unique with a system of seventeen municipal institutions. The only other cities operating more than one municipal public hospital were St. Louis with four (now only three) and Boston with three. No public hospital (under any auspices) existed in Philadelphia (which had recently closed its public facility), Honolulu, or Tulsa. In seventeen cities, hospitals were run under county government auspices, while in six, one or two combined city/county hospitals existed. Hospital authorities were responsible for public facilities in ten cities. State governments operated public general acute or chronic/rehabilitative hospitals in eighteen cities—the most frequently occurring arrangement among the fifty cities. Nearly all these state hospitals were university-affiliated. One city/county, one hospital authority, and two county facilities were also university-affiliated. In only ten cities were public hospitals operated by more than one level of government. Except for New York, the largest number of public general acute and chronic/rehabilitative hospitals operated by all levels of local and state government was five, in Memphis. No other city contained more than three such hospitals within its boundaries.

Among the fifty largest cities, municipally operated hospitals tend to be found in older cities of the Northeast and the North Central states. Hospital authorities are particularly prevalent in the South and Southwest, especially in Texas. Combined city/county hospitals are not found at all among large, old, northeastern cities. County hospitals are widely and fairly evenly distributed, as are state and university-affiliated facilities. Although psychiatric institutions were excluded from consideration here, it should be noted that responsibility for these services is almost universally a state governmental function. The role of the states in determining the boundaries and functions of local government responsibility is intimated in the patterns of distribution of the operational authority for public hospital services. Also implied are differences rooted in the age of the city and in its geographic location, variables which will be discussed in detail later in this chapter.

A further dimension of the structure of municipal public health and public hospital services is the degree of integration between the two. Historically, there has been a significant disparity in philosophy between the health department and the hospital in their approaches to health services. The traditional public health department provided services that were oriented toward population groups and that emphasized preventive activities, such as mass immunization, rodent and insect control, and monitoring of communicable diseases, as well as sanitary inspection of public facilities and of the food and water supplies. In contrast, public hospitals have developed into centers of curative medical services focused on the individual. In fact, outpatient departments and emergency rooms of municipal hospitals, especially those teaching hospitals affiliated with medical schools, have evolved into multispecialty clinic settings that have been criticized for focusing too narrowly on only one organ, system, or disease of the individual. Thus, there has developed a generalized potential conflict between the styles and objectives of the two public agencies: the public health department with its preventive, population group orientation, and the public hospital with its curative, individual or illness-based approach to health care.

In a particularly illuminating paper, William Shonick has examined the changes in the legal and functional relationships between public health departments and public hospitals in twelve urban areas since World War II. His investigation centers on the motivation, implementation, and outcome of mergers between health departments and public hospitals. The following discussion is based primarily on this study. Shonick notes:

The direct delivery of personal health services by local government agencies has been undergoing many changes in the past 25 years, affecting both the content and quantity of the services themselves, as well as the organization of the agencies delivering them. . . . two major developments after World War II were particularly important in bringing about the increased interest in mergers in the 1970s: the accelerated deterioration of the older larger cities and a growing perception in most public executive and managerial circles that local governmental consolidation was needed to increase efficiency.[2]

Among the urban areas he studied, Shonick found two major sets of health department-hospital consolidations. The first set were "loosely coupled" consolidations resulting from good government motives in or before the early 1950s. The second set were "firmly coupled" mergers taking place from about 1966 to 1974. Major changes occurred to influence these later mergers.

These events included: a rapid acceleration in the economic decline of many older large cities, a coincident acceleration in the rate of inflation, a rapid growth in the demand for local public services in the growing population "sunbelt" areas, the passage of Medicare and Medicaid and other "great society" programs of the 1960s, an expansion of enrollments in state-owned medical schools, a decline in the average daily census coupled with an increase in bed capacity of private hospitals, and demographic changes in the large cities with their accompanying political turbulence. The "later" mergers were in large part responses to these events whereas the "earlier" unifications, of course, were not.[3]

While Shonick commented upon influences and conditions affecting mergers, he was quick to point out the variation of situations from locality to locality, and emphasized that the study did not identify necessary or sufficient "causes" for mergers.

There were, however, several frequently articulated goals for mergers, three of which were efficiency-oriented and one, quality-oriented. The latter focused on improvement of care through the creation of a coordinated and comprehensive primary care system, while the efficiency goals included better management through cost control and reduced span of control, reduction of bureaucratic red tape, and improved revenue collection capabilities. Shonick found that, in general, these goals were not met, and often progress was not measured. Only Denver is cited as having achieved the quality goal of a viable, comprehensive system of regionalized health services for public sector patients. Other areas where mergers had been effected experienced moderate improvement in their primary care services, organizationally and financially, but so did areas which did not merge agencies.

Among Shonick's comments on the implementation of decreed mergers are many useful lessons. Only in the case of Denver, which merged successfully, did the impetus for merger come as much from the agencies involved as from the local government. An emphasis placed by administrative personnel on increasing collections for ambulatory care and on instituting more complex management techniques often led to criticism by health professionals that uninsured patients were discouraged from utilizing services. Obstacles to merger implementation arose from internal and external sources. The major external impediment was the lack of necessary additional dollars to expand services, along with harrassment of the new agency by local political forces. The main internal impediments included two facets of professional domain conflict.

One facet of the domain conflict was the public health-curative health rivalry. The prior existence of a highly developed Haven Emerson type standard public health department was a strong impediment to the successful implementation of a merger plan. . . . The other facet of this rivalry that impeded the development of a neighborhood-based health care system in merged agencies was the preexistence of a well established public hospital, particularly if it was associated with a dominating teaching program. The impedance took two forms: The goals of the medical teaching program were not entirely the same as those of an agency focusing on health care and service to clients; and if the teaching program was run by a medical school, especially a state-owned one, the public hospital was often faced with a takeover by the medical school. The latter eventuality became especially imminent when coupled with increasing efforts by the sponsoring local government to free its budget of the expense of maintaining the public general hospital.

Local public officials, both staff and elected, who strongly pushed mergers as a means of reducing their span of control, were quite generally unaware of the depth of the differences between the training and outlook of public health and clinical personnel, and they were equally unaware of the differences between the priorities of teaching hospitals and service hospitals.[4]

These findings are useful in considering how to formulate new strategies for approaching increased demands for publicly sponsored primary care in a context of constrained resources and calls for efficiency. Perhaps the most salient of Shonick's findings are, first, that reliable and adequate funding is the real bottom line and, second, that it is the process of working toward specific programmatic and managerial goals, rather than the decree of legal organizational form, that is important in improving local public health service delivery.

We now will examine some details of the structure of the public sector health delivery system in Cincinnati, Milwaukee, St. Louis, Baltimore, and San Jose.

Cincinnati. The city of Cincinnati has had a public health department since 1826. The department is subject to the authority of a nine-member independent Board of Health. Operating with a minimum 51 percent consumer representation, the members are appointed by the mayor for three-year staggered terms. The board is responsible for setting policy for the department, providing community input, and hiring and firing the health commissioner. Members may also assist the commissioner in budget negotiations with the city manager and may advocate health policies before the city council. Since the board's reorganization in 1971, which strengthened the role of consumers, it has become a more vital component of the health department operation.

In addition to the Cincinnati Health Department, Hamilton County also contains eight independent health departments, as well as a "catch-all" county health department. Many of the smaller health departments utilize the services of the city and county health departments on a contract basis, but prefer independence because of a state law that permits incorporated areas of 4,000 residents to receive state funding for health department activities. The Hamilton County Health Department mainly provides traditional preventive, population-based services outside the Cincinnati city limits. Cincinnati has long complained that the county does not pay for its share of health care services in the area, since many Hamilton County residents living outside the city limits utilize the city's health care services. It has been the hope of recent administrations that more county services will eventually be provided on a contract basis by the Cincinnati Health Department.

While the health department serves the city and is funded, in part, by the city, it is legally a creature of the state and its mission is defined by law. Because Ohio is a "home rule" state, in practice the Cincinnati Health Department is relatively autonomous of the state health department. Even so, the city department does administer many state-funded programs and conducts state inspection programs of hospitals and nursing homes. Most significant, the department is responsible for a network of primary care centers funded from local, state, and federal dollars. A major effort goes into personal health services, both through department-operated clinics and through centers contractually operated by community groups, an unusual arrangement. The Cincinnati Health Department is the grantee for all moneys, but consumer participation is extensive at both community-run contract centers and health department centers.

The decade of the 1970s saw a shift in orientation of Cincinnati General Hospital from an urban, public general hospital to a university medical center. The change was accomplished by a transfer of responsibility from the city to the University of Cincinnati and the subsequent transformation of the university from a municipal to a state institution. The city government does not have any direct input to hospital policy, although it lends its support in budgetary matters and in seeking favorable planning decisions. Technically, however, the city still owns the buildings and land occupied by Cincinnati General Hospital. Even though they were turned over to the state under a long-term lease, the lease protects certain city interests. For example, if the hospital were to significantly alter its mission toward the indigent, the city could take initiative to correct the situation.

An important consideration about the public hospital in Cincinnati is the degree of complexity of its administrative and financial structure. The hospital has municipal roots, serves both a city and a county population, and now is officially a state institution. Administration of the hospital is many layers removed from its trustees, with medical center, medical school, and university decision makers between. Medical staff are under the control of the medical school, creating a bipartite structure even internally. This type of complexity is to be found in varying forms in other cities, as well.

Cincinnati provides an example of a strong city health department that has entered the arena of personal health service delivery through seeking state and federal grant dollars. The county health department is a less strong, more traditional agency. The public hospital is an example of the increasing interest and power of medical education in the urban public hospital arena and of the pressure on local government to shift the burden of finance to other levels of government.

Milwaukee. The responsibility for the provision of health services to the poor and medically indigent population of Milwaukee has traditionally been assumed by the Milwaukee City Health Department and the Milwaukee County Medical Complex (MCMC). The health department interprets its role as one of providing a range of preventive and educational health services to the community. The city commissioner of health, a physician, brought to his present job the conviction that the delivery of primary care was properly an activity of the county and that the role of the city health department should be confined to preventive services. The city role is defined by him as "gap filling": the city is not *providing* care but *assuring* that it is provided.

The Milwaukee County Medical Complex includes in its organization all countywide medical and mental health services. The MCMC provides primary care and inpatient services, and also serves as the major educational facility for the Medical College of Wisconsin. The Medical College and the Medical Complex are located in Wauwatosa, a western suburb of Milwaukee, on county grounds.

In many respects the Milwaukee County Hospital shares the problems of Cincinnati General with its multiple lines of authority. While it is not unusual to find policy conflicts in any hospital among administrators, governing boards, and the medical staff, these differences are greatly amplified in public hospitals that have major affiliation with medical schools because of conflicts between service goals and teaching goals. The relationship of the Medical College of Wisconsin to the Milwaukee County Hospital has been a controversial issue. At the base of the controversy is the belief of some critics that the hospital's existence is owed to the medical school affiliation and that less expensive, more convenient care could be delivered by private inner-city hospitals with the funds that now support a suburban public hospital with a daily rate of more than $400. On the one hand, the medical school and its supporters view their contribution as meeting the health manpower needs of the state while providing a wide range of primary, secondary, and tertiary services to the immediate region. The critics, on the other hand, argue that health service needs of the community at large are subservient to the medical school's priorities, where students and faculty are concerned.

Several studies of Milwaukee County Hospital's role and operations have been undertaken in recent years, highlighting weaknesses in the administrative structure under the county's Board of Public Welfare. The following is excerpted from a position paper issued in 1979 by the county executive's office:

Like a bowl of spaghetti, Milwaukee County's Board of Public Welfare deals with hopelessly tangled and intertwined programs between social services and medical delivery systems. In the last five years, over a dozen major research efforts have called for separation of county medical services from the social programs which are largely a product of state and federal misdirection.[5]

Despite the fact that county government is responsible for reimbursing the uncollectibles at the hospital and in effect underwrites the costs of the teaching programs, county board members have nonetheless been supportive of medical school objectives because of their strong desire to keep a major medical center that also provides a sizable number of county jobs.

Milwaukee presents a case of a city with a relatively small poverty population and low demand on public health services. The city and its surrounding county have supported a costly suburban public teaching hospital to which the inner-city poor must travel. The Milwaukee Health Department is a traditional agency which has resisted becoming involved in direct primary care delivery, and pressures have not developed to force it to do so. The county has assumed responsibility for all direct personal health care delivery to the city's poor, and has coped with any criticism of the heavy involvement of the Medical College in the public hospital. This town-gown tension, characteristic of public hospital-medical school relationships, is not unique to Milwaukee, but rather is an instance of a common dilemma. Without medical school self-interest and leadership, public hospitals often deteriorate; with them, issues of governance, cost, and public accountability present formidable problems.

St. Louis. While health sector functions in Milwaukee are dispersed among agencies at different levels of local government, St. Louis is an example of a metropolitan area in which functions are consolidated in a single city agency. Since it is also a county, the city of St. Louis inherits the *de facto* responsibility of providing health care for indigent citizens through its Department of Health and Hospitals, which was created in 1958 by removing these two agencies from the cumbersome Department of Public Welfare.

The city's Department of Health and Hospitals is headed by a director who oversees two major division heads, the commissioner of hospitals and the commissioner of health. The hospital commissioner is responsible for the outpatient, inpatient, and emergency medical services provided in two acute care hospitals (in 1978; one of these, Homer G. Phillips, closed in 1979); the rehabilitative, skilled nursing, intermediate, and domiciliary services provided in two long-term care facilities; and laboratory services at the public Snodgras Laboratory. In addition to traditional public health functions such as preventive services, environmental health, operation of the Public Health Laboratory, etc., the health commissioner is responsible for personal health services offered at four (in 1978) municipal health centers.

The organizational structure of a single agency managing both health and hospitals would seem to suggest greater flexibility in the use of resources and more effective administrative control than in localities in which authority is fragmented. Nevertheless, several factors have superseded any advantage one might ascribe to the consolidated administrative authority under the Department of Health and Hospitals. One such factor is fragmented power among the city's elected leadership, which tends to limit the direction and support a strong city agency would need to make tough political decisions. And in view of the recent economic and demographic fortunes of St. Louis, these decisions have indeed been tough.

Additionally, the city's Department of Health and Hospitals labored for years under two major constraining conditions—a protracted political battle over the consolidation of its two public acute care hospitals, and a civil service salary limit of $25,000 per annum. During 1979, Mayor James Conway accomplished the consolidation of acute care services at City Hospital #1, and in August 1980, St. Louis voters eliminated the $25,000 salary limit. Each of these factors will be discussed in detail later in this chapter.

In St. Louis, the salient structural feature of the public health care sector is that the nominally unified city health and hospitals departments have no access to county resources or services, due to the status of St. Louis as an autonomous city-county separated legally and geographically from the outlying St. Louis County. The demands placed on the public sector for primary care in St. Louis have been severe, and the resources have been very limited; but the dispute over hospital consolidation has dominated health policy considerations and considerably hampered the city's ability to respond to other health concerns.

Baltimore. The city of Baltimore, like St. Louis, holds independent status; that is, it does not reside in a county. Baltimore has the oldest existing health department in the United States. The Baltimore Health Department developed traditional population-based preventive services, and also categorical programs for special population groups. The city health department in particular has expanded its involvement in the provision of personal health care services to neighborhood residents. The degree of such involvement has ranged from the actual provision of primary care services, to contractual arrangements for certain services or space, to departmental support for the establishment of private sector delivery of services. The predominant leadership philosophy, however, views the agency role as a community organizer or facilitator aiding the development and coordination of programs rather than as the provider of direct services.

The Department of Hospitals shares the responsibility in city government for the promotion of health. The department is basically an umbrella agency for Baltimore City Hospitals (BCH), which is a large municipal hospital complex located in Southeast Baltimore. Heading this department has been the City Hospitals Commission, composed of six lay members appointed by the mayor for six-year overlapping terms. While the commission has been responsible for overseeing BCH policies, the hospital director, who was appointed by the mayor (with the approval of the commission), held primary administrative responsibility. In 1981 the City Hospitals Commission was authorized to change its status to a quasi-public corporation with a newly appointed board of trustees.

Responsibility for the administration of Baltimore City Hospitals rested originally with state government. In 1935 it came under the jurisdiction of the Baltimore City Department of Public Welfare. By 1965 the municipal complex had become unwieldy, and the city voters approved the establishment of the Department of Hospitals. Since that time, the department has been faced with major budget deficits, largely due to problems related to the hospital's role as a charitable institution. Specifically, until the early 1970s, collections were given a low priority. Compounding the collections issue were low utilization rates, which resulted from at least two factors. First, BCH has not been a community hospital for the private practitioners within its geographic service area, who generally admitted patients from the area to voluntary hospitals. It has therefore lacked a community referral system. In addition, the medical staff traditionally has been drawn from academic medicine (and was therefore salaried), so that patient or third-party payment for services was not an issue of direct concern. The BCH became a teaching hospital for the Johns Hopkins Medical School in the late 1800s. The University of Maryland Medical School and BCH have also had joint programs. Since the 1950s all members of the full-time professional staff were required to hold faculty appointments at one of the two schools.

In 1972 the mayor engaged a consulting firm to address the critical issues facing the hospital, including low collections, budget deficits, unwieldy medical staff organization, and shrinking census. A resultant major recommendation was the separation of the medical staff from municipal employment procedures. Implementation of this recommendation led to the establishment of the Chesapeake Physicians Professional Association (CPPA). The formation of a unit that was financially separate from the hospital allowed for the receipt of additional third-party reimbursement for care. In other words, Medicare, Medicaid, Blue Cross, and other payors could be billed separately for physician services. Also, the development of a group practice was based on the assumption that a physician group would be able to be more responsive than the hospital had been to the needs of the community.

The CPPA was officially organized in October 1972 by 58 full-time physicians. Their aims were both to ensure the survival of City Hospitals as a teaching and patient care facility (and thus their role as medical staff) and to provide quality care at a lower cost to the city. In return for the provision of a medical and teaching staff, as well as staffing referral clinics in the community, CPPA has received $1.6 million per year from the city, an amount which has remained constant since the initial agreement in 1972. (Prior to that, the city had been paying $2.2 million per year for hospital physician services alone.) The CPPA had grown by 1978 to 90 full-time and 110 part-time physicians, in addition to more than 200 other health professional and administrative employees. Its offices are located on BCH grounds, and plans have been considered to construct new headquarters on adjacent hospital land.

The growth of CPPA and its ability to employ well-qualified personnel may be attributed in part to its association with the Johns Hopkins Medical Institutions. All full-time CPPA physicians also have full-time faculty appointments at Hopkins and are therefore approved by the School of Medicine, as well as by CPPA and the City Hospital Commission. The definition of "full-time" and concomitant responsibilities has led to contention between CPPA and some of its contractors for ambulatory medical care. The academic and research opportunities to Hopkins faculty compensate for a lower income than that which is offered by other community hospitals in Baltimore. The CPPA physicians receive an average salary of $45,000 per year (which is higher than the previous civil service salaries). All full-time physicians own one share of nonparticipating stock in the association, which entitles each to one vote when policy decisions arise. Due to the association's nonprofit status, there are no bonuses or dividends from profits.

In summary, Baltimore has an established traditional health department that has responded to increased primary care demands by providing limited personal health services. Baltimore is legally distanced from access to county resources and suffers from classic inner-city problems. Its public hospital has long been closely affiliated with two medical schools and has not been a community hospital. Financial deficits have created pressures that resulted in establishment of a novel mechanism, an independent physician group, to improve both productivity and access to additional revenues. This development was a singular response to conditions common in other cities.

San Jose. The city of San Jose does not provide health and hospital services; instead these functions reside principally with the county government, an arrangement prevailing throughout California. Although the state of California originally took primary responsibility for the health care of the indigent sick, the state Welfare and Institutions code was changed in 1931, shifting the burden to local county governments. By 1937, California counties were assigned the tasks of "providing" medical and dental care and health services and supplies to persons in need. Reaffirmed by 1975 legislation and an interpretation by the state attorney general, state law requires counties to fulfill properly and continuously their obligation to the indigent population—although each county has wide discretion over eligibility, services offered, and the manner in which care is provided.

Similarly, in the area of public health, the California State Board of Health, second oldest in the nation, over time began to share more and more responsibility with local governments. In 1947 the state legislature officially created county health departments and began to supplement local tax revenue with financial support. Again, counties vary in the extent and types of services offered to their residents.

Santa Clara, the county containing the city of San Jose, maintains both a health department and a public hospital, Valley Medical Center (VMC). The health department offers a wide range of traditional public health services, while the county hospital provides a substantial amount of primary care.

Since the health department has not assumed a major leadership role in establishing comprehensive primary care centers, the foci of political interaction in this area are the county hospital, the community clinics, and the county government. Although Santa Clara does not exert as much control over contract community clinics as does the city of Cincinnati, the nature of community health politics in San Jose has dictated an ever-growing number of linkages. For example, one community health center that was originally funded largely by the Regional Medical Program lost its funding after 1973. Prevailing upon the county for aid, it eventually became a line item in the county budget, an example of a private/public financing and administrative mix.

Valley Medical Center, like most public hospitals in California during the 1970s, faced an uncertain future as the county questioned its continuing ability to fund such enterprises. Despite its strengths as a tertiary care center with a Stanford University affiliation, its continued existence was in question until 1975, when the Board of Supervisors voted against disengaging from support of the institution.

Valley Medical Center's administrative structure, like that of other public hospitals in the five cities, can be characterized by confusing lines of authority, which have generated administrative tension. The critical points of tension involved several power centers: the hospital medical staff newly organized into a group practice; community groups and community clinics attempting to accommodate to their growing quasi-public role vis-a-vis the public hospital; the county executive struggling to define his authority over hospital administration; the hospital's chief operating officer (Director of Medical Institutions) responsible for the continuing viability of the hospital amid Proposition 13; and finally the county Board of Supervisors, a politically diverse body responsible for reconciling the multiple interests via the annual budget and decisions on overall policy.

San Jose provides an example of a young and rapidly growing urban area in a state where county rather than city government has been given legal and actual responsibility for health services for the poor. While some characteristics are familiar, among our cities the important role of community groups in providing primary care to the poor is unique to San Jose. The health department plays a major role in funding and monitoring primary care delivery as well as providing it. The public hospital demonstrates a recognized pattern of involvement with medical education and the growth of a physician group practice.

Financing of Local Government Health Services

The previous section has revealed wide diversity in the organization of local government units charged with providing health services. Cities, counties, and special districts often overlap, sometimes share responsibility, and may even compete for funds and patients. Because the structure for providing health and hospital services is so variable, the means of financing this care are necessarily even more complex. Local governments rely primarily on the property tax for locally generated revenue. In the decade prior to 1977, local governments received steadily increasing amounts of revenue from state and federal governments. The combined federal and state aid to local governments increased by 97 percent between 1972 and 1977 alone. From 1967 to 1972, federal aid to local governments increased by an average of 21.2 percent per annum; between 1972 and 1977, it increased by 29.5 percent per annum. Much of the growth in federal aid was provided through new, direct federal-to-local mechanisms, outside the traditional functional areas for which federal-to-state dollars had flowed in the past (public welfare, health, highways, and employment security). After 1972, the historic local dependence on state aid shifted, with the state proportion of all intergovernmental aid to localities dropping from 70.0 percent in 1972 to 62.5 percent in 1977 (excluding educational aid, the proportion dropped from 56.1 percent to 40.9 percent of the total). State aid to local governments increased at an annual rate of 15.3 percent between 1967 and 1972, but slowed to 11.3 percent per annum between 1972 and 1977.[6] In fiscal year 1976, intergovernmental revenue accounted for 45.3 percent of all county and 38.0 percent of all municipal general revenue.[7] A sharp reversal in the increasing reliance of local governments on intergovernmental revenue from federal sources can be expected in the new federal policy climate aimed at returning responsibility for financing of services to state and local governments.

TABLE 2.3

PER CAPITA AMOUNTS OF SELECTED FINANCIAL ITEMS FOR FIFTY LARGEST CITIES, 1977-1978

	New York	Los Angeles	Chicago	Philadelphia	Detroit	Houston	Baltimore	Dallas	San Diego	San Antonio	Indianapolis	Washington	Honolulu
Revenue													
General revenue, all sources	1,915.36	424.65	396.43	667.86	671.88	309.76	1,270.64	335.10	303.95	208.54	425.59	2,188.59	405.97
General revenue, selected sources:													
Taxes	806.40[2]	216.17[16]	211.29[17]	359.60[6]	246.75[13]	183.04[24]	339.52[7]	210.16[18]	128.04[43]	78.39[50]	141.09[38]	1,038.26[1]	202.20[21]
Property	437.14	109.73	103.12	96.06	125.49	113.83	234.27	139.04	61.35	49.23	137.14	233.06	162.08
Other	370.21	106.44	108.17	263.63	121.26	69.21	105.25	71.11	66.67	29.15	3.95	805.20	40.12
Intergovernmental revenue	907.51[2]	115.15[41]	136.71[34]	217.82[16]	330.33[10]	47.26[50]	825.85[3]	52.92[48]	115.17[40]	77.77[46]	203.38[18]	1,023.17[1]	150.92[29]
Miscellaneous general revenue	216.45	93.33	48.43	90.36	94.80	79.46	105.27	72.02	60.76	52.38	81.12	127.16	52.85
Expenditure													
General expenditure, all functions	1,628.77	334.90	377.81	603.96	517.25	294.22	1,293.94	305.53	252.37	241.95	418.69	2,146.26	441.01
General expenditure, selected items:													
Education	351.38	5.34	5.63	5.52	12.47	0.24	355.98	-	7.02	0.85	1.59	481.67	-
Highways	21.26	28.79	26.85	21.22	31.29	23.07	164.13	28.44	20.05	19.63	37.88	74.22	38.56
Public welfare	471.81	-	7.66	27.42	0.49		187.63	-	0.02	1.22	55.45	372.56	-
Health and hospitals	143.16[4]	0.91[39]	17.87[20]	55.70[14]	65.05[11]	12.16[27]	77.95[10]	5.53[33]	0.63[42]	10.55[30]	79.29[9]	166.38[2]	8.37[32]
As percent of total	8.78	0.27	4.72	9.22	12.58	4.13	6.02	1.81	0.25	4.36	18.94	7.75	1.90
Police protection	95.03	83.43	101.68	94.01	89.97	51.83	86.60	50.44	39.12	34.29	52.58	201.93	50.50
Fire protection	39.92	34.87	10.67	30.30	31.80	35.38	46.62	29.67	23.58	21.48	25.82	70.85	25.22
Sewerage	23.19	8.79	28.33	37.50	50.34	43.87	47.63	30.71	22.14	27.65	39.67	83.85	59.44
Sanitation other than sewerage	35.22	14.38	4.48	27.33	25.73	11.89	27.21	11.93	11.86	11.78	5.22	34.30	16.67
Parks and recreation	16.80	19.79	-	28.12	34.19	15.50	36.61	26.40	38.18	31.31	19.76	32.50	42.01
Housing and urban renewal	65.14	9.16	5.62	24.79	31.81	-	51.43	-	4.15	4.16	9.08	52.61	9.35

	Milwaukee	Phoenix	San Francisco	Memphis	Cleveland	Boston	New Orleans	San Jose	Columbus OH	Jacksonville	St. Louis	Seattle	Denver
Revenue													
General revenue, all sources	379.95	343.77	1,201.48	528.32	449.19	1,265.62	449.05	357.79	298.54	411.69	561.03	525.00	740.40
General revenue, selected sources:													
Taxes	124.80[46]	128.46[42]	537.32[5]	130.00[41]	150.64[33]	686.87[3]	170.65[29]	143.69[7]	127.81[44]	118.38[48]	309.62[9]	196.37[22]	285.78[10]
Property	119.82	49.38	364.24	100.75	61.87	680.59	55.75	59.42	15.87	77.25	66.04	81.15	114.79
Other	4.99	79.08	173.08	29.25	88.77	6.28	114.90	84.27	111.94	41.13	243.59	115.21	170.99
Intergovernmental revenue	191.25[20]	154.24[28]	471.53[7]	329.99[11]	193.63[19]	447.16[8]	179.08[23]	138.38[30]	91.73[44]	159.24[26]	162.30[25]	185.75[21]	246.10[12]
Miscellaneous general revenue	63.99	63.06	192.63	68.33	104.92	131.58	99.31	75.72	78.99	134.06	89.10	142.88	208.52
Expenditure													
General expenditure, all functions	348.84	360.47	1,045.36	540.94	500.18	1,224.18	413.76	328.48	309.10	411.52	511.87	476.92	735.54
General expenditure, selected items:													
Education	0.04	1.61	4.33	233.18	1.01	420.29	2.15	-	-	0.03	1.01	2.56	N.A.
Highways	40.48	45.07	24.61	30.83	38.95	28.20	28.99	29.78	26.07	20.37	19.35	40.27	24.74
Public welfare	-	0.38	216.88	1.10	2.81	6.43	5.56	-	-	7.59	6.74	-	116.16
Health and hospitals	12.48[26]	2.94[44]	143.76[3]	0.64[41]	13.77[24]	123.08[5]	19.24[17]	-	10.12[31]	56.61[16]	105.61[6]	18.67[18]	101.34[8]
As percent of total	3.57	0.08	13.75	0.12	2.75	10.05	4.65	-	3.27	13.76	20.63	3.91	13.78
Police protection	70.54	67.05	75.99	48.26	94.41	104.55	57.36	43.56	55.76	42.17	82.17	67.94	75.83
Fire protection	30.82	28.52	56.74	41.96	42.00	63.04	28.48	25.57	34.90	74.17	25.90	47.38	43.42
Sewerage	21.53	25.75	69.15	35.42	37.07	12.09	27.97	95.01	38.91	12.65	0.71	42.11	41.90
Sanitation other than sewerage	25.56	26.18	9.25	30.58	22.15	22.69	15.76	3.65	15.82	13.36	12.44	23.27	18.12
Parks and recreation	18.08	27.27	43.66	33.93	20.16	27.42	30.09	34.20	24.04	22.40	45.87	74.70	67.77
Housing and urban renewal	25.76	13.06	35.38	-	21.73	49.54	1.14	1.74	0.87	-	15.96	22.81	15.21

Revenue and Expenditure by City (dollars per capita)

	Kansas City	Pittsburgh	Atlanta	Nashville-Davidson	Cincinnati	Buffalo	El Paso	Minneapolis	Omaha	Toledo	Oklahoma City	Miami
Revenue												
General revenue, all sources	538.51	329.42	491.70	684.59	1,160.29	996.65	201.41	471.15	316.92	331.70	440.97	288.50
General revenue, selected sources:												
Taxes	272.48[11]	162.77[32]	205.98[19]	335.77[8]	239.69[15]	244.30[14]	90.60[49]	179.49[25]	136.12[39]	118.78[47]	172.31[27]	166.35[30]
Property	52.06	90.76	132.43	215.31	67.31	234.37	55.73	154.28	79.01	17.33	60.99	104.18
Other	220.42	72.01	73.55	120.46	172.38	9.93	34.87	25.21	57.11	101.44	111.32	62.18
Intergovernmental revenue	153.75[27]	137.06[32]	128.31[37]	224.21[15]	495.87[6]	673.93[4]	48.90[49]	212.89[17]	137.24[31]	129.61[36]	180.72[22]	87.00[45]
Miscellaneous general revenue	112.58	29.59	157.42	124.61	424.73	78.42	61.91	78.78	43.56	83.31	87.87	35.11
Expenditure												
General expenditure, all functions	497.13	336.65	484.46	740.29	1,101.23	905.15	181.17	494.47	299.61	376.04	410.26	320.09
General expenditure, selected items:												
Education	27.29	0.39	12.38	289.71	359.67	302.23	-	0.02	0.10	-	-	0.07
Highways	46.15	35.49	30.58	45.93	43.93	29.49	11.20	71.15	38.77	34.63	40.01	25.51
Public welfare	1.44	0.07	0.70	8.15	-	-	0.01[35]	-	0.25[36]	-	-	-
Health and hospitals	33.01[16]	0.58[43]	0.11[46]	57.06[12]	173.24[1]	2.98[37]	4.56	16.11[21]	4.50	16.09[22]	-	0.86[40]
As percent of total	6.64	0.17	0.02	7.71	15.73	0.33	2.52	3.26	1.50	4.28	-	0.27
Police protection	70.88	54.17	65.72	47.01	77.45	60.20	26.10	50.73	32.22	47.46	33.58	72.48
Fire protection	35.20	39.79	32.24	25.12	50.44	43.89	16.36	32.47	24.75	37.77	33.61	44.29
Sewerage	37.30	2.57	32.95	95.15	97.05	131.46	8.12	38.55	64.38	44.12	93.52	18.83
Sanitation other than sewerage	12.97	20.90	21.97	16.54	22.02	17.63	3.17	21.42	16.80	17.06	10.13	31.52
Parks and recreation	45.09	18.89	37.57	16.45	43.50	19.71	12.67	58.95	18.00	18.75	31.15	52.34
Housing and urban renewal	13.96	28.44	0.48	0.12	27.87	77.32	-	27.06	8.21	29.29	17.37	-

	Fort Worth	Portland OR	Newark	Louisville	Long Beach	Tulsa	Oakland	Austin	Tucson	Baton Rouge	Norfolk	Charlotte
Revenue												
General revenue, all sources	315.15	393.40	1,086.47	506.59	478.93	369.72	570.89	334.51	340.62	390.31	759.73	370.12
General revenue, selected sources:												
Taxes	135.95[40]	171.70[28]	395.92[5]	165.65[31]	175.65[26]	149.68[35]	205.59[20]	125.29[45]	150.24[34]	189.31[23]	268.60[12]	148.07[36]
Property	87.97	128.35	293.80	52.25	89.61	34.90	116.62	84.38	31.61	57.14	133.21	143.03
Other	47.97	43.35	102.12	113.40	86.04	114.78	88.96	40.91	118.63	132.17	135.39	5.04
Intergovernmental revenue	100.94[43]	137.00[33]	655.05[5]	231.13[14]	114.08[42]	130.78[35]	240.95[13]	77.48[47]	126.82[38]	124.55[39]	419.24[9]	163.88[24]
Miscellaneous general revenue	78.28	84.70	35.30	109.81	189.21	89.26	124.36	131.74	63.55	76.45	71.90	58.17
Expenditure												
General expenditure, all functions	318.16	361.75	981.29	481.18	537.94	376.78	481.45	434.50	368.16	380.68	730.47	335.22
General expenditure, selected items:												
Education	0.41	1.55	443.30	0.09	1.11	-	1.63	0.35	-	0.56	219.53	-
Highways	29.92	29.39	11.84	12.05	18.58	20.97	36.71	27.37	42.44	37.92	23.53	61.83
Public welfare	-	-	83.87[2]	-	-	-	-	1.53	-	0.04[23]	91.26[6]	-
Health and hospitals	5.15[34]	1.58[38]	13.23[25]	18.03[19]	10.85[29]	10.94[28]	-	105.00[27]	-	15.44[23]	36.34[15]	0.12[45]
As percent of total	1.62	0.44	1.35	3.75	2.02	2.90	-	24.17	-	4.06	4.97	0.04
Police protection	40.84	65.79	96.47	59.93	84.07	35.48	66.02	36.54	47.51	45.60	38.56	39.15
Fire protection	26.09	45.22	64.65	30.86	54.23	33.64	48.93	21.32	28.74	23.37	23.55	28.58
Sewerage	91.07	59.05	11.80	61.68	6.52	11.91	6.29	71.74	21.62	20.66	5.47	30.20
Sanitation other than sewerage	13.96	5.97	24.17	24.17	18.52	5.56	5.56	10.33	22.31	15.93	13.64	29.43
Parks and recreation	16.91	38.86	17.05	28.24	79.73	49.12	35.46	30.49	40.98	45.63	32.86	14.36
Housing and urban renewal	N.A.	10.38	3.77	80.51	17.25	18.70	16.34	8.35	12.48	-	112.61	12.50

SOURCE: City Government Finances in 1977-78, GF 78, No.4, U.S. Department of Commerce, Bureau of the Census, 1978.

TABLE 2.4

PER CAPITA AMOUNTS OF LOCAL GOVERNMENT FINANCIAL ITEMS FOR FIFTY LARGEST CITIES AND THEIR COUNTY AREAS, 1977-1978

	New York (city)	Chicago Cook	Los Angeles Los Angeles	Philadelphia (city)	Detroit Wayne	Houston Harris	Baltimore (city)	Dallas Dallas	San Diego San Diego	San Antonio Bexar	Indianapolis Marion	St. Louis (city)	Washington District of Columbia	Seattle King	Denver Denver	Honolulu Honolulu
Revenue																
General revenue	2,036.66	954.62	1,325.73	1,173.74	1,229.17	773.41	1,372.05	763.43	1,070.68	630.59	815.29	1,192.34	3,079.85	1,025.13	1,326.04	446.29
Intergovernmental revenue	910.12	390.17	587.51	526.08	568.96	218.96	863.72	226.14	464.41	333.45	390.61	509.03	1,640.31	399.68	441.13	191.81
From state government	756.50	263.95	487.51	340.82	400.03	168.56	555.99	179.17	369.70	236.08	271.23	233.35	—	292.39	255.14	19.42
From federal government	153.62	126.92	100.00	185.26	168.93	50.40	307.72	46.98	94.72	97.38	119.38	275.68	1,640.31	107.29	185.98	172.39
Own sources	1,126.54	563.75	738.22	647.67	660.21	554.45	508.33	537.28	606.26	297.13	424.68	683.30	1,439.54	625.45	884.91	254.48
Taxes	841.79	457.38	600.82	521.18	452.69	404.14	386.88	411.00	446.75	197.36	309.43	479.26	1,237.67	392.37	629.68	208.77
Property	448.43	351.23	351.23	192.42	377.06	343.27	260.90	340.44	376.24	166.79	304.74	212.19	288.78	255.94	360.06	168.17
General sales, gross receipts	127.73	37.04	45.12	—	—	38.76	—	40.89	42.20	23.16	—	59.58	230.27	57.02	209.18	—
Other	265.63	69.11	47.35	328.76	75.62	22.11	125.98	29.66	28.32	7.41	4.69	207.49	718.62	79.42	60.43	40.60
Charges	223.56	70.32	83.08	70.50	162.15	94.09	83.41	92.67	101.80	65.04	77.86	162.68	109.85	176.07	180.53	27.94
Miscellaneous	61.18	36.05	54.32	55.99	45.38	56.22	38.04	33.61	57.71	34.73	37.39	41.37	92.02	57.00	74.70	17.77
Expenditure																
Education	369.12	395.39	446.45	296.15	410.49	359.10	400.75	370.03	440.89	346.74	295.89	339.21	474.06	380.56	333.10	—
Public welfare	467.89	44.19	158.43[2]	42.49[28]	116.27	47.12	93.83[13]	3.18	104.63	2.71	57.34	7.99	416.33	0.16	116.53	—
Health and hospitals	151.87[3]	43.49[35]	82.43[17]	48.49	48.99	44.12[34]	156.37	45.95[32]	62.21[24]	51.50[26]	79.25[19]	128.66[5]	202.66[1]	37.57[37]	112.38	5.53[46]
Highways	40.28	33.02	33.94	40.58	100.27	37.03	95.18	40.12	30.63	18.05	36.55	25.87	81.47	45.36	77.65	32.38
Police protection	99.61	81.66	34.79	106.32	35.04	46.28	45.92	50.40	40.62	35.82	47.02	93.85	204.80	53.14	49.51	51.75
Fire protection	44.47	28.17	13.44	51.37	60.93	26.15	50.91	27.13	33.77	16.66	23.94	33.33	80.12	29.67	45.65	25.77
Sewerage	18.43	59.77	11.54	36.42	23.53	82.80	27.97	22.98	25.60	28.15	41.10	114.62	104.13	33.46	44.08	79.99
Sanitation other than sewerage	41.08	20.89	32.80	40.07	39.27	11.02	44.70	23.47	11.55	10.36	9.11	15.60	35.11	16.73	21.76	16.20
Parks and recreation	18.75	34.05	18.90	29.20	23.65	13.87	97.31	22.74	28.87	26.48	20.98	40.71	39.81	45.69	65.50	32.73
Housing and urban renewal	66.64	21.23	—	—	—	6.22	—	8.20	8.39	27.24	8.87	23.57	53.87	26.89	13.24	9.76

	Milwaukee Milwaukee	Phoenix Maricopa	San Francisco San Francisco	Memphis Shelby	Cleveland Cuyahoga	Boston Suffolk	New Orleans Orleans Parish	San Jose Santa Clara	Columbus OH Franklin	Jacksonville Duval
Revenue										
General revenue	1,198.32	951.13	1,808.36	811.04	1,076.50	1,628.26	783.48	1,295.91	759.99	798.67
Intergovernmental revenue	621.60	438.45	711.42	307.92	441.13	809.69	382.22	538.49	329.47	415.68
From state government	530.67	333.54	447.34	188.20	319.53	529.10	220.16	476.53	253.21	330.39
From federal government	90.93	104.91	264.08	119.72	121.60	280.58	162.06	61.95	76.25	85.28
Own sources	576.72	512.68	1,096.94	503.12	635.36	818.57	401.25	757.42	430.52	382.99
Taxes	394.00	351.06	792.16	313.84	468.54	673.45	275.45	595.46	301.23	208.89
Property	383.26	276.98	599.16	211.93	334.56	667.03	102.31	502.92	202.20	163.25
General sales, gross receipts	—	50.30	59.20	56.99	41.28	—	129.86	52.23	—	—
Other	10.74	23.79	134.40	44.92	92.70	6.42	43.28	40.31	99.03	45.64
Charges	130.65	83.29	208.01	139.70	119.90	117.19	97.11	101.95	84.47	125.70
Miscellaneous	52.07	78.33	96.17	49.59	46.92	27.93	28.69	60.01	44.82	48.41
Expenditure										
Education	361.07	419.73	387.06	260.53	372.37	377.20	227.15	583.03	319.82	384.66
Public welfare	144.81	1.67	172.23	1.22	57.65	7.13	7.18	112.63	63.60	7.81
Health and hospitals	150.47[4]	65.59[23]	153.50[2]	90.01[15]	103.02[11]	123.81[16]	14.17[14]	75.48[20]	25.89[44]	68.13[22]
Highways	46.02	52.44	64.91	39.77	34.88	37.12	38.98	42.55	31.10	23.96
Police protection	66.42	61.27	74.39	41.92	65.36	108.42	55.00	54.81	28.84	45.85
Fire protection	30.73	22.84	55.89	23.00	46.39	76.29	26.36	31.72	41.04	47.20
Sewerage	58.19	16.24	7.01	18.73	18.73	7.93	33.84	30.99	11.04	17.89
Sanitation other than sewerage	21.39	26.81	51.20	23.38	23.38	21.15	17.18	6.52	15.22	17.44
Parks and recreation	45.89	11.17	53.86	32.39	25.09	29.43	38.93	44.85	25.09	13.91
Housing and urban renewal	17.67	—	—	15.47	—	121.35	34.77	2.16	14.61	16.70

Top block

	Kansas City MO Jackson	Pittsburgh Allegheny	Atlanta Fulton	Nashville-Davidson Davidson	Cincinnati Hamilton	Buffalo Erie	El Paso El Paso	Minneapolis Hennepin	Omaha Douglas	Toledo Lucas	Oklahoma City Oklahoma	Miami Dade
Revenue												
General revenue	1,009.30	807.97	1,531.19	811.63	886.28	1,290.45		1,150.41	960.21	829.19	706.18	1,025.24
Intergovernmental revenue	383.10	314.48	668.25	305.05	353.64	669.04		513.81	315.19	342.95	283.63	393.16
From state government	172.17	233.86	237.09	142.12	249.76	488.05		428.52	170.94	244.13	142.74	261.88
From federal government	210.94	80.62	431.16	162.93	103.89	180.99		85.29	144.25	98.82	140.89	131.28
Own sources	626.19	493.50	862.94	506.58	532.63	621.41		636.60	645.02	486.24	422.56	632.09
Taxes	459.20	383.43	543.96	338.03	419.11	525.80		434.94	426.62	352.60	284.87	350.49
Property	241.66	291.61	416.33	213.81	282.82	367.54		416.48	364.59	229.12	174.99	286.39
General sales, gross receipts	54.32	-	71.89	77.60	16.56	126.75		-	40.03	16.35	90.89	2.46
Other	163.23	91.82	55.74	46.62	119.73	31.51		18.46	22.00	107.13	18.99	61.64
Charges	94.31	74.81	235.12	104.88	60.36	61.93		108.30	95.85	93.24	92.77	222.85
Miscellaneous	72.68	35.26	83.85	63.66	53.17	33.69		93.36	122.56	40.41	44.92	58.75
Expenditure												
Education	316.46	347.42	369.31	281.31	337.82	427.70		380.52	349.65	307.30	224.04	367.07
Public welfare	2.87	18.73	4.75	8.71	43.37	161.56[49]		129.08[21]	33.52[31]	51.70	3.51	5.49
Health and hospitals	46.40[30]	40.35[36]	111.06[10]	87.70[16]	45.72[33]	56.54[25]		72.84[21]	46.33[31]	30.29[41]	28.78[42]	101.81[12]
Highways	43.79	39.26	37.98	57.46	28.07	52.04		69.33	52.46	44.32	36.23	26.57
Police protection	73.06	39.66	63.01	46.72	48.50	43.64		46.28	37.72	55.80	32.77	69.08
Fire protection	43.30	19.67	27.41	33.71	27.91	26.18		18.51	27.07	33.04	38.71	30.01
Sewerage	49.33	19.03	48.72	64.13	42.55	133.30		25.68	73.73	46.28	12.72	69.15
Sanitation other than sewerage	10.70	13.14	24.31	17.98	12.36	12.29		10.35	16.24	15.82	26.14	26.39
Parks and recreation	33.08	20.38	36.85	17.76	20.91	22.27		47.36	22.85	15.15	15.13	45.54
Housing and urban renewal	19.81	15.34	25.65	24.40	32.77	39.88		49.85	42.73	13.44		4.65

Bottom block

	Fort Worth Tarrant	Portland OR Multnomah	Newark Essex	Louisville Jefferson	Long Beach Los Angeles	Tulsa Tulsa	Oakland Alameda	Austin Travis N.A.	Tucson Pima N.A.	Baton Rouge E.Baton Rouge N.A.	Norfolk (city)	Charlotte Mecklenburg
Revenue												
General revenue	766.01	1,204.96	1,278.75	732.01	1,325.73	738.43	1,561.10				741.83	898.43
Intergovernmental revenue	280.22	449.85	591.82	326.93	587.51	272.00	585.16				351.92	475.98
From state government	196.90	230.98	470.92	182.77	487.51	166.86	443.65				207.02	276.24
From federal government	83.32	213.87	120.90	144.16	100.00	105.14	141.51				144.89	199.74
Own sources	485.79	755.11	686.93	405.08	738.22	466.43	975.94				389.91	422.45
Taxes	289.57	519.59	537.16	270.05	600.82	330.29	763.45				301.74	326.99
Property	239.16	433.05		129.97	508.35	214.58	617.60				152.67	278.25
General sales, gross receipts	31.19	-		-	45.12	97.08	113.09				35.64	39.85
Other	19.23	86.54	67.39	140.08	47.35	18.63	32.76				113.42	8.88
Charges	154.15	167.73	53.17	86.00	83.08	76.04	133.80				57.32	67.59
Miscellaneous	42.07	67.78	29.21	49.02	54.32	60.10	78.68				30.86	27.87
Expenditure												
Education	341.95	470.29	427.31	250.82	446.45	317.07	480.70				226.12	382.72
Public welfare	3.00	7.45	206.81[27]	7.84	158.42	0.68	133.90				45.80[38]	75.80
Health and hospitals	32.77[40]	92.51[14]	48.81[27]	47.07[29]	82.13[18]	26.91[43]	114.56[8]				34.94[38]	33.98[39]
Highways	32.98	39.70	20.21	14.11	33.94	37.59	40.74				25.87	31.80
Police protection	35.11	66.22	79.72	50.85	78.22	34.67	59.67				42.92	42.13
Fire protection	18.22	33.45	51.04	16.60	34.79	25.29	35.18				23.75	26.72
Sewerage	36.30	39.57	47.62	54.91	13.44	25.45	37.02				5.97	49.11
Sanitation other than sewerage	9.96	4.17	16.25	10.35	11.54	10.75	4.63				15.06	20.72
Parks and recreation	19.08	32.31	30.15	16.60	32.80	28.45	78.91				35.41	15.89
Housing and urban renewal	1.57	22.99	36.24	16.55	18.90	27.82	19.97				-	29.51

SOURCE: Richard P. Nathan and Mary M. Nathan, America's Governments, (New York, John Wiley & Sons, 1979).

Because of differences in accounting practices, lack of uniformity in the definition of the fiscal year from locality to locality, and structural variability, assessment of local financing practices is somewhat problematic. Still, some useful comparisons can be made by examining per capita revenues and expenditures for fiscal year 1977 for the fifty largest cities (see Table 2.3).[8] These expenditure figures relate only to those amounts expended directly by the municipal government and its agencies, excluding expenditures by overlapping jurisdictions. Nevertheless, it is possible to compare per capita revenues and expenditures among cities, and to compare the proportion expended on health to that expended for other common municipal functions.

Among the fifty largest cities, the revenue raised from local taxes during fiscal year 1977 ranged from a low of $78.39 per capita in San Antonio to a high of $1,038.26 per capita in Washington, D.C. Cincinnati's per capita city tax revenue of $239.69 was quite close to the mean of $237.55. Baltimore ranked seventh at $339.52, and St. Louis ninth at $309.62. San Jose and Milwaukee, in contrast, ranked 37th at $143.69 and 46th at $124.80, respectively. The differences can be explained by a combination of at least three determinants:

- the willingness of residents to tax themselves and the local economy (general revenue derived from local sources);
- the cost of providing services in different markets due to variations in local prices for labor, materials and energy; and
- the extent to which other levels of government are willing to share costs (intergovernmental revenue) or absorb functions.

There is as much variation in the per capita amount of intergovernmental revenue received by the fifty largest cities as there is in local tax revenue. Also from Table 2.3 we see that per capita intergovernmental revenue ranged from a low of $47.26 in Houston to a high of $1,023.17, again in Washington, D.C. As Washington has neither state nor county government overlying the municipality, municipal revenue and expenditure are expectedly high for the only nonfederal jurisdiction providing services. The mean per capita intergovernmental revenue to these cities was $245.67. Baltimore ranked third with $825.85; Cincinnati, sixth with $495.87; Milwaukee, twentieth with $191.25; St. Louis, twenty-fifth with $162.30; and San Jose, thirtieth with $138.38 per capita in intergovernmental revenue. It should be noted that federal funds supporting city services are dependent on the formula factors (e.g., per capita income tax effort) used in allocating many federal programs, the perception on the part of federal agencies of the city's needs, and to some degree the enterprise and the political skill of the city in capturing grants. Thus, comparing Baltimore to San Jose, we see almost a sixfold differential in intergovernmental revenue per capita for fiscal year 1977.

Table 2.3 also indicates the priorities municipalities assign among

functional categories (education, health, etc.) within their budgetary
discretion, in terms of per capita expenditures for selected services.
We see that per capita expenditures on health and hospitals by municipal governments in fiscal year 1977 ranged from $.11 in Atlanta
to $173.24 in Cincinnati, with a mean of $35.49 for all fifty cities.
Proportional to other services, cities spent from nothing to 24.17 percent of their total general expenditures on health and hospitals. St.
Louis spent 20.63 percent, Cincinnati 15.73 percent, Baltimore 6.02
percent, Milwaukee 3.57 percent and San Jose none of general expenditure on health and hospitals.

But as noted earlier, cities often share health and hospital responsibilities with the county. San Jose, for example, does not provide
these services, but its residents benefit from the relatively generous
support of Santa Clara County. Table 2.4 therefore offers a different
perspective—financial data for all legal entities (the city, the county,
special districts) within the *geographic* boundaries of the county.[9] When
all local governmental units within the boundaries of the county containing the central city are taken into account, the financial picture
shifts. Per capita expenditures on health and hospitals by all local
units of government within the boundaries of the county containing
the central city (available for forty-six of our fifty cities) ranged from
a low of $5.53 in Honolulu to a high of $202.66 in Washington, with
a mean of $73.04. These data show Milwaukee ranking fourth at
$150.47 per capita, St. Louis fifth at $128.66 per capita, Baltimore
thirteenth at $95.83 per capita, San Jose twentieth at $75.48 per capita,
and Cincinnati thirty-third at $45.72 per capita. The discrepancy be-
tween the two data sources as to expenditures in Cincinnati is probably due to the reporting date of the 1977 transfer of the municipal
hospital's operations to the University of Cincinnati and thus to the
state government.

The information used in the above analysis was derived from the
comparative financial data on local governments published annually
by the U.S. Bureau of the Census. More detailed data on local health
and hospital finances were collected for the five cities being studied.*
The Census Bureau data provide at least a rough indication of the

---

* Several points should be raised concerning both the conceptual and practical
problems of such comparisons among cities. First, since there is wide diversity
in who delivers particular services from locality to locality, a fair comparison
of cities must take into account all levels of government that provide services.
This is not readily apparent from an examination of budgets alone. For example, it is not easy to parse out the expenditures of a county hospital or
health department serving both a city and its environs. If the focus of inquiry
is spending solely in the municipality, detailed utilization data would be
required to begin to make appropriate allocation.

Second, with respect to the Census Bureau's efforts to provide systematic
data across local governments, several problems have been cited. Perhaps

relative importance of various services within cities and across several urban areas. This has been useful in attempts to gain a better general understanding of the major determinants of municipal spending levels.

In approaching the health and hospital budgets of municipalities, one must be aware of the differences among cities in the needs of their populations and the extent to which those needs are met by the state and federal governments. With this as backdrop, budget makers must decide on the basis of local tradition and politics how far they wish to go in providing personal health services in the context of other public needs. These decisions are reflected in the health department and hospital budgets.

Table 2.5 displays health and hospital budgets for the five case study cities. These data indicate the magnitude of local spending and the relative importance of health and hospitals within the budgetary discretion of local decision makers. The total expenditure levels for public health and public hospitals for the five localities (city, county, or combination of the two, depending upon structure of responsibility) fall within a relatively narrow range, from $51.7 million in St. Louis, to $88.8 million in Santa Clara County (San Jose), with a mean of $68.5 million. Milwaukee at $61.6 million, Baltimore at $65.2 million, and Cincinnati at $75.3 million are close to the mean. Among our five cities, the greatest proportional difference is found in expenditures for the public health department, which range from only $6.9 million in St. Louis and $8.9 million in Milwaukee, to $30.6 million in Baltimore and $32.9 million in Santa Clara County (San Jose), with Cincinnati in the middle at $14.8 million. Expenditures for public hospitals ranged from $34.6 million in Baltimore to $60.6 million in Cincinnati. These figures should be compared to the per capita expenditure data presented above for proper perspective.

The dangers of facile comparisons among urban areas cannot be emphasized strongly enough. For example, the relatively high proportion of funds devoted to health and hospitals as compared to other functions in St. Louis must be seen in light of the fact that a number of nonhealth municipal functions lie outside the control of the city budget, under the authority of special districts. In Santa Clara County, mental health service expenditures are included among county health budget responsibilities; in other localities, separate mental health departments, some of which are located at the state level, perform these functions.

---

one of the chief difficulties to surmount has been the lack of uniformity in financial accounting and reporting practices among cities, leading to under- or overstatements in functional expenditure categories. The lack of standardized accounting practices, compounded by the poor quality of local government record-keeping, also increases the opportunity for error on the part of cities in reporting information and on the part of the Census Bureau in assigning costs appropriately.

TABLE 2.5

TOTAL CITY (COUNTY) BUDGETS AND PERCENT DISTRIBUTIONS
FOR HEALTH AND HOSPITALS AND OTHER MUNICIPAL FUNCTIONS, FISCAL YEAR 1977
(in 000's)

	Baltimore		Cincinnati		Hamilton County State of Ohio	Milwaukee		Milwaukee County		St. Louis		Santa Clara County	
	$	%	$	%	$	$	%	$	%	$	%	$	%
Total budget	1,258,076	100.0	206,136	100.0	-	221,228	100.0	418,423	100.0	274,932	100.0	434,924	100.0
Health & hospitals	65,188	5.2	14,764	7.2	60,570	8,916	4.0	53,689	12.8	51,901	18.9	88,809	20.4
Health	30,582	2.4	14,764	7.2	-	8,916	4.0	-	-	6,923	2.5	32,916	7.6
Hospitals	34,606	2.8	-	-	60,570	-	-	53,689	12.8	44,978	16.4	55,893	12.8
Other municipal (county) functions	1,192,888	94.8	191,372	92.8	-	212,312	96.0	364,734	87.2	223,031	81.1	346,115	79.6

NOTE: In Hamilton County, Ohio, the public hospital is part of the state university system, but also receives county tax levy ($9,155) and county welfare funds ($3,223). Figure represents hospital budget only.

TABLE 2.6

AGGREGATE AND PERCENTAGE DISTRIBUTION OF GOVERNMENT FUNDS FOR SELECTED
FUNCTIONS, FISCAL YEAR 1977

BALTIMORE

Source of payment	Total health & hospitals		Health		Hospitals		Other municipal functions	
	$	%	$	%	$	%	$	%
(Aggregate amt. in 000s) Total	65,188	100.0	30,582	100.0	34,606	100.0	1,192,888	100.0
Local	30,305	46.5	12,592[a]	41.2	17,713	51.2	740,661	62.1
State/federal	34,883	53.5	17,990[b]	58.8	16,893[c]	48.8	452,227	37.9

[a]Includes designated funds, local taxes, municipal funds, and private grants.

[b]Includes state and federal grants.

[c]Includes Medicare and Medicaid payments in 1978, and federal and state grants in 1977 (Medicare and Medicaid data for 1977 not available but local authorities maintain that they were about the same as 1978).

Despite the several caveats we have offered on the interpretation of these data, individual local budgets usefully can be viewed as political documents. In conjunction with an understanding of the institutional structures—both the delivery system and the organization of local government—budgets can provide insight into the policy options available to decision makers. Thus, in our examination of local budgets we have sought to explore the major forces behind diversity in spending among communities. The chief focus for this inquiry has been the role of intergovernmental financing as it relates to the functional assignment of responsibility for various health activities among the levels of government, and in some cases between government and the private sector.

The fiscal year 1977 budgets of the five study cities and the counties that share health responsibilities are presented in Tables 2.6 through 2.10. They are based on revenues generated from local taxes and funds received from the state and federal governments. For hospital budgets, the state/federal contribution is primarily Medicare and Medicaid reimbursement. As entitlement programs, these funds do not represent direct operational support for local government health activities, but do enable patients to purchase services that the city would in large part be obliged to provide otherwise. For health department budgets, state/federal contributions are principally in the form of categorical grants (e.g., Maternal and Child Health, family planning,

TABLE 2.7

AGGREGATE AND PERCENTAGE DISTRIBUTION OF GOVERNMENT FUNDS FOR SELECTED
FUNCTIONS, FISCAL YEAR 1977

CINCINNATI

Source of payment	Health (city)		Hospitals (state/county)		Other municipal functions	
	$	%	$	%	$	%
(Aggregate amt. in 000s)						
Total	14,764	100.0	60,570	100.0	191,372	100.0
Local	5,802[a]	39.3	30,749[c]	50.8	141,770	74.1
State/federal	8,962[b]	60.7	29,821[d]	49.2	49,602	25.9

[a]Includes general fund.

[b]Includes general revenue sharing, community development, public health research, rodent control, Maternity & Infant Care, WIC, & CETA.

[c]Includes county welfare and county tax levy, private insurance, self pays, Workmen's Compensation.

[d]Includes Medicare, Medicaid, HEW categoricals, Clinical Teaching Funds and other state and federal subsidies.

Children and Youth, rodent control, community health center) or other nonhealth specific programs, such as revenue sharing or community development block grants.

The proportion of local health department budgets that was financed by state/federal revenues in fiscal year 1977 ranged from a low of 22.1 percent in Milwaukee, which provides very little direct health care, to a high of 67.0 percent in Santa Clara County (for San Jose). The other three cities also exhibited a relatively high proportion of state/federal revenues in their health department budgets: Baltimore, 58.8 percent; Cincinnati, 60.7 percent; and St. Louis, 53.1 percent. The hospital budgets relied less heavily than the health department budgets on state/federal financing, primarily because of the availability of some private insurance and direct self-pay revenues as well as local government subvention. The state/federal contribution to hospital budgets varied from 48.8 percent in Baltimore to 67.2 percent in Santa Clara County. Total hospital budgets ranged from less than $35 million in Baltimore, with one community-level hospital, to more than $65 million in Cincinnati, with a large, highly sophisticated teaching facility. Total health department budgets were fairly low in Milwaukee (less than $7 million) and St. Louis (less than $10 million), where smaller populations and/or less extensive programs existed. Cincin-

TABLE 2.8

AGGREGATE AND PERCENTAGE DISTRIBUTION OF GOVERNMENT FUNDS FOR SELECTED
FUNCTIONS, FISCAL YEAR 1977

MILWAUKEE AND MILWAUKEE COUNTY

Source of payment	City health department		Other municipal functions		County hospital		Other county functions	
	$	%	$	%	$	%	$	%
(Aggregate amt. in 000s) Total	8,916	100.0	212,312	100.0	53,689[d]	100.0	364,734[f]	100.0
Local	6,943[a]	77.9	100,050	47.1	27,207	50.7	172,085	47.2
State/federal	1,973[b]	22.1	112,262[c]	52.9	26,482[e]	49.3	192,649[g]	52.8

[a]Includes city's general fund.

[b]Includes HEW categorical, Medicaid (EPSDT), state/federal grants and aid, and other federal revenue.

[c]Includes federal and state shared revenues.

[d]Includes Medical Complex (general hospital, rehabilitation and chronic disease hospitals and Downtown Medical & Health Services).

[e]Includes only Medicare and Medicaid payments.

[f]Includes mental health center and institution service departments.

[g]Includes Medicare, Medicaid, state funds, state/federal grants to institution service departments ($13,717), and other state/federal grants and aid for other county functions ($155,832).

TABLE 2.9

AGGREGATE AND PERCENTAGE DISTRIBUTION OF GOVERNMENT FUNDS FOR SELECTED
FUNCTIONS, FISCAL YEAR 1977

ST. LOUIS

Source of payment	Total health & hospitals		Health		Hospitals		Other municipal functions	
	$	%	$	%	$	%	$	%
(Aggregate Amt. in 000s) Total	51,901[a]	100.0	6,923	100.0	44,978	100.0	223,031	100.0
Local	20,193	38.9	3,247	46.9	20,895[b]	46.5	163,031	73.1
State/federal	31,708	61.1	3,676	53.1	24,083[c]	53.5	60,000	26.9

[a]Excludes Office of Director of Health and Hospitals ($1,299).

[b]Includes self pay and private insurance.

[c]Includes Medicare, Medicaid and other federal revenues.

TABLE 2.10

AGGREGATE AND PERCENTAGE DISTRIBUTION OF GOVERNMENT FUNDS FOR SELECTED
FUNCTIONS, FISCAL YEAR 1977

SANTA CLARA COUNTY (SAN JOSE)

Source of payment	Total health & hospitals		Health		Hospitals		Other county functions	
	$	%	$	%	$	%	$	%
(Aggregate amt. in 000s) Total	88,809[a]	100.0	32,916[d]	100.0	55,893[a]	100.0	346,115	100.0
Local	29,188	32.9	10,865[e]	33.0	18,322[b]	32.8	180,734	52.2
State/federal	59,621[f]	67.1	22,050	67.0	37,571[c]	67.2	165,381	47.8

[a]Excludes emergency medical services.

[b]Includes county subsidies and private insurance.

[c]Includes Medicare, Medicaid, and other state subsidies.

[d]Based on projected budget. Includes mental health services.

[e]Includes private insurance, self pay and county subsidy.

[f]Includes Medicare, Medicaid, HEW categorical programs and other federal revenues and state subsidies.

nati's mid-range $15 million served a small population with extensive primary care services. In Baltimore and San Jose, health departments had much larger populations to serve, as is indicated by budgets over $30 million.

The differences among local governments in the ratio of local funds to state/federal contributions can be explained in part by circumstances beyond the discretion of local officials. The level of Medicare and Medicaid reimbursement is dependent upon the characteristics of the population utilizing the hospital, as well as on the eligibility standards and reimbursement levels established by the state. Within these constraints local officials can improve collections of third-party payment through better billing systems. They also have some discretion to adjust eligibility levels and administrative procedures, which affect enrollment.

Table 2.11 presents fiscal year 1977 expenditure data on the Medicaid program for the states in which our five cities are located.[10] California had almost five times as high a total ($2,618 million) of medical assistance payments as any of the other four states, and a local share ($373.2 million) that exceeded Maryland or Missouri's total payments. Wisconsin expended more per million dollars of personal

income ($16,064) and more per beneficiary ($1,350 per family), however; it also had the most generous income ceiling ($6,300) for the
medically needy. California simply had a much larger population to
cover. Missouri registered lowest among the five states on all of these
measures. Missouri and Ohio had no medically needy program. Among
the five, only California and Maryland required local government to
pay a portion of Medicaid costs. Again, Medicaid is not primarily a
municipal responsibility, but local budgets indirectly respond to the
size and scope of the state's program. Those state programs that are
relatively generous in eligibility, benefits, and reimbursement counterbalance the need for large local subsidies to municipal or county
facilities or, as is more frequently the case, permit local officials the
option of providing more extensive services, as is true in San Jose
and Milwaukee. With a less generous program, local officials face a
larger uncovered population, demanding services from poorly reimbursed public outpatient and inpatient facilities that can barely be
maintained with local revenues, as is the case in St. Louis and Baltimore. It is also important to note that the nature of the hospital itself
dictates the overall costs and how they will be met. For instance, a
direct comparison of hospital finances in Cincinnati and St. Louis
must be accompanied by the knowledge that the former has a highly
specialized public teaching hospital under state auspices, while the
latter operates institutions conforming to the conventional image of
the distressed city hospital.

The amount of federal categorical support that appears in local
health department budgets is highly dependent upon the relationship
between the state and the local health agencies. Much of the federal
categorical money is allocated to the state, which may deliver services
itself or make grants to local health centers. Arrangements differ from
state to state and sometimes by categorical program.

Little or no third-party revenues are reflected in the health department budgets. Although many localities have become more mind-
ful of their billing practices, in the past health department
comprehensive clinics have not billed Medicare or Medicaid; or when
they have, these revenues have not been sequestered for departmental use but have been channelled instead to the general treasury.
Health department officials have been reluctant to bill for a combination of reasons: given the traditional budgeting process there has
been no incentive to increase third-party revenues; the notion of health
department care as "free care" often frustrated attempts to install
billing systems; and the reimbursement levels often did not justify
the personnel and data resources required to capture revenue effectively. These considerations are instructive in the context of the growing pressure on local governments to provide more services with
fewer resources, and of the generally articulated strategies for restructuring local health services to provide more comprehensive care more

TABLE 2.11

MEDICAID EXPENDITURES AND PAYMENT DATA FOR STATES WITH MUNICIPAL HEALTH SERVICES PROGRAM SITES

State	Medical assistance payments (FY 1977) (in millions)				Medicaid expenditure per million dollars personal income (FY 1977)		Average payment for persons eligible on the basis of receipt of AFDC[b] (FY 1977)			Income levels for medically needy with family of four (as of 7/78)
	Total medical assistance payments[a]	Federal share	State share	Local share	Total expenditure	State/local share	Families	Children	Adults	
California	$2,618.0	$1,104.1	$1,140.7	$373.2	$12,643	$6,339	$1,310	$310	$700	$5,604
Maryland	306.6	132.2	169.9	4.5	8,324	4,132	990	250	560	3,800
Missouri	188.3	109.2	79.1	-	5,689	2,240	670	150	410	*
Ohio	532.8	296.6	236.2	-	6,983	3,078	1,080	220	650	*
Wisconsin	505.4	312.3	193.1	-	16,064	6,138	1,350	370	680	6,300

[a]Expenditures may include payments to provide medical assistance to persons who are financially eligible but not categorically eligible under Title 19 or persons whose income exceeds the state income standards or the maximum level allowed for the medically needy by Title 19.

[b]Based on average number of recipients eligible during the year, rather than the total number of recipients, in order to eliminate the effect of persons coming on and off the rolls for limited periods of time.

NOTE: Asterisk signifies state has no medically needy program.

SOURCE: Health Care Financing Administration, Data on the Medicaid Program, rev. ed. (U.S. Department of Health, Education and Welfare, 1979).

efficiently. Shonick's findings about structure have particular relevance as well for financing considerations.

In summary, perhaps the most salient observation that can be made about the financing of local government health services is that the patterns and the volume of dollar flows vary greatly from locale to locale. It is generally the case that the highest levels of expenditure on health and hospitals are found in the older cities of the Northeast and North Central regions, where heavier demands are placed on the public sector, especially municipal government, by low-income populations. Local governments, city and county, have come to rely very heavily on intergovernmental revenue, whether in the form of project grants or general revenue-sharing, to finance local service delivery, and these sources are projected to shrink considerably. Local sources, primarily the property tax, will have to supply additional revenue to finance expansion or simply maintenance of local health and hospital services. Shortages of resources are likely to result in increased calls at the local level for improved billing and collections for health services, for greater efficiencies and economies in the health care system, and for shifting of responsibility for health to higher levels (county, state, federal) of government.

Underlying Forces

In this section of the chapter, we will examine the environment in which the local public health delivery system must function. At the broadest level of this discussion will be an assessment of demographic and socioeconomic trends in the urban locale. Following this information will be an evaluation of the nature and strength of minority ethnic group politics in the city as a determinant of local policy choices in the health arena. Finally, the general structure of city government will be described, by addressing first, the overall administrative configuration of municipal government, and second, the specifics of the budgetary process.

DEMOGRAPHIC AND SOCIOECONOMIC TRENDS OVER
THREE DECADES

Until 1950, most U.S. cities were growing in population. During the fifties, and with accelerating volume after 1960, most older cities lost population. In the introduction to a 1976 Urban Institute publication, *The Urban Predicament*, Gorham and Glazer identify three major demographic and socioeconomic trends:

the regional shift in population and economic activity from the Northeast and North Central regions into the West and most recently into the South; the relative economic decline and the loss of middle-income population from the major central cities in the Northeast and North Central regions; and the increasing concentration in the cities of blacks, a large percentage of whom are of low income.[11]

The older American cities, those which reached a large population size by the early part of this century, tend to have greater population density (although density is declining) and much older and more deteriorated housing and other capital stock. Most outmigration from these central cities has been of middle-income population, generally white, while the inmigration until 1970 was largely of low-income, rural, southern blacks. The first major population shift was the large-scale suburbanization within metropolitan areas. This movement to the suburbs tended to disadvantage central cities relative to their outlying counties and suburban cities in terms of tax base (both property and income) and in terms of the demands placed on central city services by a residual lower-income population. The nation's poor have shifted increasingly from nonmetropolitan areas toward central cities from the late 1950s to the present, and the poor population in central cities has become predominantly black. Some of the specific effects of suburbanization on individual cities have been discussed in earlier sections of this chapter.

The second major demographic change affecting urban health services is the declining population of the Northeast and the North Central regions since 1950. While not all cities in each region follow the growth pattern of their surrounding urban neighbors, in general the older central cities of the northeast quadrant are either shrinking or growing very slowly. Cities in the South and Southwest, particularly younger, smaller cities, tend to be growing rapidly. Cities of more than 50,000 inhabitants now have a declining share of the U.S. population and a minority of the total.[12]

In the process of evaluating the community development block grant program, Nathan and Dommel address the characteristics of declining cities:

A decline in population would not be a problem per se unless it was associated with problem conditions for the cities affected. One such condition that is particularly serious for declining cities is their relative old age. Census data are available for all cities on housing built before 1939. For central cities and suburban cities of over 50,000 population in 1973, the proportion of the housing built before 1939 was 29.8 percent for those that gained population and 58.4 percent for the losers. Although comparable census data are not available, knowledge of the cities in which Brookings field research has been conducted indicates that an aging housing stock is associated with the deterioration of related physical facilities—streets, schools, sewer and water facilities, parks.

There is also a relation between population decline and major economic variables. Declining cities had a per capita income level $300 lower than growing cities in 1970; housing values were nearly $3,000 lower. It can also be seen that between 1960 and 1970 per capita income increased almost 5 percent faster in the growing cities than in the declining cities, and home values increased nearly 6 percent faster in the growing cities.[13]

Declining cities are confronted with problematic imbalances between service demands and available resources. As George Peterson
states:

Because of their physical construction and political orientation, cities have
found it unusually difficult to reduce public service expenditures commen-
surately with declines in the number of users of those services. The simple
economics of overhead spreading then dictates that as population falls, the
per capita costs associated with city operations must weigh more heavily on
the remaining taxpayers.[14]

In contrast to the squeeze felt by declining cities, growing cities
have a better prospect, as Peterson goes on to observe:

Just as declining central cities tend to acquire increasingly costly conditions
for producing public services as a result of their population losses, growing
cities often find service provision made easier and cheaper because in an-
nexing unincorporated suburban areas they are able to acquire low-cost production conditions. The initial capital costs of installing water and sewer
networks may be greater in outlying areas (though these costs now are often
borne by the users themselves), but they are more than compensated for by
savings in police protection, urban renewal, public health and other services
where the need for public spending is reduced by low density, modern capital
stock, and the socioeconomic characteristics of the annexed population. Overhead spreading also causes population growth to lessen the per capita expenditure burden on city residents.[15]

In their approach to assessing urban decline, Nathan and Dommel
developed an urban conditions index which combined three variables:
population decline, economic conditions measured by percent poverty, and old age measured by percent of housing built before 1940.
Table 2.1 shows the urban conditions index with measures for its
three variables for the fifty largest cities.[16] Also shown is estimated
population for 1975. In parentheses after each city's score on the
hardship index is its rank among the fifty largest.

It is of particular interest that among the five study cities are those
which ranked at the top and bottom of the urban distress scale. Among
the fifty largest cities, St. Louis ranked worst (first) on the urban
conditions index with a score of 487. St. Louis, of course, is trapped
inside legal geographic boundaries and cannot tap into suburban tax
bases. It lost 30 percent of its population in fifteen years, the highest
loss among the fifty cities, and has an extremely high proportion of
antiquated housing. Cincinnati ranked eighth worst, with a score of
289. Baltimore was ninth at 249, Milwaukee twentieth at 161, and San
Jose at the bottom of the scale, best off in fiftieth position with a score
of 11. A classic example of the young, expanding, growing city, San
Jose experienced 172 percent population growth between 1960 and
1975, and only 13.9 percent of its housing stock predated 1940.

The expenditure and revenue differentials between growing and
declining cities can be seen in detail in Table 2.2 (discussed earlier in

the finance section), which shows per capita revenue and expenditure for all the fifty largest cities in fiscal year 1977. Among our five study cities, only San Jose ranks among the growing, generally well off cities. Milwaukee is perhaps less critically afflicted than others, but Cincinnati and Baltimore exhibit all the symptoms of the declining central city, and St. Louis is the nation's most distressed large city, based on its composite score on comparative indicators of urban distress.

MINORITY ETHNIC GROUP POLITICS

As has been discussed, declining central cities are associated with increasing lower-income minority populations, who represent a high proportion of the users of the public sector health delivery system. In many cities, there has been a history of health policy conflict over minority issues. In many other cities, either no specific conflicts over minority issues have arisen in the health arena, or the groups affected have been able to achieve resolution or accommodation satisfactorily. The ability of some minority community groups to build leadership and power via the federally funded community health center program served to defuse conflict over health services as well as to bring services into congruence with community perceptions of needs. In Cincinnati, Milwaukee, and Baltimore, conflict in the health arena has been minimal or has been resolved through representation and public responsiveness.

Although Cincinnati has a large black population, more than 25 percent in 1970, concentrated residentially in specific neighborhoods characteristic of central-city ghettoes, there have been no major minority group conflicts, particularly in the arena of health policy. Minority groups were involved in the People's Health Movement in the late 1960s, a movement which demanded and obtained expanded participation and services for the poor, which resulted in Cincinnati's public primary care clinic network. Inner-city neighborhoods have representation in health decision making and seem satisfied.

Less than 20 percent of Milwaukee's 1970 population was nonwhite. A special census in 1975 indicated that minority populations had increased in two inner-city neighborhoods to the following proportions: inner-city north, 56 percent black and 2 percent Hispanic; and inner-city south, 9 percent Hispanic and 3 percent American Indian. Black and Hispanic community groups have organized to provide primary health care. There have been no major health policy conflicts arising from minority group tensions.

Baltimore's nonwhite population in 1975 was more than 52 percent of the total and was primarily black. The racial composition of Baltimore is symbolic of a set of complex problems referable to its historic location along the dividing line between the North and South during the Civil War. For example, its segregation policies, such as those reflected in area hospitals, were unchanged until the 1960s. The swell of the black population and its discontent with human conditions gave impetus to the city riots following the death of Martin Luther King in 1968. Resulting programs have included an innovative city effort to rebuild and rehabilitate inner-city neighborhoods, along with business community support for the redevelopment of the downtown and harbor areas. Well-organized community associations provide a variety of services and articulate demands. It is reasonable to suggest that Baltimore in the 1970s had the more generic problems of a large urban area rather than those related primarily to racial inequalities. The health services arena was not preoccupied by any major conflicts along racial lines during this period.

Two of the five study cities, however, bear special attention: San Jose, because of the unusual degree of political power its minority groups have developed in the health arena, and St. Louis, because of an entrenched health policy conflict along predominantly racial lines.

San Jose. San Jose is unique among the study cities in that its major ethnic minority group is Chicano rather than black. In California, Chicanos and other ethnic minority groups have been politically and organizationally active, especially in the health services arena, with the establishment of community-sponsored primary care clinics. A growing minority which may in the foreseeable future become a majority, Chicanos are already demanding a greater share of political power and are able to exert increasing influence. The health care arena for those demands, however, has generally been circumscribed by the community clinic movement, where Chicano groups already hold control. The struggle will increasingly be over limited grant and reimbursement dollars. It has not resulted in any specifically racial conflicts in the health sector in San Jose.

St. Louis. St. Louis is one of the two study cities with a history of a policy of racial segregation, Baltimore being the other. This legacy has led to a health policy confrontation that has dominated health planning in St. Louis for more than a decade—an issue which city blacks see as primarily racial in nature, but which city administrators maintain is a fiscal imperative.

The city's original public hospital was City Number One (Max C. Starkloff Hospital), which dates to 1834. Due to state segregation policies, blacks were not admitted to City Hospital Number One, and what little institutional medical care was available to them was provided through private or religious facilities or through a small, overcrowded, segregated hospital operated by the city. A drive by blacks over many years for better public hospital facilities culminated in the opening of Homer G. Phillips Hospital in 1934. Until the desegregation decision of the U.S. Supreme Court in 1954, Phillips was the only public hospital facility where blacks could obtain inpatient care, and it was located in the center of what was then the major black community of St. Louis. The hospital also provided internships and residencies for black graduates of medical schools across the United States; thus a national alumni group of "Homer G." evolved.

Different staffing patterns emerged at City Number One and Homer G. Phillips. At City Number One, then the hospital for the white population, heavy reliance was placed on medical staffing by the medical schools of Washington and St. Louis universities. As a result, until the late 1970s virtually all departments and medical services at City Number One were headed by doctors who held appointments at one or the other of the medical schools, and virtually all medical staff similarly held appointments at one or both of the medical schools. By September 1980, Washington University Medical School had withdrawn from all programs except neurology and neurosurgery at City Hospital Number One, leaving St. Louis University physicians in charge of almost all departments and services. A year later, St. Louis University and the St. Louis Department of Health and Hospitals signed a memorandum of understanding formalizing their relationship, the first written agreement in their many years of shared activities.

The situation was quite different at Homer G. Phillips, where almost all departments and medical services were headed by black doctors who were in private practice, and there were few formal staff arrangements with either of the two local medical schools. Surgery, which was affiliated with Washington University Medical School, was a notable exception. Popular and professional opinion was critical of inequality of care at Phillips.

Following the end of legal segregation and separate-but-equal public facilities in 1954, City Hospital Number One and Homer G. Phillips were officially desegregated and both were theoretically open to patients and staff of any race. Nevertheless, designation of patient catchment areas for the two public general hospitals along the east-west axis of the city, which coincided with the *de facto* housing segregation pattern, perpetuated segregation in patient usage until 1966, when a court ruling overturned the policy. By the mid-1960s, for a variety of reasons, a general impression prevailed among St. Louis residents that if one's only option was a public hospital, better and more comprehensive care could be received at City Number One (which did in fact have extensive medical school affiliations and superior professional staffing) than at Homer G. Phillips. Use of Homer G. Phillips, even among blacks, tended to be restricted to the emergency room and to long-term care or conditions of a less acute nature.

As the city of St. Louis continued its population decline, it also began to lose jobs and tax revenue, precipitating growing fiscal pressure on the city. Since the budget for the two general hospitals usually constituted more than one-fourth of the city's total budget (budget debates tended to concentrate on gross expenditures while disregarding patient care revenues), pressure mounted to reduce the financial burden of the hospital operation in the city of St. Louis. Remedies advanced during the 1960s increasingly included the possibility of the city's withdrawal from direct provision of hospital services.

During the 1970s attention turned to the feasibility of consolidating services to permit closing one of the city hospitals, or even closing both and replacing them with a more modern and cost-efficient facility. As time passed consultants and elected officials began to focus on Homer G. Phillips as the prime candidate for closure or conversion to an emergency or long-term care facility. These proposals evoked outpourings of racial pride and civic concern from black leaders, who attempted to block such moves. Nevertheless, the city closed Homer G. Phillips as an acute general hospital and consolidated inpatient services at City Number One in late 1979.

During the following year, black leaders engaged in a series of protests and appeals, which appeared to be leading nowhere. But when the seemingly strongly entrenched and powerful incumbent mayor came up for reelection early in 1981, the volatility of the Homer G. issue became pronounced. A white opponent campaigning in black north St. Louis predominantly on a promise to reopen Homer Phillips and close City Number One (meanwhile emphasizing in the white south side that the incumbent intended to cut the police force) unseated the mayor in a dramatic upset. In a city where blacks now constitute 44 percent of the population, with considerable (if not proportional) political power, the hospital question, which most blacks view as a racial issue (although whites either ignore it or consider it fiscal in nature), continues to dominate not only health but most other municipal policy-making as well.

CITY GOVERNMENT

To examine the overall administrative configuration and budgetary process for each of the five study cities, the Municipal Year Book provides useful perspective on local government.[17] The process of local government is closely related to government structure. Municipal government structure reflects several characteristic forms, each associated with such variables as city age, political tradition, ethnic composition, population, and income levels. The three predominant forms of contemporary American municipal government are the council-manager form (55.5% of localities with more than 25,000 in population), the mayor-council form (39% of localities), and the commission form (6% of localities), according to a 1977 survey by the International City Management Association. Heywood Sanders notes that the council-manager model is associated with efforts to achieve efficiency and professional competence in government. This newest form is found most frequently in cities in the West—young, rapidly growing localities with developing governmental structures. San Jose is representative of this group. Cincinnati also features a council-manager structure. The mayor-council form, common in larger, older cities with ethnic diversity and strong political traditions, is found most frequently in the East. This form predominated nationwide during the 19th century and is associated with an emphasis on political leadership and conflict resolution. Baltimore, Milwaukee, and St. Louis all operate with mayor-council governments. The third form, the commission model, was associated with early 20th century reform efforts to assure accountability and honesty in government. It has been replaced widely by the council-manager form and is now no longer common. In mayor-council governments, the authority and role of the mayor may vary from weak to strong, as evidenced by length of term, veto power, and appointment power. Cities with populations less than 50,000 and those in the range from 250,000 to 500,000 generally appear to have strong mayoralties, while cities of more than 500,000 have the highest proportion of weak mayoralties. Council-manager governments generally have a mayoralty with a weak, primarily ceremonial role. San Jose and Cincinnati are examples of this group. Among mayor-council governments, Milwaukee and St. Louis have weak mayoralties, and Baltimore is representative of the strong mayoralty form.

Cincinnati. Cincinnati has a council-manager form of government, in which general policy-making responsibility is vested in an elected council, and administration is assigned to an appointed, professional administrator, the city manager. The "weak" mayor serves at the head of the council. The city manager, who serves at the pleasure of the city council, plays an important role in the operation of the city but has little direct involvement in the conduct of health department affairs. The main impact of the city administration is budgetary. This influence is exercised through the Office of Budget Evaluation and Research, which operationalizes the city council's priorities in the form of the annual budget. The city manager has a key role in relating council policy to budget evaluation and research. City managers in the past have been sympathetic to neighborhood development and the delivery of health services, a position that has been helpful in establishing the network of primary health care clinics.

The commissioner of health in Cincinnati is appointed by the Board of Health and is not a patronage appointee controlled by the mayor or any faction in the city council. This has tended to limit the influence local elected political leaders can exert over health department programs. In addition to the Board of Health and the city manager's office, the commissioner must also interact with the thirteen members of the city council. In order to cope with this bureaucratic structure, a strong, politically oriented commissioner has been viewed as desirable. Among the constraints faced by the commissioner are civil service regulations that have imposed salary limitations and inflexible job standards. These have hampered health staff recruitment for public services. This problem is common to other cities.

The Democratic coalition that dominates city politics has been generally supportive of the health department's activities—especially the network of primary care clinics—although austerity measures in recent years have cut into the city's health budget. This political support is advantageous for elected officials, since the health department has been successful in developing a strong positive image in the minds of the voters.

As has been discussed earlier, the Cincinnati General Hospital has been transferred from local to state auspices together with the medical school. The medical school traditionally has had exceptional financial support from local as well as federal sources, and some local subsidy continues.

Milwaukee. Milwaukee's civic history in the twentieth century was shaped by its adoption in the early years of the century of the principles of municipal reform and by its persistent election of officials adhering to those principles. In the tradition of reform government, Milwaukee has a weak mayoralty and a strong council as well as many appointed policy-making boards. The structure of government is riddled with provisions to avoid centralization of partisan power, including such modern day anomalies as life tenure for the chief of police.

The city's mayoralty was captured in 1910 by the Socialist party, which held the office for all but twelve years until 1960 when election of the current mayor, Henry Maier, placed the office in the hands of the Democratic party. The "Socialism" of these officials, while marking the city's approach to public services, was less striking than their devotion to principles of reform, including non-partisan administration, sound financial and budgetary procedures, fiscal solvency, procedural propriety, and, in general, government by textbook standards.

The dispersion of formal influence in the city government structure has had several results including the flow of power to strong department heads. Among these is the commissioner of health. Alliances with such department heads have been a cornerstone of Maier's skillful concentration of political power. In forging a power base, the mayor, who had inherited a capable bureaucratic structure, focused on filling "gaps" in government activity, especially gaps in those administrative units formally under his control rather than that of the common council.[18] Thus, the mayor, who is not allowed by the formal structure to formulate an executive budget, has achieved a major role in the process through close relations with the head of the Bureau of Budget and Management, a unit which has vastly increased its influence under his sponsorship. The mayor has also expanded his influence through the placement of federal categorical programs within his sphere of administrative control. Like the director of the budget, the commissioner of health is a good friend and powerful ally of the mayor.

While the structure of the city health department and the mayor's personal political strategy position the health unit well to respond aggressively to external initiatives, most medical care is beyond the jurisdiction of the city government. It is Milwaukee County which has traditionally provided and continues to provide medical services to the needy in Milwaukee. In contrast to the steady development of administrative structure in the city, the county government has faced tumult in recent years as it has tried to adapt its structure to its increasing responsibilities. The first commission to study and make recommendations for the improvement of county government was appointed in 1950. The office of the county executive was created in 1959. The newly created office was given considerable power to appoint and to prepare the budget but not to veto acts of the county board. Significantly, as Schmandt et al. point out, it did not inherit the tradition of governmental sophistication which characterized the city. They observe:

If Maier in 1960 could initially face a council that understood the role of the mayor's office . . . and, if Maier could focus his attention on those areas most susceptible to his control while knowing he had a strong and well-functioning administrative structure behind him, [the County Executive] could not. Not only was the latter faced with the necessity of working out relations with a County Board that felt it necessary to scrutinize all his actions as potential threats to the group's pre-existing prerogatives; he was also compelled to develop an effective administrative organization to overcome the disabilities inherent in the old unintegrated and "headless" system. . . . [19]

The appointment of a chief executive has not eliminated the continuing involvement and parallel power of the county Board of Supervisors in the administration of the health institutions. Problems are further complicated by the existence of a Board of Public Welfare with official governing authority over the county's health and welfare activities. This power is ambiguous, however, since the board's policies may be rejected by the county Board of Supervisors which controls appropriations to the institutions. Coupled with the supervisory role of the Medical College of Wisconsin over the educational functions of the institution's medical staffs, these governance complexities have allowed a good deal of management to reflect incompatible objectives and potential for media coverage.

St. Louis. Many of the problems St. Louis faces as a city can be traced to the decision in 1876 to separate itself from St. Louis County, which created a consolidated city/county. In addition to the fiscal problems engendered by this split, health care delivery in the city of St. Louis is further influenced by the form of municipal government prevailing under the city's basic laws. The charter for the city of St. Louis dates to 1914, and while it embodies most of the good government reforms of the turn of the century, many of these (e.g., the presence of more than fifty independent and quasi-independent boards and commissions) tend to hamper quick and effective response to the urban problems of today.

The executive is characterized as a "weak mayor" because of the lack of strong executive authority in the major areas of executive responsibility. The mayor must share budget-making authority on the Board of Estimate and Apportionment, which decides the city's budget, with two other members, the president of the Board of Aldermen and the city comptroller, both elected at large and potential political opponents of the mayor. The mayor has weak appointing power.

The legislature in the city of St. Louis is the Board of Aldermen. It is comprised of 28 members, elected by ward, and a president of the Board of Aldermen, who is elected at large.

Employment practices of the city and constraints imposed by civil service and other regulations pose serious problems not only for the health and hospitals department but also for the entire city. A city charter provision limited all salaries, from the mayor down, to $25,000 per year, until it was changed in 1980. This had been a particularly confining limit for the Department of Health and Hospitals, which had been unable to recruit and hold physicians at such a salary. Especially hard-hit were faculty-staff positions at the public hospitals (City Number One and the chronic and rehabilitation hospitals) affiliated with the two St. Louis medical schools, which raised questions about maintaining their relationship under these circumstances.

Baltimore. Baltimore, like St. Louis, is a city/county. The provisions of its charter, passed in 1964, call for a mayor-council form of government in which the mayor, president of the city council, and comptroller are elected on a citywide basis for four-year terms of office. In addition, eighteen councilmen are elected from six districts for four-year terms concurrent with the mayor's term. The city has a municipal civil service system in which most personnel below the level of department head are included.

The system does provide for the formulation of labor relations and personnel policies, and recognizes the right of employees to organize and bargain collectively. While the mayor is authorized to submit disputes to binding arbitration, the provisions of the charter do not authorize strikes by municipal employees.

In contrast to St. Louis, the city has a "strong mayor" type of government. The mayor retains the authority to veto ordinances; to make some 230 appointments, including the heads of 65 departments, agencies, commissions, and boards; and to control the Board of Estimates, which determines the annual budget. Members of the board include the mayor and two of his appointees, the city solicitor and the director of public works, as well as the comptroller and the president of the city council (who also serves as president of the board).

The budget is therefore an executive budget which the city council has the power only to reduce. It is important to note that the charter prohibits short-term borrowing, a policy aimed at preventing a fiscal crisis of the sort that has occurred in Cleveland and New York. Faced with an ever-decreasing tax base, the city has attempted to follow a fiscal policy limiting the growth of city services and encouraging redevelopment in cooperation with the business community.

The Baltimore City Health Department is one of twenty-one executive departments in the city government. The commissioner of the health department (through his deputy commissioner) is charged with the responsibility of determining the department budget which goes to the Department of Finance, another major executive department. All of the executive departments submit their budget proposals to the Board of Estimates, which then determines the yearly budget.

San Jose. In San Jose, the city government does not provide health services. Its role in health care has been limited to the functioning of its city Health Commission. A mayoral advisory panel, this body has served primarily to furnish oversight and review on those occasions in which city input was required. An Office of Intergovernmental Relations within municipal government represents the city in the development and monitoring of contracts and grants with other levels of government.

The major actors in health are located in county government and consist of the county Board of Supervisors, the county executive, the Director of Medical Institutions and the administrator of the county health department.

The Board of Supervisors, consisting of five members elected by district, is the general governing body for the county. The main duties of the board are overseeing the fiscal affairs of the county and performing various administrative and executive functions. During 1977–1978, two of the board members were generally viewed as having liberal voting records on social policy issues, two were considered conservative, and the remaining supervisor provided the swing vote.

The county executive's office is basically responsible for managing the day-to-day affairs of the county. Answerable to the Board of Supervisors, the county executive is relied upon for charting general policy directions and developing issues for the board to consider. In health, these responsibilities encompass the two major agencies, the health department and the Valley Medical Center.

Summary

This chapter has presented the city's role in the structure and financing of health care for the poor in the context of the urban environment of the 1970s. It has been pointed out that local government structure, the locus of legal responsibility for health, and the orientation of local health and hospital agencies are extremely varied from city to city. Financial commitment to health has been seen to be tied to the locus of responsibility for health and to socioeconomic trends in the city. Many lessons from earlier local approaches to reorganizing publicly sponsored primary care have been cited. We have identified potential professional and philosophical conflict among key providers in and around the public sector. An assessment of socioeconomic trends has revealed the severe strains on local resources that are likely to continue and even worsen in certain cities. And a quick look at city government and budgets has identified the major actors on the local resource scene.

The great variation at the local level implies a need for flexibility in any new strategy to improve publicly sponsored care for the urban poor. Diminishing resources dictate that existing agencies' abilities must be used, refined, reorganized, and built upon. Local health departments and local public hospitals need to be realigned in order to satisfy better the needs and demands of the urban poor for personal and preventive health services.

References

1. Richard P. Nathan and Paul Dommel, "The Cities," in *Setting National Priorities, 1978,* edited by Joseph Pechman (Washington, D.C.: The Brookings Institution, 1977), p. 289.

2. William Shonick, "Mergers of Public Health Departments with Public Hospitals in Urban Areas," Supplement to *Medical Care* 18, no. 8 (August 1980): 1.

3. Ibid., p. 26.

4. Ibid., p. 28.

5. Office of the County Executive, Milwaukee County, Wisconsin, 1979.

6. Advisory Commission on Intergovernmental Relations, *Recent Trends in Federal and State Aid to Local Governments* (Washington, D.C., July, 1980).

7. Richard Nathan and Mary Nathan, *America's Governments* (New York: John Wiley & Sons, 1979), pp. 149, 177.

8. Ibid., pp. 183–211.

9. 1977 Census of Governments, "Selected Local Government Finances by County Area," *Compendium of Government Finances.*

10. U.S. Department of Health, Education and Welfare, Health Care Financing Administration, *Data on the Medicaid Program,* rev. ed. (Washington, D.C., 1979).

11. William Gorham and Nathan Glazer, eds., *The Urban Predicament* (Washington, D.C.: The Urban Institute, 1976), p. 22.

12. Nathan and Dommel, "The Cities," p. 285.

13. Ibid., p. 286.

14. George Peterson, "Finance," in *The Urban Predicament,* ed. by Gorham and Glazer, p. 46.

15. Ibid., p. 47.

16. Paul Dommel, Richard Nathan et al., *Decentralizing Community Development* (Washington, D.C.: U.S. Department of Housing and Urban Development, 1978).

17. Heywood Sanders, "Governmental Structure in American Cities," *The Municipal Year Book*, International City Management Association (Washington, D.C., 1979).

18. Henry J. Schmandt, John C. Goldbach and Donald B. Vogel, *Milwaukee: A Contemporary Urban Profile*, Praeger Publishers (New York, 1971).

19. Ibid., p. 83.

CHAPTER THREE

Access to Ambulatory Care
for the Urban Poor

In the previous chapters of this volume, we have examined recent federal policy initiatives that have addressed the ambulatory care needs of the poor and the role of local government in delivering or facilitating the delivery of health services. In this chapter, we will explore the issue of access to ambulatory care for the urban poor. First, the concept of access to health services will be discussed in the context of its historical and political development, and an effort will be made to arrive at a general definition or philosophy of access for the purposes of this analysis. This will be followed by a comparative analysis of access in the five study cities, measured by a set of indicators. The major emphasis will be on available resources and, to the degree that the information is obtainable, on the utilization of these resources. A second area of emphasis will be the potential financial barrier to access and the degree to which this barrier appears to have been removed via certain financing mechanisms for health care for the poor. The assessment of resources will include both the public sector and private sector delivery systems, while the examination of financial access will address poverty level, enrollment in and use of public financing programs such as Medicaid and Medicare, and the local eligibility criteria, service coverage, and reimbursement levels for each program.

Access: An Effort to Define the Term

The use of the term "access" in reference to the potential or actual obtaining of health services by a population must be considered within its historical context. Although public provision of medical services to the "sick poor" in America can be traced to the municipal physicians and midwives of the colonial period, the problems encountered by the poor in obtaining health care gained salience as a public policy issue only within the newly industrialized society of the early twentieth century. In this environment of entrepreneurial private medical practice and public or philanthropic hospital development, health care in the United States evolved into a largely uncoordinated, highly pluralistic system, in contrast to the centrally financed and administered health services of some other Western nations. Federal, state, and local governments sought through specific programs to fill gaps left by the private and charitable market, attempting to target social welfare services and resource development to meet the needs of those populations identified as underserved. Such early programs as those promoting child welfare and maternal health were briefly discussed in Chapter One. A federal program which specifically addressed resource availability was the Hill-Burton hospital construction support begun in the late 1940s. Throughout the first half of the century, there seemed to be a national consensus that certain basic health services should be available to all citizens and that the public sector was an appropriate guarantor of such a minimum level of care where the private market or charitable organizations failed. Public discussion of the availability of health services became much more urgent and focused during the early period of the Great Society, as the first chapter has described.

By the 1960s it became popular to talk of improving "access" to care in recognition of the failure of government or private market efforts to address adequately the financial and resource barriers to health services. The federal government responded by enactment of financing programs (Medicare and Medicaid), programs to assess community health needs (Comprehensive Health Planning), programs to reorganize the delivery system (Health Maintenance Organizations), and programs to increase the availability of health manpower and physical resources to underserved communities (Community Health Centers, Health Professions Educational Assistance). Participation of state and local governments varied depending upon the federal program and the predilections of the individual locality. In many cases, states and localities embarked upon parallel or independent projects. In these and other programs initiated under federal, state, and local health policy initiatives, a primary objective was to improve the public's access to health services.

The use of the term "access" has been somewhat imprecise, as Aday and Andersen have aptly pointed out:

Just what the concept of access means, however, much less how it might be measured and what methods should be used to evaluate it are ill-defined at present. Thus far, access has been more of a political than an operational

idea. It has for some time been an expressed or at least an implicit goal of
health policy. However, few attempts have been made to provide formalized
conceptual or empirical definitions of access that permit policy makers and
consumers to actually monitor the effectiveness of various programs in meeting that goal.[1]

Definitions of access have been lacking, and as was seen in the
previous chapter, the web of government programs (and the variety
of ways in which it is spun out in different localities) prohibits any
easy assessment of the degree to which particular programmatic efforts have led to specific social outcomes. While in theory it would
be useful for health policy-makers in any given locale to be able to
monitor the use and the costs of specific health programs and to assess
these programmatic interventions in terms of their impact on users'
health status, in practice such evaluations have not yet become con-
ceptually clear or operationally practicable. Milton Chen and James
Bush explain some of the inherent difficulties:

Because of the lack of acceptable comprehensive measures of health status,
the distribution implications of many public programs are not clear. Since
the majority of publicly-financed health programs are in-kind transfers of one
sort or the other, their distributional impact in terms of health is not clear.
Because of a lack of viable health status measures, even the flow of federal
funds to state and local governments cannot be analyzed for the funds' distributional impact in terms of health. The interaction of the interest groups
in political exchange often obscures the distributional impact further.[2]

Apart from these problems of conceptualization and measurement,
the costs of collecting the necessary financial and utilization data on
an ongoing basis have proved prohibitive for local governmental
budgets. In fact, most local planning agencies have barely been able
to maintain current inventories of service programs, their cost, and
the volume of services delivered.

The level of the public discussion of access to health care has been
significantly advanced by the work of researchers at the University
of Chicago's Center for Health Administration Studies (CHAS). Based
on their earlier studies of utilization of health services, Lu Ann Aday
and Ronald Andersen in 1973 initiated a research project to develop
an index of access to health care. This research was funded by the
Robert Wood Johnson Foundation as an avenue to assist the Foundation in evaluating the impact of the many programs it was supporting to improve access to health services. During the first phase
of the project, the researchers carried out a thorough review of the
literature on access. Then, drawing upon the diverse, limited, earlier
discussions of the topic, they analyzed individual indicators and syn-
thesized a variety of approaches into a coherent conceptual framework
for considering access as it can be affected by health policy. Subsequently, with their colleague Gretchen Fleming, Aday and Andersen
refined their conceptual framework and used the access-to-care measures they had developed in a national population survey, which ex-

amined the equity in access to health care of the major U.S. population groups.[3] They are currently performing a parallel evaluation of the Municipal Health Services Program (MHSP), which will use the methodology to measure changes in access to care that result from implementation of the program in the five study cities. The remainder of this section will be based on the conceptual framework and definition of access developed at the Center for Health Administration Studies.

The researchers themselves best summarize their theoretical framework:

Our approach to the study of access to medical care implies that characteristics of the delivery system (the availability and distribution of health care providers and facilities, for example) and characteristics of the population-at-risk in an area (their age, health status, insurance coverage, and income levels, for example) reflect the probable or *potential* levels of access to medical care whereas utilization and satisfaction measures may be considered indicators of actual or *realized* access to services. Health policy efforts such as the large-scale federal financing initiatives or the hospital-based group practices the Robert Wood Johnson Foundation has funded represent efforts to impact on the characteristics of the delivery system itself (by providing more convenient facilities) or of potential users of the system (by eliminating the financial barriers to care) and thereby ultimately influence the probability of individuals' entering the system and their subjective evaluations of how satisfactory they found the experience of care seeking to be.[4]

The basic definition of access offered by the researchers is "those dimensions which describe the potential and actual entry of a given population group to the health care delivery system." [5] This multifactor definition of access takes into account the numerous diverse yet valid approaches to the concept and makes it possible to evaluate the impact of health policy decisions not only on structural or resource inputs, but also on process and outcome measures.

A brief summary follows of some operational indicators of the framework for assessment of access. In the balance of the chapter, data will be presented for some of these operational indicators, principally those referring to characteristics of the delivery system. Two major groups of indicators are associated with this access framework, those related to potential access and those related to realized access. The indicators of potential access include characteristics of the delivery system, such as measures of the volume and distribution of personnel and facilities, and of organization of the system. Other indicators of potential access are characteristics of the population-at-risk, including such predisposing factors as health care beliefs, education, age, sex, race, and ethnicity; such enabling indicators as income levels, insurance coverage, and place of residence; and such need characteristics as illness symptoms and disability days.

The second major group of indicators are those that refer to realized access. Objective indicators of realized access are measures of utilization of health services, categorized by type of service, by site, by purpose, and by time interval. Subjective indicators of realized access are measures of consumer satisfaction. Included are general attitudes and specific evaluations of care received.

A final major issue to be accounted for in the evaluation of access is the degree to which any variation in access levels among population subgroups is equitable. As defined by the University of Chicago researchers, "equity is present when services are distributed on the basis of people's need for them," rather than on the basis of such characteristics as race, income, or place of residence.[6] The 1975–1976 national population survey they conducted measured equity of access for population subgroups by examining the patterns of utilization of health services during reported episodes of need.

The CHAS study concluded that the evidence from the national survey suggests that progress has been made in the past fifteen years in access to services and in the equity of access among subgroups of the population. It determined that only about 12 percent of the population surveyed had no regular source of medical care. This translates, however, to an estimated 26 million persons with no regular point of entry to the system, persons who receive less care than need would indicate and whose care is inconvenient and unsatisfactory. The study also concluded that approximately 22 million persons under the age of 65 have no insurance coverage for health services of any type, including publicly financed welfare services. These groups are generally young, often urban, frequently employed in blue collar jobs and constitute the population often referred to as "working poor." This group utilizes services at a lower rate than need would dictate. Overall findings indicate, however, that the distribution of hospital and physician services is equitable across groups and relative to need and that, over time, access for the elderly and the poor, for nonwhite and for rural farm populations, has improved substantially since 1963. This would seem to validate the achievements of the federal financing and delivery mechanisms that were developed to improve access for the elderly and the poor in the past decade and a half, particularly Medicare and Medicaid. Nevertheless, specific subgroups in the population still rank lower on certain indicators of both potential and realized access to health services. These include specific ethnic groups: individuals of Spanish heritage and rural and urban blacks; the rural population in general; older children and young adults; and the working poor.[7] Several of these groups are concentrated in the central cities, and issues of access remain important in our assessment of care for the urban poor.

Despite the advances described above, caution has been expressed over prematurely drawing the conclusion that the poor are now adequately served. For example, although low-income groups now surpass the affluent in mean number of physician visits annually, questions of use relative to need have been raised. Other caveats have been identified that center on certain groups of the poor who have not benefited equally in the progress of the past decade because of ex-

. clusion from Medicaid, continued discrimination, or cultural barriers. Additionally, there is concern about the locus and nature of care that may be masked by a simplistic interpretation of general utilization trends. That the poor frequently use emergency rooms (ER) and out-patient departments (OPD) rather than family doctors, that waiting times for care are lengthy, that they receive few preventive services and undergo a large volume of surgical procedures led several ob-servers to argue for continued, if not augmented, efforts to further enhance equity of access.

This section has presented a useful format developed by Aday, Andersen, and Fleming to define access and to operationalize meas-urements of access by the use of several indicators previously iden-tified in the literature. While the study described is much more exhaustive than the assessment presented here of access in the five cities can be, the following sections of this chapter will attempt to relate available resources, utilization, and financing data to the con-ceptual framework enunciated above.

Characteristics of the Health Care Delivery System

A major set of indicators for potential access are embodied in the characteristics of the health care delivery system, the most evident group of which are the available resources themselves and their dis-tribution. Evidence of realized access lies in utilization statistics for the available components of the delivery system. Assessments of ac-cess, of the quality and nature of health care the poor receive in cities, ultimately come down to the behavior of specific institutional pro-viders in a particular locality—whom they treat, whom they don't treat, and what kind of care is delivered.

To gain better insight into how the poor fare in local health care delivery systems, we will examine the major public sector and private sector providers in the five study cities, with special attention to the low-income neighborhoods involved in the demonstration project. We will approach these different groups of providers as generic classes to be compared across the five cities, and then by way of summary attempt to show how they fit together in each of the cities to create a unique set of circumstances that characterize the local environment. For purposes of simplification, the private sector will be considered to consist of private physicians and private (voluntary and for-profit) hospitals, which will be discussed first. The public hospital and public health department clinics will be considered next as the public sector component of the health system. Finally, community health centers will be identified separately, although there is often considerable over-lap between public and private sector activity in this provider cate-gory, as well as great diversity in service mission, ranging from comprehensive to special purpose programs. Public health department clinics in some cities are federally funded with community health center grants. Programs that overlap will be identified whenever possible. A series of city maps showing MHSP sites, target neighborhoods, and major health service providers is found on pages 195–99.

THE PRIVATE SECTOR: PRIVATE PHYSICIANS

According to recent figures, the majority of Americans prefer to receive their ambulatory care from office-based physicians. Data published by the National Center for Health Statistics on physician visits in 1975 indicate that 77.7 percent of the visits (excluding telephone contacts) took place in physician offices (including prepaid group), while 14.8 percent took place in hospital clinics or emergency rooms.[8] The data from the National Health Interview Survey for 1978 indicate that 76.1 percent of the reported visits (excluding telephone contacts) took place in physician offices (including group practices and clinics), while 15.5 percent took place in hospital clinics or emergency rooms.[9] Although the proportion of care taking place in hospitals has been increasing steadily, it is clear that the private physician's office, whether solo or group practice, is still the predominant model for ambulatory care delivery in the United States. Hospital-based ambulatory care is more heavily represented in Standard Metropolitan Statistical Areas (SMSA) in terms of place of residence and in the Northeast in terms of geographic region.[10] These facts reflect a phenomenon common to the private physician market in low-income urban areas: poor urban neighborhoods generally have few office-based physicians in practice.

The use of private practitioners by the poor depends upon at least three major factors: the presence of the physician in the community; the physician's willingness to treat poor patients, which is closely related to the expected level of remuneration for the services; and the ability and motivation of the patient, in the absence of nearby practitioners, to travel to other areas of the city for care. The former Department of Health, Education and Welfare (HEW), as part of the documentation of eligibility for funding National Health Service Corps (NHSC) sites, developed mechanisms for designating health manpower shortage areas and medically underserved areas based on such general criteria as the following:

- available health resources in relation to the size of the area and its population, e.g., physician-to-population ratio;
- health indices for the population of the area, e.g., infant mortality rate;
- economic factors affecting the population's need and demand for health services, e.g., percentage of the population below the poverty level; and
- demographic characteristics that affect the need and demand for health services, e.g., percentage of the population over age 65.

Table 3.1 presents by degree of severity the number of sites which had been designated as primary care health manpower shortage areas

TABLE 3.1

PRIMARY CARE HEALTH MANPOWER SHORTAGE AREAS, NATIONWIDE,

BY DEGREE OF SHORTAGE, AUGUST 31, 1978

Degree of Shortage Group[a]	Metro	Nonmetro	Total	Percent of all areas
1	120	305	425	38%
2	90	182	272	24
3	42	180	222	20
4	43	154	197	18
TOTAL	294	821	1,116	100%

[a](1) indicates most severe shortage; (4), least severe.

TABLE 3.2

PRIMARY CARE HEALTH MANPOWER SHORTAGE AREAS, FIVE CITIES

AUGUST 6, 1979

State	County	Service area	Degree of doctor shortage[a]
California	Santa Clara	Loma Prieta School District	2
Wisconsin	Milwaukee	Inner City North (Milwaukee)	1
		Inner City South (Milwaukee)	3
Ohio	Hamilton	East End (Cincinnati)	2
		Winton Hills (Cincinnati)	1
		Price Hill/Fairmont (Cincinnati)	1
		Lincoln Heights (Cincinnati)	2
Maryland	Baltimore	North Central Baltimore	1
		O'Donnell Heights	1
		Cherry Hill	1
		Constant Care Service Area	2
		East Baltimore	2
		West Baltimore	3
		Northwest Baltimore	1
		Hampden/Woodberry/Remington	3
Missouri	St. Louis City	Southeast St. Louis	3
		North St. Louis	2

[a](1) indicates most severe shortage; (3), least severe.

SOURCE: U.S. Department of Health, Education and Welfare, Health Resources Administration, "List of Health Manpower Shortage Areas Designated under Section 332 of the Public Health Service Act," Federal Register, August 6, 1979.

nationwide as of mid-1978. Among the five cities involved in the Municipal Health Services Program, seventeen communities had been designated as primary care health manpower shortage areas, as shown in Table 3.2.

Another approach to assessing physician resources is to compare overall physician-to-population ratios for urban areas. The American Medical Association collects and annually updates information on physicians in practice by county, state, census division, and region, as well as by specialty and professional activity. While information corresponding to city boundaries is not available, the county data can still be useful. Table 3.3 presents physician-to-population ratios for the counties in which the fifty largest cities are located. County population is estimated for December 31, 1975, and physician complement is the reported number of nonfederal physicians engaged in patient care as of December 31, 1976. The range is from 92 physicians per 100,000 population in El Paso, to 621 per 100,000 in the borough of Manhattan in New York. It must be noted, however, that urban centers are area markets for medical services and generally serve outlying suburban and rural patients as well as central city populations. In addition, those cities (counties) which rank unusually high on this distribution are almost all (St. Louis, Boston, San Francisco, Washington, Baltimore) independent cities which are not part of a county that extends into suburban areas, or cities which dominate the overlying county in terms of both space and population. Cities in the Southwest, which have been gaining population rapidly in recent years, tend to exhibit lower county physician-to-population ratios than other regions.

Cincinnati. Cincinnati's primary care manpower problems in the inner city are indicative of the conditions extant in many poor urban areas. Private physicians have long since abandoned practices in economically depressed neighborhoods. In the Madisonville area in 1977 there was one part-time physician near retirement who had been ill for several years, a full-time podiatrist, and a full-time pharmacist located directly next door to a city clinic. In the Winton Hills site, one physician and a pharmacist associate have continued operating several blocks from the new health center. In Avondale, only one physician would accept new Medicaid patients.

Milwaukee. Milwaukee provides a concrete example of the type of analysis involved in achieving federal designation of a community as a health manpower shortage area. The Southeastern Wisconsin Health Systems Agency (HSA) in 1977 calculated the availability of primary care physicians in Milwaukee's inner-city north and inner-city south, areas which roughly coincide with the two target areas of the MHSP. The task involved determining the number of *office-based* primary care practitioners (general practice, family practice, obstetrics, gynecology, pediatrics, and internal medicine); estimating the number of ambu-

TABLE 3.3

NONFEDERAL PATIENT CARE PHYSICIAN-TO-POPULATION RATIOS FOR THE COUNTY AREAS
OF THE FIFTY LARGEST CITIES, DECEMBER 31, 1976

City (County)	County patient care physicians Dec. 31, 1976	County resident population Dec. 31, 1975	County physician-to-population ratio (per 100,000)
New York (five counties)*	18,732	7,509,300	249
Chicago (Cook)	9,657	5,337,600	180
Los Angeles (Los Angeles)	13,162	6,936,200	189
Philadelphia (city)	4,295	1,804,100	238
Detroit (Wayne)	3,355	2,256,000	148
Houston (Harris)	3,315	1,973,200	168
Baltimore (city)	3,182	826,400	385
Dallas (Dallas)	2,342	1,407,500	166
San Diego (San Diego)	2,644	1,609,100	164
San Antonio (Bexar)	1,300	930,800	139
Indianapolis (Marion)	1,565	798,200	196
Washington (District of Columbia)	2,491	713,900	348
Honolulu (Honolulu)	1,029	710,500	144
Milwaukee (Milwaukee)	1,741	1,031,200	168
Phoenix (Maricopa)	1,941	1,237,800	156
San Francisco (San Francisco)	2,875	660,200	435
Memphis (Shelby)	1,443	744,900	193
Cleveland (Cuyahoga)	3,397	1,587,500	213
Boston (Suffolk)	3,333	720,500	462
New Orleans (Orleans Parish)	1,402	575,200	243
San Jose (Santa Clara)	2,253	1,218,700	184
Columbus, OH (Franklin)	1,530	866,600	176
Jacksonville, FL (Duval)	733	565,800	129
St. Louis (city)	2,434	520,000	468
Seattle (King)	2,476	1,149,600	215
Denver (Denver)	1,971	501,900	392
Kansas City, MO (Jackson)	1,044	641,800	162
Pittsburgh (Allegheny)	2,893	1,519,600	190
Atlanta (Fulton)	1,760	587,200	299
Nashville-Davidson (Davidson)	1,113	455,800	244
Cincinnati (Hamilton)	1,876	890,200	210
Buffalo (Erie)	1,890	1,092,100	173
El Paso (El Paso)	400	432,200	92
Minneapolis (Hennepin)	2,147	922,200	232
Omaha (Douglas)	930	421,500	220
Toledo (Lucas)	843	484,800	173
Oklahoma City (Oklahoma)	1,065	557,900	190
Miami (Dade)	3,378	1,464,400	230
Fort Worth (Tarrant)	799	733,600	108
Portland, OR (Multnomah)	1,585	545,600	290
Newark (Essex)	1,908	891,300	214
Louisville (Jefferson)	1,300	711,500	182
Long Beach (Los Angeles)	13,162	6,936,200	189
Tulsa (Tulsa)	608	418,600	145
Oakland (Alameda)	1,852	1,108,300	167
Austin (Travis)	507	368,900	137
Tucson (Pima)	882	455,200	193
Baton Rouge (East Baton Rouge Parish)	445	319,300	139
Norfolk (city)	598	397,500	150
Charlotte (Mecklenburg)	564	380,900	148
*Bronx County	2,289	1,379,000	165
Kings County	4,199	2,432,700	172
New York County	8,724	1,404,300	621
Queens County	3,038	1,963,500	154
Richmond County	482	329,800	146

SOURCE: American Medical Association, Physician Distribution and Licensure in the United States, 1976 (Dearborn, Ill.: Center for Health Services Research and Demonstration, 1977).

latory primary care visits to hospital outpatient departments, emergency rooms, and walk-in clinics made by inner-city residents, to obtain a full-time equivalent (FTE) approximation of *hospital-based* physician care; and finally deriving population-to-physician ratios. The analysis revealed that for inner-city north there were a total of 20 FTE physicians, of which 11.33 FTEs were hospital-based; for inner-city south, there were only 12 FTE physicians, of which 0.56 FTEs were hospital-based.

The population-to-physician ratios produced were as follows:

Inner-city north	5301 : 1
Inner-city south	4050 : 1
Contiguous area (remainder of Milwaukee County)	1480 : 1

Although the county area contiguous to the inner city reported 586 FTE physicians (eighty of whom were located within the nearby central business district), the HSA argued that problems of access remained for inner-city residents. The downtown physicians generally serve the affluent, mobile population of the metropolitan area, including the 45,000 workers from the county-at-large who commute daily to the central business district and account for an estimated 30 percent of the physicians' patient load.

The HSA also cited physical, social, and transportation barriers to the use of these contiguous physician resources. Physicians are concentrated in a relatively small area bounded by an industrial plant, recreational sites, and luxury high-rise apartments, all of which tend to reinforce the linguistic, economic, and social isolation of poor and minority groups within the population. It was also argued that limitations of the public transportation system inhibited easy access, since travel from the inner-city north or inner-city south to the downtown area, outside of normal business hours, often requires at least one bus transfer and approximately ten to fifteen minutes of combined waiting time, in addition to actual travel time.

St. Louis. Health manpower data collected in the cities of St. Louis, Baltimore, and San Jose reveal, with some variation, conditions similar to those in Cincinnati and Milwaukee. Unlike Milwaukee, where the physician supply remained concentrated within the city, St. Louis experienced a 20 percent loss of its physician supply between 1960 and 1978, while the supply in surrounding areas in St. Louis County grew by nearly 300 percent. Nonetheless, the HSA estimated that the city managed to retain 631.5 FTE primary care physicians, resulting in the highly favorable population-to-physician ratio of 885 to 1. Closer inspection, however, revealed that the majority of these physicians were hospital and medical school-based, while the two MHSP target areas had a paucity of office-based primary care physicians: the northern region, with 48 practitioners, had a population-to-physician ratio of 4602 to 1, and the southeastern region, with 43 practitioners, had a ratio of 3767 to 1.

In evaluating the distributional aspects of the physician supply, the St. Louis HSA noted the high concentration of physicians affiliated with the city's two medical schools and the fact that many of them were engaged in teaching and research rather than in direct patient care to the local community. Furthermore, they pointed to the problem of the aging physician population, especially in low-income areas. A household survey provided evidence that almost half of those interviewed said their usual source of health care was a physician sixty years of age or older, while 28 percent were seeing physicians who were in their fifties.

Baltimore. Baltimore has also experienced the problem of losing older physicians to retirement, physicians who are often not replaced. When new physicians do locate in the area, they may not accept Medicaid recipients or patients who can afford only modest fees. In Southeast Baltimore, the focus of the Municipal Health Services Program, 58 percent of the population reported private, office-based physicians as their usual source of health care in a 1977 survey.[11] In view of the dominance of this usual source of care, the loss of physicians through death and retirement is perceived as a serious problem. In 1977, Southeast Baltimore had 39 primary care physicians for its 120,000 residents, a ratio of 3,079 persons per physician. Residents of Southeast Baltimore report unusually high reliance (52 percent) on physicians within their community, although they travel out-of-area for hospital care. This is contrasted to findings in two other disadvantaged Baltimore neighborhoods, East Baltimore and Lower Park Heights, with even more limited physician resources, where much lower use of private physicians is reported and less care is obtained in-area.

In 1979, the Baltimore City Medical Society initiated a survey of all licensed physicians in Baltimore to collect reliable information on the amount and characteristics of ambulatory care provided by private office-based practitioners. The resulting study provides one of the few really thorough assessments of the role of private physicians in providing primary care for a major U.S. city. The study found that an adequate amount of ambulatory care services was available to and received by Baltimore residents, but that services are not uniformly available across neighborhoods. Baltimore residents received less primary care and more specialty care than the national average. Black residents received much less office-based care and more institutional-based care than whites. Private office-based physicians provided 62 percent of the ambulatory care received by Baltimore residents and had the capacity to provide considerably more care, if there were increased demand and a removal of social and financial barriers.[12]

This study, sponsored by private medicine, began to address the influence on availability of care of the increasing supply of physicians in a city which has major medical training programs.

San Jose. One gross measure of physicians' willingness to serve the poor is the number of practitioners participating in the Medicaid program. The California Department of Health, for example, has compared the ratio of primary care physicians participating in Medi-Cal to Medi-Cal population with the ratio of physicians to patients in the private sector in Santa Clara County. The department asserts that to bring the physician-to-population ratio in the primary care portion of the Medi-Cal program in the county into parity with the physician-to-patient ratio in the private (non-Medi-Cal) sector, 109 more primary care physicians would be needed. Despite the difficulties of using the private sector as a standard for comparison, these figures are at least indicative of potential limits on access for Medi-Cal patients to private office-based care.

As these data seem to suggest, it is difficult to give any standard interpretation to individual physician-to-population ratios without taking into account the multiple factors dictating current utilization patterns. In this regard, it is important to distinguish the mere *presence* (potential access) of physician resources from the actual *availability* (realized access) of those resources to a specific population. Realized access is contingent upon the willingness of physicians to serve poor patients as well as on the propensity of patients to seek services from these providers.

It is difficult to predict the health care resource utilization patterns of communities simply from statistics on income, health status, and reported presence or absence of private physicians in the immediate vicinity. Many residents of low-income communities report private physicians as their usual source of health care and apparently are as willing as middle-income persons to travel out of the neighborhood to patronize the health care provider of their choice. In some cases, long-time residents of a community continue to see a physician even though his practice has been relocated in another neighborhood. Residents of urban communities which could be described as medically underserved may in fact use the services of private physicians in other communities and may have established patterns of health care utilization that may not warrant change.

A telephone interview survey of the resident population of the service areas of sites selected for participation as Municipal Health Services Program clinics, which was carried out by University of Chicago researchers, established that private physician usage was by far the predominant mode of health care for these communities. In each case, neighborhoods were surveyed which had been identified by local policy-makers as medically underserved. Reported reliance on private physicians or other noninstitutional providers as the regular source for care ranged from 57.5 percent of those surveyed in St. Louis to 71.1 percent of those surveyed in Cincinnati. This category was four to five times the size of any other reported source, including public hospital or clinics, private hospital OPD or ER, and MHSP center.[13] No information is currently available as to income level or insurance status by source of care for the surveyed community population. Any reductions in the coverage that has enabled low-income persons to use the private physician market may have an effect on provider participation and patient utilization patterns. It is clear, however, that in low-income or medically underserved communities, the overwhelming preference is still for the private physician.

THE PRIVATE SECTOR: VOLUNTARY HOSPITALS

A conventional misconception about urban health services is that the poor and near-poor, unable to obtain care from the few remaining community practitioners, are left with no alternative except to seek treatment at public hospitals and neighborhood health centers. Yet a significant proportion of the disadvantaged population do receive ambulatory care from voluntary hospitals.

There are a variety of reasons why these hospitals are willing to treat patients who may not be able to pay the full cost of services or for whom Medicaid reimbursement does not cover costs. First, the institutional mission of some hospitals—hospitals with particular religious affiliations or those that have special ties to the local community—may be oriented toward and dedicated to serving the indigent. Second, academic medical centers that have remained in inner-city areas often sponsor primary care and specialty clinics in order to provide comprehensive care, as well as to strengthen their teaching programs. Third, in many cities, hospital reimbursement regulations tie payments to occupancy rate. Thus, since outpatient clinics are viewed as major inpatient feeders, they fill beds which, if empty, would generate financial penalties. Many community hospitals remaining in the inner city have a limited population to draw upon, and their institutional survival may depend on maintaining a respectable occupancy rate even in the face of growing deficits.

Cincinnati. The role of the voluntary hospitals varies considerably from city to city and within a city among neighborhoods. There are thirteen private general acute hospitals in the Greater Cincinnati area. All provide emergency room services, and six provide organized outpatient clinical services, as shown in Table 3.4. For the most part the services are prenatal, postpartum, infant, dental, nutrition, podiatry, family planning, home health, pharmacy, and health education. Some of the financial support for these clinics is provided by the Community Chest, welfare agencies, Medicare, and Medicaid programs.

Hospitals in Cincinnati are poorly distributed. Seven hospitals,

TABLE 3.4

CINCINNATI VOLUNTARY HOSPITAL UTILIZATION DATA

Hospitals	Beds[a]	Admissions[a]	Occupancy rate[a] (percent)	OPD visits[b]	ER visits[b]
Voluntary					
Bethesda North	234	7,062	91.0	-	41,429
Bethesda Oak	492	18,982	86.4	11,377	24,758
Children's Hosp. Med. Ctr.	310	15,288	85.5	83,973	64,337
Christ	665	22,113	83.6	6,559	17,276
Deaconess	278	9,635	82.4	-	11,381
Good Samaritan	746	25,933	84.7	17,266	22,904
Jewish of Cincinnati	637	21,770	85.2	11,316	23,571
Otto Epp Memorial	80	N.A.	N.A.	-	4,083
Our Lady of Mercy	159	6,837	89.3	549	21,801
Providence	359	13,863	85.2	13,590	33,632
Shriner's	30	445	83.3	2,231	-
St. Francis	254	7,147	82.3	-	16,143
St. George	84	3,689	89.3	-	24,928
Public					
Cincinnati General	615[c]	19,915[c]	80.2[c]	16,653	95,329

[a]American Hospital Association data for 1978.

[b]Central Ohio River Valley Association Health Systems Agency data for 1977.

[c]American Hospital Association data for 1980.

comprising the majority of area beds, are located in an area with a 1.5 mile radius located north of the downtown business district and referred to locally as "Pill Hill." Overt competition among these hospitals is largely controlled by an effective hospital council, but Cincinnati is regarded by some planners as seriously over-bedded, and the potential for inter-hospital conflict is real and increasing.

Competition for patients in Cincinnati varies according to the socioeconomic class of patients. Competition among area private hospitals for paying patients is becoming more heated as the fully insured population continues to move farther from the centralized cluster of private hospitals, although occupancy levels have remained higher than 80 percent. It is reflected in the aggressive recruitment of admitting physicians, and in the many emergency departments that have been established throughout the city. In the past, the voluntary hospitals (except for Children's Hospital) have for the most part left the care of indigents to the health department and the public hospital. A new-found interest in the indigent population of Cincinnati as a source of potential inpatients is not restricted to General Hospital and Children's Hospital. Several private hospitals in Cincinnati had, by 1978, initiated discussions with the commissioner of health on a very tentative basis regarding potential linkages between clinic sites and neighborhood hospitals. If the purchasing power of indigent populations does not deteriorate extensively due to reductions in Medicaid benefits, the private hospitals in Cincinnati, in order to improve census, may be prepared to pursue these patients more aggressively.

Baltimore. In Baltimore, voluntary hospitals play an important primary care role for some disadvantaged neighborhoods. As is pointed out in Table 3.5, almost three-quarters of the population in East Baltimore view voluntary hospitals as their usual source of ambulatory care, with the Johns Hopkins Hospital providing the largest proportion of visits.[14] In Southeast Baltimore, target area of the Municipal Health Services Program, less than 30 percent of the population rely on hospital-based ambulatory care, while nearly 60 percent report the private physician as their usual source of ambulatory care. Two of the communities in the Shapiro study are low-income minority neighborhoods which have been the target of earlier federal and local strategies to improve availability of health services. The third, Southeast Baltimore, is a white working-class neighborhood, which until the MHSP was initiated had not benefited from public strategies to increase access to health care. Among the five demonstration cities, Baltimore is unique in targeting a white community for MHSP services, having in the past addressed the health care needs of ethnic minority groups via other programs.

The history of federal health policy initiatives in Baltimore illustrates a voluntary hospital role quite different from that in Cincinnati, a role in which public and private sectors worked in partnership to improve

TABLE 3.5

USUAL SOURCE OF AMBULATORY CARE, SELECTED BALTIMORE NEIGHBORHOODS
(in percentage)

Source of Care	East Baltimore	Southeast Baltimore	Lower Park Heights
Hospitals, total percentage	74.6	28.9	43.5
The Johns Hopkins Hospital	60.4	10.0	*
Baltimore City Hospitals	*	11.5	*
Sinai Hospital	*	*	21.8
Other hospitals	14.2	7.4	21.7
Community clinics	8.3	6.2	18.3
Private physician	11.8	57.8	30.3
No usual source	5.4	7.3	8.0

NOTE: Asterisk signifies included with "other hospitals."

SOURCE: Sam Shapiro, Pearl S. German, Donald M. Steinwachs, Elizabeth A.
Skinner, and Gary A. Chase, Relationship of Resources to Health
Care Behavior in Disadvantaged Populations (Baltimore, Md.: The
Johns Hopkins University Health Care Research and Development
Center, 1978).

access to care for the indigent. At the same time that Medicaid and
Medicare provided coverage for the care of dependent populations
in the private sector, other Great Society programs also stimulated
voluntary hospital participation in providing health services for the
poor. Funds from the Office of Economic Opportunity (OEO) enabled
the development of the First Maryland Health Care Corporation, a
program modeled on the American Hospital Association "Ameri-
plan", that established a community health network in West and
Northwest Baltimore. In 1967, Provident Hospital (located in West
Baltimore) and the health department obtained an OEO grant to establish a neighborhood health center. Additional community programs developed in the early 1970s with the support of the health
department include: the Mercy-Southern Health Care Center, a joint
project with Mercy Hospital, planned with residents of South Baltimore; the Northwest Health Services Corporation; the North Central
Health Corporation; the Park Heights Community Health Center, in
cooperation with Sinai Hospital (located northwest of the city center);

the Homestead-Montebello Community Health Center, in coopera-
tion with Union Memorial, North Charles General, and Good Sa-
maritan hospitals (in the northern part of the city); West Baltimore
Community Health Corporation, in cooperation with Bon Secours
Hospital; and the East Baltimore Medical Plan, established by the
Johns Hopkins Hospital.

Thus it is evident that in Baltimore, the voluntary hospitals have
played a major and assertive role in providing ambulatory care for
the urban poor not only in emergency rooms and outpatient departments, but also in neighborhood primary care clinics. Table 3.6 shows
voluntary hospital utilization data for Baltimore. Given an increasing
proportion of poor and minority citizens in Baltimore as total numbers
shrank, it is not surprising that voluntary hospitals showed concern
over their decreasing service populations and began competing for
patients rather early. The Johns Hopkins Hospital in particular became
a major primary care resource for the poor black population, as is
shown in Table 3.6, partly because of its location. Competition within
the voluntary hospital sector and between public and private sectors
is evidenced further by the development of as many as nine health
maintenance organizations (HMO) in Baltimore as of early 1980, each
of which aims to capture part of the inpatient market for its referral
hospital(s).

St. Louis. St. Louis is also a city where declining population and
increasing proportions of poor and minorities have caused established
hospitals to compete for patients and sometimes to fail financially due
to growing debt from unrecompensed care. Between 1960 and 1978,
St. Louis lost more than half its hospital bed capacity as population,
facilities, and health personnel migrated to St. Louis County. The
number of general hospitals in St. Louis dropped during the same
period as voluntary hospitals merged, changed auspices, or closed
entirely, while the county suburbs' resources grew as hospitals relocated outside the city.

An overview of recent voluntary hospital utilization is presented
in Table 3.7. These changes paralleled the city's loss of 40 percent of
its population between 1950 and 1978. These figures are particularly
significant in view of the fact that delivery of health care in St. Louis
tends to be hospital-oriented. A substantial proportion of ambulatory
patients in St. Louis is treated in the outpatient departments of large
general hospitals, including the university hospitals (Barnes, St. Louis
Children's, St. Louis University, and Cardinal Glennon Children's),
the major teaching affiliates (Jewish and Deaconess), and the city
hospital clinics. Each of these facilities handled more than 23,000 visits
in 1978, and all have many specialty clinics, frequently staffed by
house officers. The Greater St. Louis Health Systems Agency noted
in its 1978 Health Systems Plan that Medicaid patients in the city (but
not elsewhere in the region) made more visits to outpatient depart-

TABLE 3.6

BALTIMORE VOLUNTARY HOSPITAL UTILIZATION DATA

Hospitals	Beds[a,b]	Admis-sions[c]	Occu-pancy rate[a] (percent)	OPD visits[a]	ER visits[a]
Voluntary					
Bon Secours	217	5,481	75.6	29,342	22,263
Children's	126	2,683	53.0	14,200	-
Church	310	9,362	89.7	26,889	22,992
Good Samaritan	235	5,257	77.9	19,242	1,965
Greater Balt. Med. Ctr.	401	19,829	89.7	56,564	33,177
Johns Hopkins	1,081	33,476	83.2	373,013	83,718
Lutheran	194	4,780	76.7	13,709	22,052
Maryland General	351	12,344	81.9	88,052	25,809
Mercy	328	11,652	85.0	105,611	27,762
North Charles General	142	4,143	87.7	20,907	6,953
Provident	271	6,527	77.0	26,095	30,054
Sinai	516	18,496	87.7	37,307	63,616
South Baltimore General	384	15,043	83.7	24,786	37,920
St. Agnes	463	17,825	87.0	49,822	57,096
St. Joseph	442	16,657	86.7	44,946	33,458
Union Memorial	415	14,247	86.1	32,699	36,979
University of Maryland	681	19,175	74.8	198,923	52,188
Public					
Baltimore City	332	10,090	78.7	100,991	52,863

[a]Maryland Hospital Association data for 1977.

[b]December 1977 bed count.

[c]American Hospital Association data for 1978.

ments and emergency rooms than to physicians' offices and community health centers in 1978. There may be less competition among St. Louis's voluntary hospitals than one would expect, however, because of the relative scarcity of private facilities. Private hospitals, with their outpatient departments, have migrated to the suburbs in significant numbers, so that except for the university teaching hospitals, no private OPD or emergency room has sufficient patient volume to constitute real competition with the public facilities and community health centers.

Milwaukee. In Milwaukee, the circumstances are somewhat different. Milwaukee's Health Systems Agency estimated in 1978 that overbedding in the metropolitan area exceeded 900 medical and surgical beds. A very considerable proportion of the unused capacity was in seven acute care general hospitals, located close to the old central business district, where occupancy rates were between 50 percent and 70 percent in 1978, as seen in Table 3.8. The clustered hospitals are contained within an area twenty-three blocks long and four blocks wide. Only one hospital had relocated to the suburbs by 1977.

The remaining hospitals have competed vigorously for patients, with varying success. They have employed a variety of strategies, including expansion of tertiary services (four of the seven hospitals offer open-heart surgery), expansion of emergency room services, establishment of links with outlying community hospitals, creation of feeder clinics in rural areas and small cities, construction or renovation of facilities, and construction of professional office buildings. In Milwaukee, black physicians do not limit their practices to any particular hospital, but many have admitting privileges at these seven hospitals close to the inner city.

While some voluntary hospitals have reluctantly assumed the role of primary care provider through their emergency rooms and clinics by dint of demographic shifts within their service areas, others have begun to come to terms with this role by restructuring their operations and establishing linkages to community and government programs. For example, in Milwaukee, Mount Sinai Hospital, in cooperation with a community-based organization (Inner City Development Commission), garnered federal grant funds to establish neighborhood health centers, one of which was incorporated into the Municipal Health Services Program. The welfare and survival of the voluntary hospitals have been a concern of strong private interests in the city, and regulatory and planning agency recommendations for consolidation, merger, or closing of services have generated constant controversy.

San Jose. San Jose, perhaps because it is a much younger city which has just recently grown quite large, has a much smaller philanthropic institutional infrastructure. The city had only five voluntary hospitals in 1978, all with emergency rooms and most offering organized outpatient department services, as shown in Table 3.9. Nonetheless, the

TABLE 3.7

ST. LOUIS VOLUNTARY HOSPITAL UTILIZATION DATA

Hospitals	Beds	Dis-charges	Occu-pancy rate (percent)	OPD visits	ER visits
Voluntary					
Alexian Brothers	198	5,397	74.4	-	10,857
Barnes-Washington Univ.	1,208	40,468	82.9	98,891	45,785
Bethesda General	150	2,724	54.4	-	1,399
Cardinal Glennon Mem. Children's	190	9,558	82.5	37,003	51,957
Central Med. Ctr.	116	3,402	79.1	747	5,802
Deaconess	505	15,718	86.5	8,016	15,096
Incarnate Word	340	9,462	80.5	-	11,931
Jewish of St. Louis	628	17,613	78.4	24,153	25,930
Lindell	81	1,407	39.0	4,310	-
Lutheran Med. Ctr.	425	10,903	74.0	34,200	62,071
St. Louis Children's	182	8,029	88.1	42,821	33,907
St. Louis University	362	9,227	68.9	18,540	18,104
St. Louis Little Rock (Compton Hill)	260	3,616	41.4	48,499	-
St. Luke's	383	6,599	49.7	13,036	15,960
Public					
Max Starkloff City	550	9,463	41.5	76,327	74,456
Homer G. Phillips	432	11,292	61.7	79,605	56,798

SOURCE: Missouri Center for Health Statistics data for 1978.

TABLE 3.8

MILWAUKEE VOLUNTARY HOSPITAL UTILIZATION DATA

Hospitals	Beds[a]	Admis-sions[a]	Occu-pancy rate[a] (percent)	OPD visits[b]	ER visits[b]
Voluntary					
Columbia	406	11,116	72.7	42,248	20,423
Deaconess	290	7,955	63.4	26,257	3,105
Family	181	6,978	66.9	2,596	2,631
Lakeview	118	3,738	55.9	5,607	-
Lutheran	320	6,211	57.5	8,991	-
Milwaukee Children's	186	8,081	65.2	66,677	41,218
Mount Sinai	376	12,294	68.6	34,787	27,140
Northwest General	169	5,615	62.7	5,309	11,222
St. Anthony	104	2,905	56.7	3,042	10,102
St. Francis	250	9,307	80.2	2,480	3,311
St. Joseph's	571	18,249	72.3	12,331	32,689
St. Luke's	553	16,387	81.4	22,167	47,407
St. Mary's	300	12,032	88.7	22,908	25,253
St. Michael	405	12,814	78.5	72,122	43,872
Public					
Milwaukee County Medical Complex	517	13,876	75.3	152,333	79,424

[a]American Hospital Association data for 1978.

[b]Milwaukee Health Systems Agency data for 1977.

TABLE 3.9

SAN JOSE VOLUNTARY HOSPITAL UTILIZATION DATA

Hospitals	Beds[a]	Admis-sions[a]	Occu-pancy rate[a] (percent)	OPD visits[b]	ER visits[b]
Voluntary					
Alexian Brothers	180	9,284	79.4	21,517	51,036
Good Samaritan	389	17,722	66.4	1,826	27,363
O'Connor	302	13,219	77.8	21,341	29,672
San Jose	417	16,126	70.5	19,971	35,394
Santa Teresa	105	5,166	61.6	N.A.	30,287
Public					
Valley Medical Center	445	11,579	61.9	93,435	49,360

[a]American Hospital Association data for 1978.

[b]Hospital administration data for fiscal year 1978.

voluntary sector has played a role in providing care for the poor, evidenced by the fact that each of the five provided more than 25,000 emergency visits, many of which constituted primary care services for Medi-Cal patients. O'Connor and San Jose hospitals also have made significant efforts to develop ambulatory care programs to serve those in need and to provide referral and back-up services for many of the community-based neighborhood health centers. For example, the initial San Jose Municipal Health Services Program proposal designated San Jose Hospital as the provider of hospital care for the downtown San Jose target area. Among the initiatives of this community hospital is a family practice program intended to accommodate about 8,000 visits a year in addition to approximately 60,000 in the OPD and ER. The strong community health center orientation in San Jose has fostered other linkages between such facilities and community hospitals to provide back-up services. One example is the arrangement between Gardner Health Center and O'Connor Hospital to provide certain specialty services for Gardner patients. O'Connor and San Jose hospitals, especially, compete for patients with the public hospital, Valley Medical Center. The voluntaries in San Jose and in neighboring areas of Santa Clara County are suffering from low occupancy rates—no hospital exceeded 77 percent occupancy in 1977—despite the population growth in the county.

To summarize, the role of voluntary hospitals in providing ambulatory care for the urban poor varies from city to city. Table 3.10 shows the volume of voluntary and public hospital beds and OPD and ER visits relative to city population in the five study cities. The bed-to-population ratio ranges from a low 2.5 (voluntary) or 3.3 (total) beds per 1,000, in San Jose, to 10.5 (voluntary) or 12.0 (total) beds per 1,000, in Cincinnati. St. Louis also registers high with 9.5 (voluntary) or 11.4 (total) beds per 1,000. Milwaukee, with 6.3 (voluntary) or 7.1 (total) beds per 1,000, and Baltimore, with 7.7 (voluntary) or 8.1 (total) beds per 1,000, are intermediate in rank. Cincinnati also reported the highest ratio of emergency room visits: 973 per 1,000, with 76 percent of these in the voluntary hospitals. St. Louis, second highest in volume of ER visits, 819 per 1,000, had the lowest proportion taking place in the voluntary sector—69 percent. Baltimore, third with 717 ER visits per 1,000, relied most heavily on voluntary hospitals, which provided 91 percent of ER visits. In Milwaukee, voluntary hospitals provided 77 percent of the 522 ER visits per 1,000. San Jose reported the lowest utilization of ER visits, 401 per 1,000, with 78 percent provided in voluntary hospitals. Baltimore's hospitals reported by far the highest volume and ratio of outpatient visits, almost 1,500 per 1,000, with 92 percent provided in voluntary hospitals. While 90 percent of Cincinnati's OPD visits took place in voluntaries, the volume and ratio were second lowest of the five cities, indicating much heavier reliance on emergency room care. In both Milwaukee and St. Louis, voluntary hospitals provided 68 percent of OPD visits, volume was just under 500,000 total OPD visits, and ratios of OPD visits were somewhat higher than emergency visits per 1,000 population. San Jose was lowest on every measure of hospital-based care. A lower ratio of visits, 284 per 1,000 population, took place in outpatient departments than in emergency rooms. Only 41 percent of these were in voluntary hospitals.

While no specific data are available as to the proportion of hospital-based ambulatory care that is provided to the poor, it may be inferred that large volumes of OPD and ER visits indicate heavy utilization by low-income patients, who are unable to obtain care from private physicians and use the hospitals as primary care resources. As it has been pointed out, hospitals, including voluntaries, are major providers of ambulatory care in Cincinnati, St. Louis, and Baltimore; in Milwaukee and San Jose, voluntary hospitals provide a much lower volume of care per 1,000 population, indicating a reliance on other sources of primary care, either private physicians or community clinics. In all five cities, falling inpatient occupancy rates may be influencing voluntary hospitals to undertake more aggressive marketing among new populations, including the poor. The burgeoning of primary care

TABLE 3.10

VOLUNTARY AND PUBLIC HOSPITAL BEDS, EMERGENCY VISITS, OUTPATIENT VISITS, AND RATIOS TO POPULATION, FIVE CITIES

City and auspices	General hospital beds	General hospital beds per 1000 population	ER visits	ER visits per 1000 population	OPD visits	OPD visits per 1000 population
Baltimore						
Voluntary	6,557	7.7	558,002	655 (91%)	1,162,107	1,364 (92%)
Public	332	.4	52,863	62 (9%)	100,991	119 (8%)
Total	6,889	8.1	610,865	717	1,263,098	1,483
Cincinnati						
Voluntary	4,328	10.5	306,243	742 (76%)	146,861	356 (90%)
Public	614	1.5	95,329	231 (24%)	16,653	40 (10%)
Total	4,942	12.0	401,572	973	163,514	396
Milwaukee						
Voluntary	4,229	6.3	268,373	403 (77%)	327,552	492 (68%)
Public	517	.8	79,424	119 (23%)	152,333	229 (32%)
Total	4,746	7.1	347,797	522	479,885	721
St. Louis						
Voluntary	5,028	9.5	298,799	569 (69%)	330,216	629 (68%)
Public	982	1.9	131,254	250 (31%)	155,932	297 (32%)
Total	6,010	11.4	430,053	819	486,148	926
San Jose						
Voluntary	1,393	2.5	173,752	313 (78%)	64,655	116 (41%)
Public	445	.8	49,360	88 (22%)	93,435	168 (59%)
Total	1,838	3.3	223,112	401	158,090	284

SOURCE: Compiled from Tables 3.4, and 3.6 through 3.9.

training programs in many teaching facilities may also encourage both public and voluntary hospitals to be responsible for increasing provision of primary care.

THE PUBLIC SECTOR: THE PUBLIC HOSPITAL

In view of the apparent service gaps left by the private medical market, where do the urban poor receive medical care? Perhaps chief among the resources for those who cannot avail themselves of private medical care is the public hospital. In this section, the role of the public hospital in providing ambulatory care to the urban poor will be discussed, a role which is characterized in the following statement from the report of the Commission on Public-General Hospitals:

In the nation's 100 largest cities, there are 90 public-general hospitals. Although these hospitals represent only 9.3 percent of the community hospitals in these cities, they are large, with an average of more than 500 beds, and deliver 13.2 percent of all inpatient services and 28.9 percent of all hospital outpatient services in these cities. In some of these cities, they deliver as much as one-third of all inpatient care and one-half of all outpatient care.[15]

Among the public hospitals in the five study cities, there are both common features and some quite distinctive characteristics. In two cities municipal government operates the public facilities (Baltimore and St. Louis); in two, public hospitals are county facilities (Milwaukee and San Jose); and in one, a hospital which previously had been operated by the municipal government as part of a city university (University of Cincinnati) has been taken over together with its parent university by the state government. In each of the five cities, the public hospitals fulfill some of the critical roles identified by the Commission on Public-General Hospitals. First, they provide a substantial proportion of the city's institutional-based health services. Second, they provide services, such as sophisticated emergency and trauma care, treatment of medical-social problems such as drug and alcohol dependency, highly specialized diagnostic and therapeutic care, and high volumes of primary care for the poor, that are simply unavailable elsewhere. Third, they are a major teaching resource for all types of health professionals. Fourth, in most cases they eliminate the financial, geographic, and social barriers to care faced by poor and minority population groups. Finally, at least in theory, public hospitals are publicly accountable and are direct tools of public policy. In the remainder of this section, more of the distinctive characteristics of the public hospitals in the five study cities will be discussed.

Baltimore. Baltimore's public hospital was founded in 1773 as the county almshouse in midtown Baltimore. It was renamed Baltimore City Hospitals (BCH) in 1925 and was relocated in the eastern outskirts of the city. By 1935, BCH's mission was restricted to medical care, eliminating its orphanage, asylum, and jail functions, and until the mid-

1960s it primarily provided care to the city's indigent black population, many of whom resided in East Baltimore. After Baltimore hospitals were integrated during the 1960s and Medicare and Medicaid removed some of the financial barriers to care, utilization patterns of Baltimore residents changed markedly. The East Baltimore black population sought care closer to home at the Johns Hopkins Hospital, and Baltimore City Hospitals was essentially left without a service community.

Until 1973, BCH was staffed by physicians who were employed by the city as civil servants. The institution had been a teaching hospital for the Johns Hopkins School of Medicine since the nineteenth century, as well as for the University of Maryland Medical School. Since the 1950s all physicians who were members of the full-time professional staff at BCH were required to hold faculty appointments at one of the two medical schools. In the early 1970s, BCH fit several of the stereotypes of the urban public hospital. With a medical staff that was heavily involved in academic medicine and research, BCH lacked a community physician referral system, and did not serve as a community hospital for its surrounding geographic area. It had a deteriorating physical plant, increasing budget deficits due to both managerial shortcomings and the large volume of free care it provided, and a public image which made it unattractive to new service populations. Thus, the institution faced critical problems in terms of low utilization and low collections of revenue. These difficulties led to the introduction in 1973 of an innovative staffing mechanism.

In response to the recommendation of a study group on the critical issues facing BCH, the medical staff was separated from the municipal civil service system that governed hospital employment. As Chapter Two described in detail, Chesapeake Physicians Professional Association (CPPA), a nonprofit, private group practice, was formed by the existing BCH medical staff to provide, under contract with the city, all medical and teaching services at BCH and to staff referral clinics in the community. Since its establishment, CPPA has attempted to expand the services at BCH and in the community, while maintaining the cost of its services to the city at its 1973 dollar level.

Declining utilization of Baltimore City Hospitals motivated an initial unsuccessful effort by CPPA to encourage community physicians to refer their patients there. In addition, CPPA developed outreach programs, including primary care satellite clinics and health maintenance organizations. By 1977, CPPA operated three HMOs (the Greater Dundalk Medical Center, the Chesapeake Health Plan, and the Metropolitan Baltimore Health Plan ["Care First"]) and a medical center for ambulatory care, the Southeast Community Medical Office. At BCH, CPPA has sponsored the development of the neurology, emergency medicine, and child psychiatry services, as well as centers for the treatment of alcoholism, drug abuse, and renal disease. These services are viewed by CPPA members as strong sources of patients for BCH in the future.

TABLE 3.11

BALTIMORE CITY HOSPITALS OUTPATIENT SERVICES

1970-1980

| | Number of visits | |
Year	OPD	ER
1970	122,498	92,462
1971	116,537	79,264
1972	100,984	50,722
1973	104,517	51,295
1974	101,054	52,976
1975	107,656	54,096
1976	102,936	48,909
1977	100,991	52,863
1978[a]	66,256	36,413
1979[a]	57,949	33,665
1980[a]	74,203	49,317

[a]Data for fiscal year, not calendar year.

SOURCE: Maryland Hospital Association, Inc., Annual Statistical Report, 1971, 1972, 1973, 1974, 1975, 1976, 1977; Baltimore City Hospitals data for fiscal years 1978, 1979, 1980.

In summary, it is reasonable to suggest that CPPA has contributed to stabilization of Baltimore City Hospitals. The occupancy rate of inpatient services has remained higher than 70 percent since 1974, one year after the CPPA hospital contract, and rose to 77 percent in 1977. It is important to point out, however, that the reported number of hospital beds decreased during that time. Therefore, it is difficult to specify to what extent CPPA has actually effected higher utilization rates. Table 3.11 provides an indication of changes in hospital outpatient utilization since 1970. Although difficult to document, it is possible that some patients who had been utilizing the BCH emergency room may now be receiving care under CPPA sponsorship in the community. The apparent success of such public hospital-based group practices as CPPA at BCH led in the late 1970s to much debate over the advisability of following this strategy in other public hospitals, such as those in New York City.

Cincinnati. The present mission of Cincinnati General Hospital with respect to the city's indigent population has also been shaped by historic circumstances. In drafting the charter of the city of Cincinnati in 1924, the councilmen assumed a responsibility to assure the care of the medically indigent of the city, although the Cincinnati General Hospital was also to be considered a teaching institution. Therefore, the language drafted in the charter placed the hospital's administrative and executive activities under the city manager, while the medical activities (teaching and nursing) became the responsibility of the board of trustees of the University of Cincinnati. In the 1960s, the city, perceiving that third-party payors had relieved them of the need to provide health care to the medically indigent, transferred authority for the Cincinnati General Hospital to the board of trustees of the University of Cincinnati.

As was pointed out in Chapter Two, the role of Cincinnati General Hospital shifted during the 1970s from that of municipal hospital to that of university medical center. As the primary teaching hospital of the University of Cincinnati College of Medicine, its outpatient services are oriented toward teaching and research and rely on clinic patients to carry out these activities. The hospital's functions have been dominated by the faculty of the College of Medicine, which has been highly independent and powerful. In the past there has been friction between the College of Medicine and private practitioners, the city health department, and representatives of the indigent population of Cincinnati. But in the mid-1970s, the college and Cincinnati General Hospital responded to public pressure to place more emphasis on the amenities and quality of care in the emergency department and the outpatient clinics. The hospital has also been more responsive in providing back-up specialty and inpatient care for patients referred from the health department's primary care clinics. Cincinnati General Hospital provides a full range of outpatient services, from primary medical care to quite esoteric subspecialties.

In 1978 the hospital terminated its pediatric service. All pediatric patients, including patients from the primary care network, who come to General Hospital, are now referred to nearby Children's Hospital for care. The Cincinnati Children's Hospital is also affiliated with the College of Medicine. Traditionally, it had a public posture similar to that of the Cincinnati General Hospital, but during the mid-1970s it also became more community-oriented and engaged in more cooperative ventures with the health department's clinics.

Ambulatory care utilization data for Cincinnati General Hospital for 1974 through 1980 are displayed in Table 3.12. After several years of decreasing utilization, visit volume began increasing again in 1978 and has continued to grow.

St. Louis. In Chapter Two, a detailed history of the St. Louis public general hospitals was presented, explaining the racially based conflict which has persisted for more than a decade in response to the city's effort to consolidate acute inpatient care in a single facility. Until 1979, St. Louis continued to operate two public general hospitals, Max C.

Table 3.12

CINCINNATI GENERAL HOSPITAL OUTPATIENT SERVICES

1974-1981

	Number of visits	
Year	OPD	ER
1974	154,235	127,389
1975	145,606	127,285
1976	138,546	119,436
1977	116,653	95,329
1978[a]	128,071	86,994
1979[a]	136,755	81,755
1980[a]	148,307	82,018
1981[a]	160,549	N.A.

[a]Fiscal year data.

Starkloff Hospital, known as City Number One, and Homer G. Phillips Hospital, traditionally the hospital where black physicians could practice and—prior to 1966—where most black patients were treated. As the result of constantly weakening utilization levels at both hospitals and growing budget deficits, health policy from the late 1960s on focused upon recommendations that St. Louis cease operating hospitals altogether or consolidate the two acute facilities into one. Since Starkloff was the only hospital with a strong affiliation with the two medical schools in St. Louis and hence was able to offer a more complete range of services in a slightly better physical plant with superior equipment, the choice was made by the mayor in late 1976 to close Phillips. Although three successive mayors dating back to 1969 (Cervantes, Poelker and Conway) had considered closing one or more of the city's hospitals, it was not until mid-1979 that a decision was both made and implemented.

Mayor Conway ordered and carried out the closure of inpatient services at Homer G. Phillips in 1979, amid a vocal protest from the black community that persisted for more than a year after the consolidation. Although the supporters of Phillips were not able to organize an effective movement to halt Conway's plan or force him to reverse his decision, by the spring of 1981 the campaign for the Democratic nomination in the mayoral primary had taken on the character of a new battle over Homer G. The mayor's opponent, a white alderman, campaigned in the black community on a promise to reopen Phillips and close City Number One, and in the white community

TABLE 3.13

ST. LOUIS PUBLIC HOSPITAL OUTPATIENT SERVICES

1973-1980

| | Number of visits | | | |
| | Max C. Starkloff | | Homer G. Philips | |
Year	OPD	ER	OPD	ER
1973	84,491	73,504	76,858	82,147
1974	84,863	70,331	77,623	75,248
1975	83,488	79,587	81,118	71,572
1976	87,407	84,209	79,486	66,091
1977	78,010	80,819	67,336	58,326
1978	76,327	74,456	66,654	55,647
1979	77,648	73,719	55,288	33,818
1980	74,306	74,682	50,846	18,791

the opponent emphasized Mayor Conway's decision to cut the police budget. The outcome of these two strategies was a stunning upset of the incumbent mayor in the Democratic primary and the continuing domination of St. Louis politics and budget discussions by the Homer G. Phillips issue.

The two acute care facilities in St. Louis had, as was noted, been experiencing falling utilization rates (Table 3.13). City residents made heavy use of the public hospital emergency rooms for primary care, largely because of the lack of private physicians in poor neighborhoods. Although clinic utilization remained fairly stable at both hospitals and high rates of emergency room use continued at Starkloff, there was a significant decline in emergency room visits at Phillips from 1973 to 1980. Possible explanations for this drop in emergency room use may be the presence of two health centers located within a relatively short distance of Homer G. Phillips (St. Louis Comprehensive and the North Kingshighway health centers) and the continued controversy surrounding the quality of care and ultimate survival of the hospital. Nonetheless, it is clear that the public hospital ambulatory services are a major resource for poor patients in St. Louis.

Milwaukee. The Milwaukee County Hospital began operations in the 1880s as a facility for Milwaukee County's indigent population. Along with a variety of other medical and social institutions including the zoo, the hospital was located on a large tract of county-owned property, the "county grounds", lying in what is now a western suburb of Milwaukee. The hospital relied in its early years on donated medical services by the faculties of two medical schools which in 1913 merged to form the Marquette University School of Medicine. Over the years, a strong relationship evolved between the medical school and the county's medical institutions which came collectively to be incorporated as the Milwaukee County Medical Complex (MCMC). The medical school's faculty became the full time staff of the MCMC, responsible to the county for patient care and to the medical school for education. Although the MCMC has continued to the present to serve primarily a low-income population, the continued expansion of educational activities also resulted in the institution's development into the area's principal tertiary care center, serving the specialized needs of patients of all income levels.

Several major changes took place in the years following 1967. The medical school was separated from Marquette University, which could no longer support it financially. Under new state-county sponsorship and funding, it began plans for construction of new facilities next to the hospital on the grounds of the Milwaukee County Medical Complex. Construction began in 1976, enabling the college to relocate to its new buildings in 1978. At this same time, plans for a new, privately sponsored teaching hospital, Froedtert Memorial Lutheran Hospital, came to fruition. Construction of this facility, completed for a 1980 opening, was also on the grounds of the MCMC. Thus, by 1980 a newly housed medical school was operating on the county grounds with two physically and functionally connected teaching institutions.

The expansion of inpatient capacity on the county grounds was based more on the projected needs of the medical college for teaching beds than on the demand of county residents for care at that site. However, in spite of the thirty minute travel time by car and an even longer travel time by bus from the downtown area, Milwaukee County Hospital has traditionally functioned as a source of primary care through its emergency department, outpatient clinics and other services and has provided inpatient services for the majority of Milwaukee's poor and medically indigent population.

Table 3.14 shows the trends in utilization of the emergency room and outpatient department of Milwaukee County Hospital (as well as its satellite facility, Downtown Medical and Health Services [DMHS], within the city proper) from 1974 to 1980. The number of patient visits to the OPD clinics, the ER, and the DMHS satellite declined steadily during this period, with ER utilization dropping by almost 50 percent, from 62,584 visits in 1974 to 33,879 visits in 1980. The proportion of county hospital ambulatory services provided to inner-city residents also declined, from about 45 percent in 1974 to only 35 percent by 1978. In 1976, more than 60 percent of the ER visits, however, were from inner-city residents. The ambulatory services of the county facilities are more frequently utilized by those residing in the inner-city north than in the inner-city south.

Although the public hospital serving Milwaukee residents provides

TABLE 3.14

MILWAUKEE COUNTY HOSPITAL OUTPATIENT SERVICES,

1974-1980

	Number of visits		
Year	OPD	ER	DMHS[a]
1974	142,258	62,584	56,133
1975	144,808	53,616	56,866
1976	140,637	51,548	59,451
1977	133,960	49,776	46,093
1978	128,135	41,788	47,088
1979	131,622	39,159	45,581
1980	134,186	33,879	46,468

[a] Downtown Medical and Health Services.

TABLE 3.15

VALLEY MEDICAL CENTER OUTPATIENT SERVICES

FISCAL YEARS 1976-1981

	Number of Visits	
Year	OPD	ER
1976	84,837	46,862
1977	93,280	49,399
1978	93,435	49,360
1979	87,602	43,842
1980	88,629	44,310
1981	93,350	47,158

relief from some financial barriers, the problem of distance remains. It has occasionally been suggested that the county should contract for services for the indigent with the downtown voluntary hospitals that are nearer the residences of those needing care. The county facility is also experiencing low occupancy and growing financial deficits, and has come under considerable criticism because, as the result of its sophisticated teaching capabilities, it has the highest per diem cost of any Milwaukee hospital.

San Jose. Santa Clara County Valley Medical Center (VMC), the county hospital, is one of six acute care hospitals in San Jose and one of fifteen in Santa Clara County. In San Jose, only the Veterans' Administration Hospital is larger. Valley Medical Center provided 49,360 emergency visits in 1978, second only to Alexian Brothers, a voluntary hospital. Recent ambulatory utilization data for VMC (Table 3.15) indicate a modest increase in volume. In its role as one of the teaching hospitals for Stanford University's medical school, VMC serves to some degree as a regional academic medical center, offering specialty services not provided by other hospitals in the city of San Jose. It thus serves the county and region, rather than its immediate community only, and hence competes with hospitals throughout the Santa Clara area. Within San Jose, VMC is in direct competition with San Jose Hospital, the largest voluntary facility in the city.

It has been the policy of Valley Medical Center to provide services to everyone, regardless of ability to pay. It serves the highest proportion of Medi-Cal recipients and medically indigent of any San Jose hospital. Valley Medical Center's public image is that of hospital of last resort for the poor, and serious physical deficiencies contribute to its difficulty in competing for private patients. Thus, in fiscal year 1976, 59 percent of VMC's inpatients were Medi-Cal recipients, while only 21 percent were privately insured, and 10 percent were uninsured. The insured private and uninsured self-pay patients account for 25 percent of VMC hospital revenues, compared to 60 percent for other hospitals in the area.

The low percentage of private patient revenues can be seen in Figure 3.1, which shows the payor mix for the major departments. The greatest percentage of Medi-Cal patients is found in the maternity (72 percent), pediatric (66 percent), and nursery (70 percent) departments, indicating the dependence of the local poor on the public hospital for primary care. A study of patient origins performed by the county found that two-thirds of VMC's emergency room and outpatient clinic users live in a geographic core area adjacent to VMC. It was also revealed that nearly half the county's Medi-Cal eligible population resides in this core area, which partially explains the high proportion of Medi-Cal and indigent users of VMC. Patients from outside the core area include Medi-Cal eligibles, the indigent, and individuals seeking specialized services, such as rehabilitation and burn treatment, not available elsewhere in the county, and neonatal services, offered only at VMC and Stanford.

The future financial viability of VMC will depend heavily upon the county's ability to utilize its general fund to reimburse the hospital for uncollectible bills and VMC's ability to generate capital revenues in order to bring the facility into compliance with accreditation standards and physical code provisions, including earthquake resistance.

Our review of the public hospital system in each of the five cities has revealed major similarities. The problems of Valley Medical Center, relating to its physical plant, resemble those of the St. Louis City Hospital. Low occupancy, highly specialized and costly teaching programs, and growing financial deficits (until 1981) are common to both VMC and the Milwaukee County Hospital. The medical school/teaching hospital relationship complicates public policy at all five public hospitals. In San Jose and in Baltimore, the public hospital medical staffs have formed group practices, and although the experience in San Jose is as yet insufficient to draw any conclusions, in Baltimore the CPPA has apparently had a stabilizing influence on the public health care delivery system. In all five cities, the public hospitals play a major role in the provision of ambulatory care services to the urban poor, although the structure and quality of these services have been subject to criticism. A persistent and generalized trend of decreasing visits in both the outpatient clinics and the emergency rooms, which has been evident over a period of several years, appears to have been reversed in Cincinnati and San Jose since 1978, and possibly in Baltimore as of 1980.

FIGURE 3.1

PERCENT OF VALLEY MEDICAL CENTER PATIENTS BY PAYOR CLASS (1975-1976)

	Medicare	Medicare/MediCal	MediCal	Private Insured	Uninsured	Other
Medical	12	28	39	10	7	4
Surgical	9	10	42	26	9	5
Rehabilitation	12	5	39	38	4	2
Pediatric			66	21	8	5
Maternity			72	13	13	2
Nursery			70	14	12	2
Total inpatient	6	8	51	21	9	4
Emergency	3	6	40	44*		7
Main outpatient clinic	4	11	55	21*		9

Highlights:

Rehabilitation has the highest percentage private insured (38%) and lowest percentage uninsured patients (4%) of all inpatient departments.

Maternity has highest percentage MediCal patients (72%).

NOTE: Asterisk signifies data not available for uninsured patients.

SOURCE: Inpatient—PAS Discharge Abstracts, 1975-1976 (Tabulation by Center for Urban Analysis). Emergency and outpatient—VMC Revenue Classification Report, 1975-1976.

THE PUBLIC SECTOR: THE PUBLIC HEALTH DEPARTMENT

Local public health departments in cities all over the country have traditionally provided a mix of preventive and categorical personal health services, including immunizations, tuberculosis and sexually transmitted disease control, prenatal and postpartum care for mothers, family planning, well-baby care, and community health nursing, along with the various environmental and sanitation functions which are population-oriented rather than individual-oriented. In some cities, public health departments have taken a more direct and active role in the provision of comprehensive ambulatory care services, sometimes in conjunction with private sector providers, sometimes using federal Community Health Center funding. In other cities, health departments have maintained a more traditional role, merely acting as a facilitator or guarantor of services that continue to be provided in the private sector. In general, relationships between public health departments and public hospitals have been characterized by less than ideal cooperation and/or integration of services, as was discussed in Chapter Two. Some illustrations of the variety of clinic services provided by the health departments in the five study cities follow.

St. Louis. The four municipal public health clinics in St. Louis at the start of the MHSP demonstration were typical of those in many American cities. They included the Kingshighway, South Grand, 13th and Wyoming (Wohl South), and Courtney health centers. The clinics provided public health nursing, maternal and child health, family planning, infant and child health, child dental health, immunization and communicable disease control, tuberculosis control, lead poisoning control, and family counseling programs. Utilization statistics for the four clinics are shown in Table 3.16.

The Kingshighway and the 13th and Wyoming centers are both two-story structures built during the late 1940s. Residents of Kingshighway's service area in northwest St. Louis are predominantly black and poor, and show some of the worst health status characteristics in the city. They rarely use private physicians and rely primarily on municipal services. The decline in usage of the Kingshighway facility is in all likelihood due to two factors: continuing migration patterns, which are now producing a decline in population in some of the black portions of north St. Louis and, perhaps even more important, the inauguration of the HEW-funded St. Louis Comprehensive Health Center, which is located approximately three blocks west of the Kingshighway Municipal Center in a large, physically attractive, modern clinical facility.

The 13th and Wyoming Center is adjacent to the Busch Brewery in nearby south St. Louis, and it is also located between, or adjacent to, several poor white neighborhoods in St. Louis. Unfortunately, the location of a major superhighway immediately to the west of the health center has now effectively cut it off from potential clients to the west. The combination of the gigantic brewery complex immediately to the north of the center and the highway to the west, combined with an unusual street pattern leading to the center itself, create significant access problems.

Low utilization at the South Grand center may be related to the deteriorated and ill-designed physical plant, as well as to its location in the southwest quadrant of St. Louis, the home of a relatively af-

Table 3.16

CLINIC AND CONFERENCE ATTENDANCE AT ST. LOUIS PUBLIC HEALTH CENTERS,

SELECTED YEARS

Clinic	1973	1974	1977
Kingshighway	30,306	28,918	27,282
South Grand	14,665	13,669	8,569
13th and Wyoming	13,678	11,467	9,999
Courtney (Jefferson Cass)	25,725(JC)	22,817(JC)	18,060(Courtney)

SOURCE: Annual Reports, Division of Health Public Health Nursing Service,
St. Louis Department of Health and Hospitals, 1973, 1974 and 1977.

fluent, predominantly white, elderly population with the city's highest overall health status. The population uses private physicians and health facilities located in the suburbs.

The Courtney Health Center was the only public clinic built under the auspices of the Model Cities program as a comprehensive OEO-style health center. It became the administrative and financial responsibility of the city health department in 1974 when Model Cities funding ended. The building is of innovative and functional design, with 54,000 square feet of patient care space. Although originally a comprehensive center, in 1978 Courtney was providing only traditional categorical services. The center also includes a pharmacy, a business office, and a medical records system. Utilization has dropped and is a continuing problem. Located in an area of progressive abandonment, this newest and most comprehensive clinic in the city's municipal system serves a catchment area with a declining population and therefore a declining patient pool.

Cincinnati. In Cincinnati prior to 1965, the delivery of primary health care services by the health department was organized under five district physicians. Services were restricted to maternal and infant care, and the district physicians were supported by five health department-operated clinics (12th Street, Muhlberg, Shoemaker, East End, and Madisonville), which were located in depressed areas of the city. These sites were nominally well-baby clinics.

Since 1965, health department-sponsored delivery of primary health care services has expanded considerably. It has become department policy to provide a full range of medical services under public health auspices. The five original clinics have grown to thirteen health centers, and the eight additional clinics that were initiated at various times under many different funding authorities now operate under contract with the health department. All are under the coordination and/or control of the Cincinnati Health Department, and comprise the Cincinnati Primary Health Care System (CPHCS). Obstetrics and gynecology or general practice is available at each clinic, and the majority offer a broad range of physician services, including family practice, general practice, obstetrics and gynecology, pediatrics, and internal medicine. Table 3.17 indicates the range and volume of services provided at clinic sites.

The Madisonville area is one of the MHSP target communities. It is the primary service area for the Braxton F. Cann Memorial Medical Center, a health department clinic, which also draws significant numbers of patients from the adjacent neighborhoods of Oakley and Kennedy Heights. Oakley is still predominantly white, while Kennedy Heights and Madisonville are racially mixed. In the last two decades these working-class neighborhoods have undergone substantial population turnover that has resulted in increasing numbers of welfare recipients, and a growing dependent elderly and youth population.

A second target area is that served by the Winton Hills Medical Center, a community-operated clinic serving the predominantly black, highly transient population of the Winton Hills public housing project and a few patients from the nearby community of Winton Place, a predominantly white, working-class community which has little association with Winton Hills. The Winton Hills adult population is largely comprised of female-headed households with a few elderly residents. Sixty percent of the residents are younger than eighteen and 31 percent of them receive welfare.

Avondale is the third target neighborhood. It is the primary service area for the health department's Avondale (Catherine Booth) Clinic. The Catherine Booth Clinic is primarily an obstetrics/gynecology and pediatrics facility; however, it does provide diagnostic, nutrition, and pharmacy services. The clinic is within walking distance of the Cincinnati General Hospital and in a sense, therefore, competes with the primary care services offered at the hospital. Despite the limited schedule and range of services, the clinic appears to draw patients from all over the city—in particular women whose mothers had received perinatal services there. The Avondale service area underwent rapid transition and physical decay in the 1950s and 1960s. The population has declined from its peak in the 1960s, after severe urban riots destroyed parts of the area. The population is predominantly black and younger than the city average, and has growing numbers of welfare recipients. Adjoining neighborhoods are predominantly white, stable, working-

TABLE 3.17

HEALTH CENTER MEDICAL ENCOUNTERS FOR
CINCINNATI PRIMARY HEALTH CARE SYSTEM, 1976

Clinic	General medical	Pediatrics	Ob/Gyn	Other specialties	Surgeon	Psychiatrist	Physician extender	Nurse	Other medical provider	Total
West End	18,072	*	1,600	964	---	220	1,824	52	672	23,504
Lincoln Heights	5,824	2,652	948	1,488	---	---	1,712	1,124	2,932	16,680
Walnut Hills/Evan.	4,472	4,340	4,236	---	---	---	6,496	4,000	1,000	24,544
Winton Hills[a]	---	888	---	---	---	---	---	---	---	7,728
East End	2,645	2,784	1,467	---	---	---	---	1,362	---	8,258
Mt. Auburn	5,000	5,904	1,526	---	---	---	---	---	---	12,430
12th Street/ Findlay Market	11,028	7,736	3,192	524	372	652	1,556	8,684	2,516	36,260
English Woods	2,320	1,518	---	---	---	---	---	---	---	3,838
Millvale	3,294	3,975	2,190	1,117	---	---	---	---	602	11,178
Muhlberg	759	4,403	2,673	---	---	---	---	---	---	7,835
Catherine Booth/ Avondale	383	2,292	3,330	---	---	---	---	---	---	6,005
Cann/Madisonville	2,293	3,536	2,538	272	---	---	---	---	---	8,639
Burnet & Melish (include physicals)	10,738	---	---	---	---	---	564	---	---	11,302
Price Hill	2,623	6,373	1,741	---	---	---	---	---	---	10,737
Total	50,994	46,402	25,441	4,365	372	872	12,152	15,222	7,722	188,938

aThere is no breakdown available for Winton Hills. The 888 pediatric encounters were in the Cincinnati Health Department clinic held in the Winton Hills facilities.

NOTE: Asterisk signifies pediatric encounters are included in the general medical encounters.

class communities with a disproportionate number of elderly and also with expanding welfare populations.

Baltimore. The Baltimore City Health Department, which has not directly operated comprehensive primary health centers, has served primarily to funnel public moneys to clinics managed under other auspices. In the earlier section on Baltimore's voluntary hospitals, the health department's role in securing federal grants in cooperation with private institutions was described. Children and Youth (C&Y) moneys, Maternal and Infant Care (MIC) funds, and other categorical primary care programs have been located in hospitals, satellite clinics, and community-sponsored clinics with health department facilitation. District health centers have carried out traditional public health services in the past, and have for the most part served poor black communities outside the target area for the MHSP, Southeast Baltimore. In 1977, the Baltimore City Health Department provided 11,650 prenatal, 44,200 family planning, and about 36,000 child health visits under its own auspices. Through five C&Y centers cosponsored by hospitals, more than 100,000 medical and dental visits were provided in 1977.

In Southeast Baltimore, the MHSP was launched in a former health district building, the Bank Street Clinic, which was transformed into a comprehensive primary care clinic to serve the Highlandtown/Canton/O'Donnell Heights communities. These areas consist of predominantly white, ethnic, blue-collar, low-income neighborhoods which are quite stable. Highlandtown contains Baltimore's oldest section, with rowhouses and marble steps. Canton contains industrial areas, and a large proportion of its population are long-term homeowners. O'Donnell Heights is a public housing project. Belair/Edison is the site of another MHSP clinic. It is the northernmost area and covers several communities. Three of these are housing projects and one (Hollander Ridge) is the site for a satellite clinic. These communities contain largely a white, ethnic population, and account for about one-third of the residents in the total Baltimore MHSP target area. The North of the Park area is due east of the Johns Hopkins Hospital (and the downtown area) and is a more racially mixed community than either Belair/Edison or Highlandtown/Canton, although still primarily white. One part of this community is located in the catchment area of Johns Hopkins, while its southern census tracts are close to Church Hospital. No municipal primary care clinic had existed in this area prior to the MHSP.

Milwaukee. Like Baltimore, the Milwaukee City Health Department had not taken responsibility for direct provision of comprehensive primary care services, limiting its mission instead to preventive services. In the case of Milwaukee, the city has generally relied upon the county for direct personal health care delivery. The health department has seen its role as that of a screening agency for the purpose of identifying needs and assuring that patients are referred to the appropriate facility for services. The one major publicly sponsored ambulatory care resource in the city has been Downtown Medical and Health Services. This clinic was formerly a municipal hospital (Downtown Emergency Hospital) that closed in the late 1960s, after population shifts and the implementation of Medicaid and Medicare had caused drastic drops in utilization. The Milwaukee County Hospital established DMHS in 1972 for the delivery of primary care services. The service program of DMHS included a 24-hour walk-in clinic, family-oriented primary care, a hypertension detection and treatment center, mental health services, in-house clinical laboratory, and x-ray and pharmacy services. It was managed by the County Hospital, which served as the principal back-up facility for specialized diagnostic and treatment services and inpatient care. In 1976 the county attempted to establish a southside MHS to provide services similar to those at DMHS. The proposal was approved by the county board, but no funds were appropriated. Subsequent to this aborted effort to establish a southside clinic modeled upon DMHS, both sites were incorporated in the proposal developed for the MHSP.

San Jose. The city of San Jose does not have a public health department. Public health services are the responsibility of the Santa Clara County Health Department, which has provided only traditional preventive services rather than direct personal health care. It is the county hospital that delivers publicly sponsored primary care, not only on-site but also in two small satellite clinics, which operate five days a week. The East Valley Clinic averages 100 patient visits daily, or 27,000 a year, and the South Valley Clinic handles about 35 visits a day, or 9,500 a year. The county also subsidizes to some degree the operations of several community-sponsored clinics, although contractual control is not nearly as direct as that in Cincinnati.

It can be noted in summary that the roles of public health departments in the delivery of ambulatory care to the urban poor vary from virtually no role, as in San Jose, to that of major provider, as in St. Louis and Cincinnati. In Baltimore and Milwaukee, the health departments have served more as facilitators to funnel public moneys to private providers than as major providers themselves. Some types of nongovernment providers will be examined in the next section.

COMMUNITY-BASED SERVICES: COMPREHENSIVE HEALTH CENTERS

The term "community health center" is generally used to describe ambulatory care programs operated by nonprofit community-based organizations rather than by private physician groups and located independently of hospitals. The term is often associated with programs based on the Office of Economic Opportunity neighborhood health center model, whose history was described in detail in the first chapter. Many comprehensive community health centers continue to be funded by the federal government through the Bureau of Community Health Services (BCHS) of the Department of Health and Human Services (HHS). These centers represent a mix of public and private initiative, generally being operated by private, nonprofit community corporations, but funded substantially by public moneys, often including state and/or local categorical grants. As of 1979, 190 community health centers in urban areas had been funded under the authority of Section 330 of the Public Health Service Act.

The typical community health center is described as having eight to ten physicians, supplemented by middle-level practitioners and support personnel, and is designed to provide, at full capacity, approximately 10,000 users with comprehensive primary care services. The following are primary care services that federally funded centers are required by statute to provide:

- diagnostic, treatment, consultative, referral, and other services rendered by a physician or a physician extender;
- diagnostic laboratory and radiological services;
- preventive health services, including nutritional assessment, medical social services, well-child care, immunization, etc.;
- emergency medical services;
- transportation services as required for patient care;
- preventive dental services; and
- pharmaceutical services.

These centers are usually sponsored by community-based organizations. The administrator of the clinic reports to a governing board, at least 51 percent of whose membership consists of consumers who are residents of the community. The great majority of centers are independent of local government. There are exceptions, however.

Cincinnati. In Cincinnati, all federal community health center funding is consolidated and routed through the city health department via contracts with the community-based centers. The contract clinics in Cincinnati represent a hybrid between the standard health department primary care clinic and the independently operated health center. Data on visit volume in the six contract clinics in Cincinnati are shown in Table 3.17. The contract community health centers are the West End, Lincoln Heights, Winton Hills, East End, Mt. Auburn, and Walnut Hills-Evanston clinics, which provided a total of more than 90,000 visits in 1976.

San Jose. San Jose has one major HHS-funded neighborhood health center, the Alviso Family Health Foundation, which handled about 60,000 visits in 1978 at an annual budget of $4.5 million. In that year Alviso operated two satellite clinics in addition to its large, modern, comprehensive main facility, serving a patient population that is approximately 50 percent Chicano and includes all area ethnic groups. Partly funded by Santa Clara County, Alviso also sponsors a prepaid health plan and uses several area hospitals, including Valley Medical Center, for back-up services.

The Alviso center is characteristic of the strong community health center presence in California. Having begun as a small, community-based program, it has grown and matured, adapting to a changing environment by diversifying its services, its financing mechanisms, and its patient population. Community health centers in California have established strong client constituencies and have developed considerable political lobbying skills, both at the local level, where they have sought county government allocations, and at the state level, where they have been able thus far to advance their interests within the health system. The socioeconomic and demographic characteristics of San Jose, a rapidly growing community with an expanding job market (in contrast to the deteriorating older cities represented by the other four demonstration sites), may constitute a more favorable environment for the development and growth of community health centers. The orientation of the early OEO model to meeting the needs of particular ethnic groups that are underserved as the result of language and cultural barriers is especially pronounced in many California clinics.

St. Louis. In 1977, there were four federally funded comprehensive community health centers in St. Louis: Grace Hill (sponsored by a settlement house of long standing), St. Louis Comprehensive (originating as an OEO-Model Cities clinic), Yeatman, and its satellite, Yeatman-Union-Sarah. In fiscal year 1976, Grace Hill provided 7,091 patient visits, St. Louis Comprehensive provided 31,183 patient visits, and Yeatman-Union-Sarah and Yeatman together provided 17,000 patient visits, for a total of at least 55,000 visits.

Baltimore. The federally funded community health centers in Baltimore are all closely associated with cooperating back-up voluntary hospitals, as was noted earlier. They were developed as independent community-based entities, however, and are not treated administratively as hospital cost centers. As of 1977, there were five health centers funded by BCHS, which supported about half the operating expenses of each. These were Constant Care with 42,246 visits a year, the Park Heights Community Health Center with 10,243 visits, the North Central Health Plan with 19,000 visits, the West Baltimore Community Health Corporation with 32,090 visits, and the East Baltimore Medical Plan with 49,714 visits a year. None of the HHS health centers served the communities of Southeast Baltimore, since all had been developed to meet the needs of poor black residents and were located in other neighborhoods.

Milwaukee. Milwaukee's ambitious OEO-sponsored Cream City Health Center failed to survive the many financial, programmatic, professional, and political stresses affecting neighborhood health centers, as Chapter One described in detail. No Federally funded OEO-model community health center was operating in Milwaukee in 1978, although Federal support had been requested and approved for at least two clinic sites, including the Mount Sinai Hospital satellite clinic which later was incorporated into the Municipal Health Services Program.

A detailed discussion of the history, development, and interrelationships of the federally sponsored community health centers in each city is found in Chapter One.

COMMUNITY-BASED SERVICES: ALTERNATIVE
HEALTH CENTERS

Other types of community-based health centers are not funded by the Bureau of Community Health Services as comprehensive centers, although in some cases they may receive limited support from local government and qualify for state or federal categorical grants. Many were developed around a specific program, such as family planning and maternity care, or in response to perceived needs of a specific population subgroup, such as an ethnic or linguistic minority or a feminist or gay clientele. Others were founded in response to dissatisfaction with the cost, quality, or cultural insensitivity of local private health care providers. Some of these independent clinics ultimately became HHS centers, but others have maintained independence in the belief that they offer a necessary alternative service delivery mode. A tremendous variation exists in scope of services, sponsorship, source of funding, and size. Brief mention will be made of some of the alternative community-based health centers serving the populations of the five study cities.

St. Louis. In St. Louis, three non-HHS health centers were operating in 1978. Carondelet was founded in 1969 on the south side of the city by university students together with a neighborhood group and relied heavily on volunteer personnel and diversified funding in 1978. Cochran Gardens, a community-run program in a downtown public housing project, and the People's Clinic in the central west end were almost completely volunteer efforts as of 1978.

Milwaukee. Milwaukee's Southside Community Health Clinic, sponsored by the Latin American Civil Liberties Union, has provided mainly adult dental services to a Southside Spanish-speaking clientele. The 16th Street Community Health Center also serves a predominantly Spanish-speaking clientele, providing about 6,000 health care visits and another 4,000 information and referral visits a year. Combining funding and volunteer services from a wide variety of sources, the center provides general medical care, basic preventive and well-child care, family planning, nutrition education, and a variety of health screening and information services. Among the supporters/participants are the city health department, Planned Parenthood, the Comprehensive Employment and Training Act (CETA), St. Mary's Hospital Family Practice Program, the Supplemental Nutrition for Women, Infants, and Children (WIC) program, United Way, and the Community Services Administration. The Guadalupe Children's Medical-Dental Clinic, sponsored by volunteer physicians with local private funds, also serves the city's Spanish speaking population primarily with child care but also with some maternity services.

Cincinnati. In Cincinnati, formerly independent clinics, whatever their original source of funding, now operate under contract with the Cincinnati Health Department.

Baltimore. Baltimore has a complicated mix of funding sources, sponsorship, and programs represented in its various primary care clinics. Nearly all are associated to some degree with a hospital, are supported by one or another federal categorical funding package, and/or participate in one of the many competing prepaid health plans in Baltimore. Map 6 (pages 200–201) shows more than thirty clinics of various types which operated in Baltimore in 1978. None, however, was located in Southeast Baltimore, the MHSP target area.

San Jose. In California, which has had a strong orientation toward independent community clinics, at least two types of developmental patterns have produced the current array of facilities. The "free clinics" of the hippie, Haight-Ashbury counter-culture movement of the late 1960s grew out of the medical, drug abuse, and counseling needs of those who either could not afford treatment elsewhere or felt that traditional providers were inappropriate and incapable of treating them (especially for drug-related problems). Since then, free medical clinics have maintained their youth orientation, but some have expanded to include family medical care in low-income neighborhoods. Because these clinics were almost totally volunteer organizations, financing, staffing, and service delivery have tended to be very unstable.

Borrowing in part from the idea of free clinics and in part from the federal neighborhood health center model, a different type of grass-roots health care delivery organization developed in some minority communities. These were called "community clinics" to distinguish them from the white, middle-class, youth-oriented "free clinics." With a different ideological base, they saw themselves not so much as alternatives but rather as the basic source of medical care in the underserved minority community.

In San Jose, such a clinic is the Gardner Community Health Center, in operation since 1972, and a participating site in the MHSP. The Gardner Clinic was the result of several years of effort by community leaders to gain low-cost family medical care for one of the poorest and most medically underserved communities in San Jose and Santa Clara County. Originally staffed by volunteer physicians, it grew into a comprehensive ambulatory care facility that provided about 8,000 visits a year by 1978. Gardner is partially financed by Santa Clara County funds, but collects about half its revenues from patient and Medi-Cal billings. Gardner's history has been shaky, with temporary closures in the past due to money shortages or inability to recruit physician staff. Providing family-oriented care, Gardner uses both a local voluntary hospital and Valley Medical Center for back-up specialty and inpatient services.

The role of community-based primary care clinics is subsidiary to that of private physicians or of hospital clinics in all five cities in terms of total volume of services. Federally funded community health centers provided from about 55,000 (St. Louis) to over 100,000 (Baltimore) visits in 1977. Alternative community-based centers added between 10,000 and 25,000 visits per city, except in Baltimore, where the volume was probably considerably higher although specific figures are not available. The relatively small absolute volume of care provided by community-based primary care centers may understate their importance for those patients who rely on them as a regular source of care. In California, community-based primary care centers represent the major resource for specific population subgroups, generally low-income ethnic minorities, who use virtually no other primary care providers. The access of such subgroups could be seriously affected by the loss of these resources.

Financial Barriers to Access and Corrective Mechanisms

One of the most frequently identified barriers to access to services is the financial barrier faced by those who cannot afford the cost of care. Perhaps the most significant public policy initiatives in the health field during the past two decades have been those programs that attempted to remove the financial barrier: Medicaid for the poor and Medicare for the elderly. In Chapter One, a detailed history of Medicaid was presented, overall conclusions as to its effectiveness were drawn, and broad comparisons across states and cities were made. The variability among states in eligibility standards, service coverage, and reimbursement levels of the Medicaid program was discussed. In this section, specific data by state and city or county as to eligibility, covered services, enrollment and expenditures under Medicaid and Medicare will be presented.

The Medicaid program's operations are summarized in a Medicaid/Medicare Management Institute publication:

Medicaid is designed to provide medical assistance to those groups or categories of people who are eligible to receive cash payments under one of the existing welfare programs established under the Social Security Act; that is, Title IV-A, the program of Aid to Families with Dependent Children (AFDC), or Title XVI, the Supplemental Security Income (SSI) program for the aged, blind and disabled. In general, receipt of a welfare payment under one of these programs means automatic eligibility for Medicaid.

In addition, States may provide Medicaid to the "medically needy," that is, to people who fit into one of the categories of people covered by the cash welfare programs (aged, blind, or disabled individuals, or members of families with dependent children when one parent is absent, incapacitated or unemployed), who have enough income to pay for their basic living expenses (and so are not recipients of welfare) but not enough to pay for their medical care.

It is important to note that Medicaid does not provide medical assistance to all of the poor. Low income is only one test of eligibility. Resources are also tested. And most importantly one must belong to one of the groups designated for welfare eligibility to be covered.

Title XIX of the Social Security Act requires that certain basic services must be offered in any State Medicaid program: Inpatient hospital services, outpatient hospital services, laboratory and X-ray services, skilled nursing facility services for individuals 21 and older, home health care services for individuals eligible for skilled nursing services, physicians' services, family planning services, rural health clinic services, and early and periodic screening, diagnosis and treatment services for individuals under 21. In addition, States may provide a number of other services if they elect to do so, including drugs, eyeglasses, private duty nursing, intermediate care facility services, inpatient psychiatric care for the aged and persons under 21, physical therapy, dental care, etc.

States determine the scope of services offered (they may limit the days of hospital care or number of physicians' visits covered, for example). They also, in general, determine the reimbursement rate for services, except for hospital care, where States are required to follow the Medicare reasonable cost payment system unless they have approval from the Secretary of Health, Education, and Welfare to use an alternate payment system for hospital care. Since July 1, 1976, they have been required to reimburse for skilled nursing facility and intermediate care facility services on a reasonable cost-related basis.

Since states generally determine the eligibility level for the welfare programs (they set the AFDC level, and determine the amount of supplement, if any, to the basic Federal SSI payment), they exercise a great deal of control over the income eligibility levels for Medicaid. If they cover the medically needy, they may establish the income level for eligibility at any point between the cash assistance eligibility level for an AFDC family (adjusted for family size) and 133-1/3 percent of the payment to such an AFDC family. All of these variations—in benefits offered, in groups covered, in income standards, and in levels of reimbursement for providers—mean that Medicaid programs differ greatly from State to State.

Medicaid operates as a vendor payment program. Payments are made directly to the provider of service for care rendered to an eligible individual. Providers must accept the Medicaid reimbursement level as payment in full. Individuals, however, are required to turn over their excess income to help pay for their care if they are in a nursing home. Copayments may also be required.

Many members of the Medicaid population are aged or disabled and are also covered under Medicare. In cases where this dual coverage exists, most State Medicaid programs pay for the Medicare premiums, deductibles and copayments, and for services not covered by Medicare.

States participate in the Medicaid program at their option. All States except Arizona currently have Medicaid programs. The District of Columbia, Puerto Rico, Guam and the Virgin Islands also provide Medicaid coverage.[16]

California and Wisconsin are among the states with the most generous Medicaid programs in the country. As of 1979, each provided not only basic services but the full array of optional services (except private duty nursing in California) to people eligible for federally supported financial assistance as well as to others in the medically needy categories described above. Maryland also provides Medicaid to the medically needy, and covers, in addition to basic services, clinic services, drugs, prosthetics, eyeglasses, emergency care, optometrists' and podiatrists' services, and care for the aged in tuberculosis and mental institutions. Missouri and Ohio fall at the lower end of the scale in range of services and eligibility. Both serve only individuals who receive federally supported financial assistance. Ohio has expanded the range of services for this group to include all the elective services except tuberculosis hospital care for the aged and various screening, preventive, diagnostic, and rehabilitation services not otherwise covered. Missouri, the least generous state of the five, has added drugs, dentistry, optometry, emergency care, intermediate care, and care for the aged in tuberculosis or mental hospitals. All five states place certain limitations on services, such as requiring prior authorization for skilled nursing or intermediate care admissions, for certain hospitalizations and for certain services or procedures.

The federal contribution to state Medicaid expenditures was 50 percent for California and Maryland, 55 percent for Ohio, 59 percent for Wisconsin, and 61 percent for Missouri in 1979. Inpatient hospital services in Ohio and Missouri were reimbursed under Medicaid by the same standards used for Medicare. California, Maryland, and Wisconsin, however, had developed approved alternative cost-related reimbursement mechanisms. Outpatient hospital services were reimbursed in Wisconsin according to Medicare standards; California set a maximum fee schedule; Maryland determined a reasonable cost; and Missouri and Ohio set reasonable and/or customary charge levels. Physician services were generally reimbursed according to state-determined fee schedules (California, Maryland), or state-determined reasonable charges (Missouri, Ohio), while Wisconsin selected the

TABLE 3.18

ANNUAL MEDICAID ENROLLMENT AND EXPENDITURES BY CITY OR COUNTY

Year	Baltimore (city only) Fiscal year		Cincinnati (Hamilton County) Calendar year		Milwaukee (Milwaukee County) Calendar year		St. Louis (city only) Fiscal year		San Jose (Santa Clara County) Fiscal year	
	Average enrollment per month	Total expenditures for year	Average enrollment per month	Total expenditures for year	Average actual users per month	Total expenditures for year	Average actual users per month	Total expenditures for year	Average enrollment per month	Total expenditures for year
1975	225,512	$100,016,139	69,600	$38,658,200	N.A.	N.A.	35,029	$26,412,624	116,431	$ 76,380,563
1976	232,495	117,711,822	70,800	49,169,000	N.A.	N.A.	38,747	31,515,085	114,189	90,279,522
1977	223,255	122,698,212	65,600	53,120,100	80,143[a]	N.A.	37,901	36,442,020	113,056	106,020,466
1978	211,047	133,643,254	60,050	57,990,600	107,192	$164,686,945	33,663	41,786,790	110,609	119,921,345
1979	202,742	152,887,592	57,000	64,548,000	101,972	167,232,661	30,730	44,189,802	102,318	123,051,667
1980	206,350	183,529,878	59,340	76,745,500	62,716[b]	142,852,929	32,041	63,008,577	100,830	143,006,288

[a]Based on last three months only.

[b]Understated due to exclusion of five months' data on those eligible under Supplemental Security Income only.

lowest of actual, median, or reasonable charge or the 1974 rate for service. Missouri was most restrictive of the five in its reimbursement to providers, and Wisconsin least restrictive.

The average Medicaid enrollment or number of users for the five cities or the counties in which they are located, and the total annual Medicaid expenditures for the city or county, are shown for the years 1975 through 1980, in Table 3.18. Baltimore contains more than half of Maryland's Medicaid recipients, one reason why its enrollment exceeds so dramatically that of the other cities. More than 25 percent of Baltimore's population received Medicaid benefits each year during this entire period. The lower eligibility levels and more restrictive benefits and reimbursement in Missouri and Ohio are evident in these figures.

Table 3.19 shows the proportion of the low-income population covered by Medicaid in each of the five cities or its county area as of 1975, based on population and poverty estimates and average monthly enrollment figures. This measure of the success of the state Medicaid programs in removing financial barriers to access for the poor indicates minimal achievement by Missouri, which covered only approximately 31 percent of St. Louis's poor. It shows good performance by Ohio and Wisconsin, and a surpassing achievement by Maryland and California, according to the then-current measure of poverty.

The Medicare program, or Health Insurance for the Aged and Disabled, covers all persons over age 65, all disabled persons who are entitled to Social Security cash benefits or railroad retirement benefits, and certain additional categories for hospital benefits. All these persons plus others who wish to participate voluntarily may be covered in the Supplementary Medical Insurance Program, which requires payment of monthly premiums. Also covered are persons under 65 who require treatment for end-stage renal disease.

Hospital insurance benefits include inpatient hospital care, skilled nursing facility care, and posthospital home health care. There are limitations as to number of days covered, as well as deductibles and copayments required of the beneficiary. Supplementary medical insurance benefits include physicians' services, hospital outpatient services, and certain medical supplies, tests, procedures, etc. This program also imposes deductibles and copayments upon the beneficiary. Providers are reimbursed by the Medicare program on a reasonable cost basis. Table 3.20 shows the number of persons enrolled and the reimbursement under Medicare for persons over 65 and for disabled persons in each of the five cities (or counties) in 1977.

Since Medicare is a federally administered program with uniform eligibility, benefits, and reimbursement rules, access of the elderly and disabled should be uniform from city to city. The few elderly who are not eligible for Medicare may be eligible for Medicaid if they meet the income standards, and a fairly large number of persons nationwide are covered under both Medicaid and Medicare. No city-

TABLE 3.19

MEDICAID ENROLLMENT COMPARED TO POVERTY POPULATION,
1975

	Estimated poverty population 1975	Average Medicaid enrollment 1975	Medicaid beneficiaries as percent of poverty population
Baltimore	136,000 (S.E. 16,000)	225,512	166%
Cincinnati	83,000 (S.E. 16,000)	69,600	84%
Milwaukee	69,000 (S.E. 11,000)	80,143[a,b]	116%
St. Louis	114,000 (S.E. 18,000)	35,029[b,c]	31%
San Jose	37,000 (S.E. 17,000)	116,431[a]	315%

[a]Enrollment or user data is for whole county.

[b]Data is for actual users rather than enrollment.

[c]St. Louis data for 1977, based on last three months only.

NOTE: The estimated poverty population is based upon the Spring 1976 Survey of
       Income and Education (SIE), a nationwide sample of households. The SIE
       is designed primarily to produce data for states. Such sub-state area
       data as is presented here is subject to high sampling errors and must be
       interpreted with caution. Poverty figures with standard errors higher
       than 15% of the estimates themselves should be considered highly
       unreliable. However, the estimates can provide a rough indication of
       the size of the poverty populations of the five cities.

SOURCE: Individual state Medicaid agency communications; U.S. Bureau of the
         Census.

or county-specific data are available for this group of beneficiaries.
Many of the elderly in nursing homes, however, are patients who
have exhausted their Medicare benefits and who, upon subsequent
exhaustion of their personal income and assets (spend-down), have
become eligible for Medicaid.

This section has presented data on the impact in each of the five
study cities of programs designed to remove financial barriers to health
care for the poor (Medicaid) and the elderly (Medicare). While Medicare benefits are distributed fairly evenly and equitably across the
five cities, it can be inferred that there remain many poor or near-
poor persons, particularly in St. Louis, who are uncovered or inadequately covered for needed health services. The decline in Medicaid
enrollment since 1975, at the same time that economic conditions have
worsened, reinforces this conclusion. In view of the constraints of
federal budgetary policy as of the early 1980s, this trend is not likely
to be reversed, at least for the short term.

TABLE 3.20

MEDICARE ENROLLMENT AND REIMBURSEMENT BY CITY OR COUNTY,
HOSPITAL AND/OR MEDICAL INSURANCE, 1977

	Persons 65 and older		Disabled beneficiaries	
	Enrollment	Reimbursement	Enrollment	Reimbursement
Baltimore (City)	99,241	$ 96,107,088	11,529	$ 14,357,390
Cincinnati (Hamilton County)	103,020	83,642,003	10,842	10,856,489
Milwaukee (Milwaukee County)	117,909	107,157,292	10,592	13,512,301
St. Louis (City)	81,636	66,111,738	7,768	7,354,447
San Jose (Santa Clara County)	84,632	66,865,085	10,502	12,397,880

SOURCE: U.S. Department of Health, Education, and Welfare, Health Care
Financing Administration, Medicare, 1977, Section 1.1,
"Reimbursement by State and County," HCFA Publication No. 03001
(12-78).

Summary

In seeking commonalities across the MHSP cities, one can discern
some general patterns of the potential and realized accessibility of
health services for the poor, despite the overall diversity in the configuration of health resources. By way of summary, we will point out
some of these commonalities and then note characteristics unique to
each city.

The degree to which private sector resources are accessible to the
poor is difficult to quantify city by city. It is clear from University of
Chicago findings that many residents of neighborhoods identified by
local policy-makers as medically underserved are finding private physicians whose services they are able to use. We do not yet know
whether the uninsured, low-income groups in these neighborhoods
are able to receive services from private physicians. Limited information is available as to the willingness of private physicians to treat
Medicaid patients. A 1977 survey by the Cincinnati Health Department indicated that of 300 private, office-based, primary care physicians in Cincinnati, only 20 percent would accept new Medicaid patients,
although 74 percent would accept new non-Medicaid patients. Recent
data released by the New York State Department of Social Services

revealed that during 1980–1981, only 32 percent of all licensed and registered physicians in New York City were actively participating in the Medicaid program.[17] Nonetheless, private physicians continue to be the provider of choice for the majority of residents in the MHSP target neighborhoods studied.

The role of nonpublic hospitals in caring for the poor is difficult to assess in view of the limitations in the availability and quality of hospital data on the characteristics of their patient populations. Because of financial pressures, without the last-dollar subsidies from city revenues which public hospitals depend upon, or special grants, these hospitals are reluctant to accept uninsured patients and must structure their outpatient programs to minimize services to this group. Nevertheless, in the course of fulfilling their service mission or of trying to maintain inpatient census, voluntary institutions have absorbed a certain amount of bad debt, in some cases, from the provision of a substantial volume of care to the city's indigent population. This situation was particularly evident in Baltimore, where, from the late sixties on, voluntary hospitals have worked in partnership with the local health department to pursue neighborhood health center grants or to cooperate with community-based health centers, and have also provided large volumes of emergency room care. The innovative rate-setting mechanisms of the Maryland Health Services Cost Review Commission, which provides for the distribution of hospitals' bad debts across all third party payors and providers, have enabled voluntary institutions to provide more free care to indigents. In St. Louis, radical demographic and socioeconomic shifts have caused the relocation of voluntary hospitals and private physicians to the suburbs, leaving the public sector and a number of financially pressed private facilities to cope with the growing burden of the inner-city poor. Milwaukee's and Cincinnati's voluntary hospitals, which hitherto had little interest in serving the poor, are seen in a period of shrinking census to be prepared to compete vigorously for new patient populations, including the Medicaid eligibles. Private practitioners and voluntary hospitals in San Jose play a relatively limited role in caring for the poor. In the context of contracting financial resources for the poor, a growing role for the private sector is likely to be limited to cases where low occupancy threatens institutional survival.

Given the large volume of ambulatory care they provide to the Medicaid and indigent populations in each of the cities, public hospitals appear to be a mainstay of medical care for those who remain outside the private medical market. The critical role of the public institution in each of the five cities has been described, in terms of the sheer volume of care produced, their relationship to local medical schools, and the specialized services they provide that are unavailable from other hospitals. Their continuing importance in the arena of health care resources for the urban poor seems inevitable, particularly in the context of future cuts in the existing financing mechanisms, which permit the poor access to the private sector.

Health centers operated by local public health departments have played a relatively small role in terms of volume of care for the poor. Their traditional emphasis on preventive services has been important, however, given the lack of preventive services in many other contexts. Among the cities, the primary health care functions of the health department vary dramatically—from San Jose, where such services are virtually nonexistent, to Cincinnati, where all primary health care clinics, including federally funded community health centers, are co-ordinated through the city health department's Primary Health Care System.

Community health centers, both comprehensive federally financed clinics and smaller, more narrowly focused alternative health clinics, play some role in each city in providing care for the poor. While limited information is available as to the volume of services they deliver in the five cities, national studies have found that community health centers offer reasonably high-quality ambulatory care, mainly to groups who would otherwise lack access to such services. As the brief descriptions of the various clinics indicate, neither the demography of urban neighborhoods nor the availability of different kinds of health resources remains static. While these currents affect the public hospital, the community clinic is even more sensitive to the changing environment, and its viability often depends upon its ability to adapt.

Our limited assessment of the performance of the major federal financing mechanisms in removing financial barriers to care indicated that large numbers of the poor and the elderly have achieved improved access to services. Nonetheless, it appears that the distribution of Medicare benefits is more equitable than that of Medicaid benefits, and that for some groups of the poor, particularly in St. Louis, financial barriers to access remain. These problems are likely to intensify as entitlement programs are cut in the future.

References

1. Lu Ann Aday and Ronald Andersen, *Access to Medical Care* (Ann Arbor, Mich.: Health Administration Press, 1975), pp. 1–2.

2. Milton Chen and James Bush, "Health Status Measures, Policy, and Biomedical Research," in *Health: What Is It Worth?*, edited by Selma Mushkin and David Dunlop (New York: Pergamon Press, 1979), p. 35.

3. Lu Ann Aday, Ronald Andersen and Gretchen Fleming, *Health Care in the U.S.: Equitable for Whom?* (Beverly Hills, Calif.: Sage Publications, 1980).

4. Ibid., p. 25.

5. Ibid., p. 26.

6. Ibid., p. 41.

7. Ibid., pp. 231–48.

8. National Center for Health Statistics, *Physician Visits, Volume, and Interval Since Last Visit, United States—1975*, Vital and Health Statistics, Ser. 10, num. 128 (Department of Health, Education and Welfare).

9. National Center for Health Statistics, *Health: United States, 1980* (Department of Health and Human Services no. [PHS]81–1232).

10. National Center for Health Statistics, *Physician Visits . . . . , 1975.*

11. Sam Shapiro, Pearl S. German, Donald M. Steinwachs, Elizabeth A. Skinner, and Gary A. Chase, *Relationship of Resources to Health Care Behavior in Disadvantaged Populations* (The Johns Hopkins University Health Care Research and Development Center, 1978).

12. Baltimore City Medical Society, *Baltimore Primary Care Study Report,* 1981.

13. Ronald Andersen and Gretchen Fleming, "Evaluation of Municipal Health Services Program" (University of Chicago, Center for Health Administration Studies, 1981, unpublished).

14. Shapiro, et. al., *Relationship of Resources.*

15. Report of the Commission on Public-General Hospitals, *The Future of the Public-General Hospital: An Agenda for Transition* (Chicago: Hospital Research and Educational Trust, 1978).

16. Medicaid-Medicare Management Institute, *Data on the Medicaid Program, 1979 Edition* (rev.) (Washington, D.C.: Department of Health and Human Services, Health Care Financing Administration).

17. New York State Department of Social Services, Division of Medical Assistance, *Utilization of Health Services by New York City Medicaid Recipients, 1979–80,* 1981.

CHAPTER FOUR

Current Issues in Providing Urban Ambulatory Care: The Public Hospital and Neighborhood Clinics

In view of the differences among cities in the array of inner-city providers, the distribution of responsibility among government agencies, and the results of past strategies to address access barriers, one might anticipate diversity as well in how the cities define their current problems and priorities in providing health services. While urban health policy-makers across the country are confronted by many of the same types of problems, the interplay of local forces produces unique circumstances that require solutions tailored to specific community needs. In this chapter, we will examine some local perceptions of the major issues facing each city's health service delivery system and municipal health services in general.

We will address two major sets of issues: the status of the public hospital and the provision of neighborhood-based ambulatory care. Under these headings, generic issues common to many metropolitan areas can be identified.

During the past two decades, many local governments became engaged in dialogues, sometimes acrimonious, about their appropriate role in guaranteeing health care for the poor. These debates often focused on the public hospital, due to commonly occurring fiscal, management, and quality problems. Such difficulties are to some degree rooted in the shortcomings of specific federal programs, as well as changes in medicine and society that are national in scope. These external forces, however, are modified by local urban circumstances, such as the role of interest groups, degree of community support, and presence of competition from the voluntary sector.

From the previous chapters' review of past attempts to bring ambulatory care closer to the poor, some generally applicable points are worth keeping in mind. The first involves the mutability of the urban scene. Very little remains static in the urban environment: neither demography, nor the level of interest or focus of community politics, nor the external forces that create both opportunities and impediments for social action.

Second, as important as questions of auspices, affiliations, and organizational structure may be, certain forces operate to shape the environment and prospects of both the public hospital and neighborhood-based ambulatory clinics. These public facilities face many of the same impediments to financial viability and efficient management: the need for stable funding to care for patients without third-party coverage; difficulties in recruiting and retaining quality personnel; the challenge of aligning the size and scope of clinic operations with a realistic assessment of likely patient utilization; and, finally, the problems of balancing the needs and demands of the community, the professional staff, and local government.

The following sections will seek to identify generic problems of public hospitals and neighborhood health care and to enrich the picture with concrete illustrations from the five cities participating in the Municipal Health Services Program (MHSP). The aim will be to understand better how local circumstances lead to the unique prescriptions for action chosen by each city in addressing similar problems.

The Status of the Public Hospital

In April 1980, the following article appeared in the St. Louis *Globe Democrat*:

Study to Consider New Medical Center

A local architectural and planning firm will study the feasibility of building a municipal medical center that eventually could replace City and Homer G. Phillips hospitals.

The City's Board of Estimate and Apportionment Tuesday approved a $50,000 contract with the firm, Hellmuth, Obata & Kassabaum Inc.

Comptroller Raymond T. Percich voted against the study, later reiterating his position that the city should get out of the hospital business and contract with private hospitals to provide indigent care.

Dr. R. Dean Wochner, city director of health and hospitals, said the study is meant to assist a special task force already studying the question of whether a new hospital could and should be built. Mayor James F. Conway supports the concept of a new medical center.

Wochner said the study, which is expected to take six months, would consider construction of such a complex and the feasibility of new construction at City Hospital or at Phillips. The firm's planners also are to formulate an interim renovation program for City Hospital, which would continue as the city's general hospital until a new hospital could be built.

The quandary in which St. Louis found itself with respect to public hospital services is not unlike that in many American cities. That a city can simultaneously be considering a massive investment of new resources and a total disengagement might be construed as an indication of a uniquely confused health politics arena. Nevertheless, it is illustrative of the debate on the mission and future of public general hospitals, which has been taking place nationwide in recent years. While a responsibility as guarantor of health care for the poor is commonly mandatory for local governments across the country, as Chapter Two elucidated, the means by which that responsibility is to be carried out has generated heated debate in many localities.

Although the debate continues at one level of intensity or another in most areas, during the 1970s certain significant localities, such as Philadelphia and San Diego County, either closed their public hospitals or turned them over to a local medical school to become university teaching hospitals. This section of the chapter will identify the major issues confronting public hospitals and discuss the history and problems of hospital operation in each of the five cities participating in the Municipal Health Services Program.

MISSION AND PHILOSOPHY

The debate over the future role of public general hospitals had generated sufficient concern by 1976 so that a national Commission on Public-General Hospitals was established by the Hospital Research and Educational Trust "to examine how the public-general hospitals carry out their public mandates and to explore their roles in the development of future health care delivery systems."[1] The commission considered the possibility that there was in fact *no* further role for the public-general hospital, and in most urban health systems adherents of this view can be found. Advocacy of a total withdrawal by local governments from direct operation of health services facilities represents one extreme in the continuum of positions on the issue. In general, those who argue for withdrawal would prefer to see the local government contract with private providers for health care for the indigent. Although the commission concluded that there was a future role for public hospitals, it conceded that individual localities had to assess their own health systems and political environments and come to decisions based on local factors.

Justification for the position that public hospitals are no longer needed derives from the enactment of Medicare and Medicaid, which theoretically should have removed financial barriers to access. It has been argued that Medicaid and Medicare changed public hospitals from institutions serving only the indigent into facilities that compete with private hospitals. For example, in New York City during the decade following Medicaid and Medicare, the municipal hospital system's share of services dropped from 23 percent to a low of less than 17 percent of inpatient days. Significantly, the greatest loss was among the elderly, who represent 37 percent of all hospitalized patients. The municipal system's share of patients older than age 65 decreased from 33 percent before Medicare to 13 percent in 1975. While the municipal hospitals provided more than 63 percent of all hospital services to welfare recipients in 1961, their 1975 share of Medicaid admissions was just over 43 percent.[2] Nonetheless, the municipal hospitals provide a disproportionate amount of the hospital care for the poor, particularly for those "medically indigent" or "working poor" who have no third-party coverage or whose coverage is inadequate. This shift in the role of New York's municipal hospitals is not dissimilar to changes in other cities' public facilities.

The decline in overall inpatient utilization at public hospitals has led to the further argument that tertiary care costs generated by the resultant underutilized facilities have become a fiscal drain on local government. Contracts with private hospitals could provide care more efficiently, this line of reasoning goes. Such an approach was taken by Multnomah County, Oregon, which eliminated its public hospital and secured federal funding to support prepaid ambulatory care for the indigent, with local physician groups and hospitals providing services under contract to the county board of health. On a broad scale, questions as to the comparative costs of public sector and private sector care for the indigent have not been satisfactorily answered. Questions of comparative quality of care also remain, although critics of the public hospital decry the "two-class system" of medical care and call for voluntary hospitals to take over contractual responsibility for direct provision of services or operation of the public facility.

Cincinnati provides an example of the case where a municipality has turned over operation of its public hospital to a state university medical school. As noted in earlier chapters, the Cincinnati General Hospital now is under the authority of the University of Cincinnati College of Medicine, although the city continues to own the land and buildings. The transfer was to some degree rationalized by the assumption that Medicaid and Medicare had eliminated the need for a city hospital. The teaching interests of the College of Medicine provided the impetus for undertaking the shift in auspices. The administrative relationships formed to accommodate such linkages are complicated. The result is often a trade-off between the resources and presumed high quality of care that come with substantial medical school involvement and a more single-minded mission of service to the disadvantaged.

In two other cities, San Jose and St. Louis, the debate over continued operation of the public hospital has been long and acrimonious. In both localities, out-moded physical plants that would require substantial investments to renovate or replace have precipitated a series of studies prepared over nearly a decade by various ad hoc committees and private consultants. In both Santa Clara County and St. Louis, there have been advocates of building a new facility as well as proponents of the disengagement of local government from operation of hospital facilities. Fierce political battles have been waged over the issue.

In Santa Clara County, a coalition of labor and community groups has been able to force votes by the county Board of Supervisors pledging to continue Valley Medical Center (VMC) as a county facility, but accreditation problems due to code deficiencies keep resurrecting the issue. San Jose voluntary hospitals have begun to emerge in direct competition with VMC for services and patients, while tertiary care costs at the public facility have prompted both criticism and support of the need to continue operation of the facility.

In St. Louis, one elected official or another has advocated nearly every option for the public hospitals. Two successive comptrollers have opposed city operation of general acute hospital services. Some members of the Board of Aldermen also favor contracting with private hospitals for care of the indigent. Mayor Conway pressed consolidation of the two general acute hospitals and succeeded in closing Homer G. Phillips, only to lose the 1981 mayoral election to a candidate whose platform was to reopen Phillips and close Max C. Starkloff (City Number One). One major constituency for public hospital services in St. Louis is the black population which primarily uses the services. The other is the St. Louis University Medical School, for which City Hospital Number One is an important teaching resource. The general population is apathetic about hospital services, although the southside white residents support the public long-term care facility where many of their elderly receive care. Although years of successive studies led to the closing of Phillips Hospital, as of 1981 a new consultant was assessing the potential for reopening Phillips and closing Starkloff, and the cost of getting out of the hospital business altogether.

The future of Milwaukee County Hospital has been a continuing topic of debate since the mid-1970s, engaging officials at the city, county, and state levels; health professionals at both public and private institutions; community agencies and organizations concerned with the delivery and cost of health services; and the community at large. Of the hundreds of articles appearing in the press speaking to every aspect of local health-related activities, many focus on the problems and future of the County Hospital. The issue of the teaching and research activities of the Milwaukee County Medical Complex (MCMC) predominates in the discussion. As has happened in other cities, a seemingly endless series of studies was commissioned over the past several years, four within a single 14-month period in 1978–1979. Criticism of administration and financial management was widespread, but the loudest complaints were voiced over the extremely high unit costs of service at the public facility (higher per diem rates than any local hospital) which, located outside the city, is far from the indigent population it is intended to serve. It has frequently been argued by representatives of inner-city neighborhoods that Milwaukee County could discharge its obligations to provide medical care for the indigent more conveniently and more efficiently through contract with voluntary hospitals in the inner city. The study which appeared to present Milwaukee policy-makers with the most politically feasible plan of action was prepared by a former president of the Medical College of Wisconsin, who was able to incorporate recommendations made by local officials and area health professionals. This study, known as the Carley report, noted administrative and financial improvements made between 1975 and 1976 and recommended that Milwaukee County Hospital remain open as a public general, teaching, and tertiary care hospital if additional needed changes were made in its governing structure, management practices, and relationship with the Medical College of Wisconsin. The report stressed that the County Hospital's central role as a teaching, research, and tertiary care center must be taken into account when questioning its future:

Equalled perhaps by only one other medical center in the entire state (University of Wisconsin Hospital, Madison), it serves a far larger population and its combined teaching and service delivery role in the future is predicted to be much larger than any other medical center in the entire state.[3]

Although not all debate has been stilled, the Medical College of Wisconsin provides such a strong constituency for the hospital that it is likely to remain in its current role for the foreseeable future. The one potential change could be a shift in the auspices of operation from the county to the Medical College, as happened in Cincinnati and other localities.

While the role of the public hospital as teaching institution predominated in discussions of Milwaukee health policy, in Baltimore this issue was only one of several concerning the future of Baltimore City Hospitals (BCH). A major long-range planning study was commissioned by the mayor in January 1979, at the same time that the Maryland Health Services Cost Review Commission conducted its own review of the public hospital. The mayor's committee study, known as the Kearney Report, was initiated in response to perceived changes in BCH patient activity that had so clouded the mission of the hospital that the city was forced to reevaluate the nature of its own commitment to the institution.

The Kearney Report approached the sensitive topic of BCH's mission by recognizing that the institution assumes multiple roles. As a public general hospital it assures access to all citizens regardless of minority status or ability to pay, and offers special services not available through other community facilities. As a community hospital it serves "private" patients who have the means to avail themselves of other hospitals but choose BCH because of easy access, personal preference, and physician referral. As a tertiary care institution it serves the region by providing complex, expensive services such as burn care, neonatal intensive care, renal dialysis and kidney transplants, and psychiatric inpatient services. Finally, as a teaching and research center, the city hospital has ties to Johns Hopkins and the University of Maryland medical schools. A review of BCH's patient population characteristics vis-a-vis other area hospitals revealed to the authors of the Kearney Report that the institution's role of "hospital of last resort" no longer applied. The committee could not find strong justification for BCH's continued existence as a public general hospital. Although it did not call for closure, it saw BCH's future role as a community hospital for the surrounding area. Teaching and research activities also could be carried on by the hospital under an altered mission. The voters of Baltimore in 1980 approved a measure authorizing establishment of an independent public benefit corporation for the public hospital. The board of directors for the new entity was appointed early in 1981, but had not by the end of the year dealt publicly with the issue of BCH's mission.

Central to the issue of a public hospital's role is the scope of services it offers to its patients. The Commission on Public-General Hospitals found that public hospitals, especially those in urban areas, provide many services beyond the scope of a community hospital, such as a large volume of sophisticated emergency and trauma care, a variety of highly specialized diagnostic inpatient and outpatient services, and the kinds of programs that deal with medical-social problems, such as alcohol and drug abuse and mental illness. And of course, the public hospitals provide a disproportionate amount of all hospital-based ambulatory care.[4] The public hospital's role in providing sophisticated trauma care and esoteric subspecialty services is fostered by the close relationships between public facilities and medical schools which use them as teaching hospitals, a relationship to be discussed in greater detail below. The tertiary care role of the public hospital has meant a major investment in expensive technology and the manpower to manage it, which has led to high operating budgets and unit costs in the public facility and accordingly the need for greater subsidies from the local government to cover deficits. Some critics argue that the appropriate role for the public hospital is as a community-level facility, leaving costly tertiary care to university medical centers or local voluntary hospitals. The degree to which this argument is heard may be related to the degree to which competition has emerged among the providers in a locality for patients or for marketable services. In some localities, the public hospital is the only facility offering many tertiary-level services, and in such areas its role is probably less likely to change, especially if it serves as a major teaching resource for a local medical school. However, as hospital costs continue to rise and further strains are placed on local governmental revenues, high-cost services in a public hospital may be a major target of budget cutters, and local health policy-makers will no doubt have to face a debate on the appropriate scope of public hospital services.

The issue of scope of services has been central to debates of public hospital mission in Milwaukee, where the tertiary care service costs have been perceived by taxpayers as an unfair drain, by voluntary hospitals as unfair competition, and by health planners as unreasonable duplication of services. Santa Clara Valley Medical Center has faced similar but much less pronounced criticism of tertiary-level service costs, partly because it is not the primary teaching hospital for a medical school and does not offer quite as wide a range of services. In Cincinnati, debate over scope of services never became heated due to the transfer of Cincinnati General Hospital to the College of Medicine. Baltimore City Hospitals and St. Louis City Hospital Number One, while offering some tertiary-level services, come closer to the community hospital model. On the other hand, Cincinnati General Hospital and Milwaukee County Medical Complex are major teaching and research institutions. However, the issue of scope of services has arisen in policy discussions in each locality.

Fundamental to the issue of hospital mission is the mix of patients by payor class. As has been mentioned, public hospitals which were historically the provider of last resort for the indigent have become, through the availability of third-party financing for many of the poor and most of the elderly and through the revolution in medical technology, providers of certain tertiary services for all types of patients, competing in some cases with the private sector. Indeed, as lengths of stay and occupancy rates have fallen among public and voluntary hospitals, some health policy analysts have called for public institutions to alter their missions and become more competitive for private patients by setting up private practice programs, prepaid health plans and other such mechanisms. The Commission on Public-General Hospitals strongly recommended a variety of such shifts, stating that the public general hospital's future depended upon its ability to become a broadly based community resource.[5] Tentative movement in this direction can be discerned in Baltimore and San Jose.

The mission of the public hospital continues to be the focus of intense debate in many localities. In the current context of reductions in federal aid to states and localities, additional constraints on the ability of states and localities to raise taxes, and heightened demands on local government services, this debate can be expected to intensify, especially in fiscally distressed urban areas. The constituencies which support public hospitals will become more visible and important to their survival. Community groups, which become most articulate in times of crisis, may play important roles, but many community groups formed to respond to health care crises are too transient to maintain lasting influence.

Treating local government as an actor in the debate over public hospital survival, we must re-emphasize the diversity of structure and responsibility among localities. Throughout the various public hospital profiles in this chapter, the tension among government officials has been a consistent element. This tension has been most evident in St. Louis between the mayor and comptroller, and in Milwaukee among a variety of state, county, and city power centers. For public officials, the critical elements to weigh in formulating a position are the constituencies that are the basis of their political support, the fiscal responsibilities their office carries, their flexibility to maneuver within budgetary constraints, and the broader concerns of the agencies they manage.

Among the groups which represent potentially strong allies of the public hospital against threats of closure are employees and medical staffs. Even though public employee unions have shown their muscle in such places as New York City, they are not universally powerful factors. To date, unions have played only a minor role in the public hospital controversies in the five demonstration cities. Nevertheless, a serious threat of closing is the sort of event that may spark greater activism. Baltimore City Hospitals, for example, can probably expect increased union activity from civil service employees as concern mounts over possible conversion to a community hospital.

Along with unions, organized medical staffs will have their say in deliberations. In Valley Medical Center and Baltimore City Hospitals, the incorporated medical staffs are of particular importance, since they are identifiable organizational entities whose interests are at stake in negotiations over the conversion of the public hospital.

As we have noted, the attitudes of other providers toward the public hospital must be taken into consideration. There are two sets of views about conflict and accommodation between the public and voluntary sectors. On one hand, the two sectors may be seen as competitors fighting for a limited supply of patients in an overbedded community. The markets in San Jose and Milwaukee to some extent fit this perception. On the other hand, the public hospital may provide a useful alternative for patients the voluntary hospitals would prefer not to treat: uninsured patients, Medicaid patients in states with poor reimbursement, and patients that are "socially" unacceptable, such as drug addicts, alcoholics, and the homeless. Thus, in St. Louis and Cincinnati the voluntary hospitals have not supported moves to terminate public hospital services. Because the state of Maryland incorporates bad debts into its rate-setting mechanism and because of BCH's unique patient population, its relationship with the voluntary hospitals is atypical for a public institution. Finally, as we have seen, a medical school affiliation is a major source of support for, as well as criticism of, the public hospital. Because this relationship is so influential and so frequent, it will be addressed separately in the following section.

THE MEDICAL SCHOOL AFFILIATION

In earlier sections, it has been described how the public hospital in each of the five cities is linked with one or more local medical schools. Among the study cities, Cincinnati and Milwaukee have the strongest relationships—the University of Cincinnati College of Medicine actually operates Cincinnati General Hospital, while the Medical College of Wisconsin is dependent upon the Milwaukee County Medical Complex as its major teaching facility. Valley Medical Center in San Jose, Baltimore City Hospitals, and St. Louis City Hospital Number One are important affiliates but are not the primary hospitals upon which Stanford, Johns Hopkins, the University of Maryland, or St. Louis University rely. The relationship between City Hospital Number One and St. Louis University became much stronger in the past few years as Washington University withdrew from its limited affiliation with the public facility. In 1981, the first formal memorandum of agreement between St. Louis University School of Medicine and the public hospital was signed. Table 4.1 shows the relationships between the public hospitals and the local medical schools in each city.

The relationship between a public hospital and a medical school has been variously praised as the hospital's means of survival and castigated as the source of some of its most intractable difficulties. While there are numerous problems presented by medical school domination of public hospitals in terms of governance, management, costs, and service to the poor, there are also considerable advantages to be derived from such affiliation. Perhaps chief among the benefits is an alliance with a powerful interest group—an especially potent political tool when the school depends primarily on the hospital for teaching and research opportunities. In the opinion of some observers, there seems to be a direct relationship between the long-term security of a public hospital's operations and the local medical school's commitment to the institution. This favorable outlook does not necessarily imply a continuation of its original governance; indeed, in several cases the municipal or county institution has been transferred to the public medical school (Cincinnati: University of Cincinnati College of Medicine; Kansas City: University of Missouri, Kansas City, School of Medicine; Newark: College of Medicine and Dentistry of New Jersey, New Jersey Medical School; San Diego County: University of California, San Diego, School of Medicine; Seattle: University of Washington School of Medicine; Toledo: Medical College of Ohio at Toledo). Critics contend that this trend decreases public accountability and the likelihood that services will be responsive to com-

TABLE 4.1

RELATIONSHIP BETWEEN PUBLIC HOSPITAL AND LOCAL MEDICAL SCHOOL
IN SELECTED CITIES AS OF 1981

Medical School	Baltimore Baltimore City Hospitals	Cincinnati Cincinnati General Hospital	Milwaukee Milwaukee County Medical Complex	St. Louis City Hospital Number One (Max Starkloff)	San Jose Santa Clara Valley Medical Center
Johns Hopkins University School of Medicine (private)	Strong affiliation; hospital is not school's primary teaching facility.				
University of Maryland School of Medicine (public)	Limited affiliation				
University of Cincinnati College of Medicine (public)		Major affiliation; hospital is school's primary teaching facility.			
Medical College of Wisconsin (private)			Major affiliation, hospital is school's primary teaching facility.		
St. Louis University School of Medicine (private)				Strengthening relationship; first formal affiliation contract 1981; not school's primary teaching facility.	
Washington University School of Medicine (private)				Limited affiliation; school has withdrawn most of its limited programs in recent years. (Homer G. Phillips Hospital now closed, had no strong medical school affiliation.)	
Stanford University School of Medicine (private) (Palo Alto)					Strong affiliation; hospital is not school's primary teaching facility.

munity concerns. But while there is no guarantee that medical schools can successfully address the endemic problems of public hospitals or that the services will satisfy public desires, medical schools tend to have great credibility in the local political arena, and their support adds to the rationale for maintaining public subsidies.

The influence of a close affiliation with a medical school on the actual delivery of ambulatory care to patients of the public facility has been widely discussed. The traditional outpatient department of a teaching hospital has been characterized as providing overspecialized, impersonal, fragmented, and episodic care focused on organ systems or diseases rather than patients. The public hospitals in the five study cities operate between 25 and 53 separate outpatient clinics. Although an objective of many public health professionals has been to coordinate care between the neighborhood clinic and the public hospital, William Shonick found, in his study of mergers of public health departments with public hospitals, that:

> One of the important forces impeding service integration appeared to stem from the imperatives of medical education carried out in the public hospital, especially when such education stressed highly technologic subspecialty training. Two distinct aspects are involved—the effects on the actual nature of the service to patients and the taking over of ownership of the public beds by the medical school. With respect to the first aspect, we observed that referrals from the neighborhood health centers to the public hospitals were equally as haphazard in the merged Boston and Los Angeles areas as in the unmerged Chicago locale. The influence of the medical teaching program operated by an outside agency, especially a medical school, proved to be an equally strong deterrent to establishing an integrated system whether the neighborhood health centers were under a formally decreed "merged" system or not. The specialty orientation of these teaching programs and their staffing—interns, residents and their teachers—militated everywhere against a close tie with neighborhood-based medical staff and the day-in, day-out performance of "garden variety" medical chores.[6]

Shonick further commented:

> With respect to the second aspect, the closing or taking over of the ownership of the public hospital, this happened in a number of places . . . the fundamental cause of this behavior seems to be a steadily declining source of "teaching material" for medical schools and teaching voluntary hospitals. This decline is due both to a decline in overall census in the private hospitals since about 1960 as well as the increased teaching patient needs of expanding medical schools. Without the presence of a patient-needy medical school, difficulty in financing the hospital did not seem to result in its being "given away".[7]

Shonick tends to side with the consumer advocate or community representation groups who are most critical of the medical school involvement with the public hospital. On the other hand, such groups as the Commission on Public-General Hospitals find that the nation's public general hospitals serve an invaluable role in training physicians and other health professionals (they accounted for 40 percent of all medical and dental residents in 1978), that the teaching programs in urban public hospitals contribute heavily to the quality of care in these facilities, and that the educational and research roles are important enough to be continued and fostered by governments at all levels.[8] The importance of medical education and its reinforcement of quality are fairly generally accepted. It is the costs of training and research, as well as the personal impact on the patient, that generate criticism at the local level.

Milwaukee has been identified as a locale where the teaching and research costs have created a county facility with the highest unit costs in the region. Opposition to these costs is expressed by the local tax-paying public and by elected officials. Milwaukee voluntary hospitals complain of shrinking census at the same time that inner-city patients are required to go out of town to the county hospital, despite the fact that the voluntary hospital costs are much lower. They would also like a greater share of the high technology in order to compete more successfully for services and patients.

Concern about the high cost of medical education prompted a special study which was requested by the Wisconsin Hospital Rate Review Committee. The investigation was conducted by a task force composed of representatives of business, labor, hospitals, medicine, and education. Its report on the costs of medical education recovered from inpatient revenues at twenty Wisconsin hospitals was released in 1979. Because of the difficulty of determining the amount of the many other related costs, the study considered only the salaries and fringe benefits paid to medical school faculty and resident physicians in hospital training programs who were compensated by the hospitals. Due to further difficulty in calculating the division of residents' time between patient care and education, the minimum cost of educating physicians was estimated at between $10.7 million and $20.8 million at these twenty hospitals. If it were assumed that 100 percent of a faculty member's or resident's time was used for educational purposes, Milwaukee County Hospital, the major training ground for the Medical College of Wisconsin, spent 11 percent of its total 1979 operating budget of $72 million for medical education. Eleven percent of $423, the average daily charge at the time of the study, amounted to $46.

The Carley Report, a consultant's study of the Milwaukee County Hospital, explicitly called for legislative action to provide state support for the costs of medical education now borne directly by patients and indirectly by county taxpayers. Similar calls have been made by groups in other cities such as San Jose. The teaching hospital must balance the need to encourage a flow of complicated and unusual cases deemed necessary for the teaching mission of a university medical center with the need to attract large numbers of patients who have adequate third-party insurance coverage to pay for the full cost of care.

The Cincinnati General Hospital faces the same problems of accommodating its multiple roles in order to maintain financial viability, and its survival is also closely related to its relationship with Cincinnati's private hospital sector. The General Hospital now finds itself in a position where cooperation and competition must be cleverly balanced. The pressures forcing cooperation among Cincinnati's major private hospitals spring mainly from the necessity to share the costs of expensive technological development and implementation of new tertiary care capacity. While the College of Medicine might prefer to have all such programs concentrated within the University Medical Center complex, the cost would likely be prohibitive, but more importantly, local voluntary hospitals are aggressively pursuing their individual goals as regional tertiary referral centers. Regional and state planning agencies, as well as the Ohio Board of Regents which sets policy for the University of Cincinnati, have supported the position that the University College of Medicine must conduct its medical education programs in association with Cincinnati's private hospitals.

The last fifteen years have witnessed an increasing scale of involvement by medical schools with public hospitals in the conduct of their teaching programs, and in many cases this has led to the takeover of public hospital plant, program, and management. This trend may not continue in the future, however. Increasing competition from the voluntary hospitals for high technology and super-specialized services may impel medical schools in some areas to spread their teaching activities more widely among area facilities. Milwaukee and Cincinnati already exhibit pressures in this direction. Nonetheless, medical education is likely to remain a major force affecting urban public hospitals, particularly those institutions which serve as the primary teaching resource for the local medical school.

THE STRUCTURE AND DELIVERY OF PRIMARY CARE IN PUBLIC HOSPITALS

In earlier chapters of this volume, reference has been made to the many deficiencies attributed to the delivery of ambulatory care services in public hospital emergency rooms (ER) and outpatient departments (OPD). These deficiencies are succinctly summarized below:

Ambulatory health services have been criticized for lack of high quality care, minimal academic involvement, fragmentation of services, over-specialization and unresponsiveness to patients' needs . . . the outpatient department of the municipal hospital involved in this study exemplified many of the difficulties encountered in providing health care in an urban center. Patient care was fragmented, episodic, disease-oriented, and lacking in adequate follow up. Health services were provided in a variety of clinics that were staffed by physicians who worked a limited number of hours on a fee per session basis. Additional staffing was provided by house staff members who were largely unsupervised during their limited participation in the OPD.

As a result, responsibility shifted from resident to resident with no single physician assuming continuing responsibility. The facility, staff, and program of the OPD were neither adequate to cope with the volume of service demanded nor prepared to supply good quality care and house staff education. House staff supervision was inadequate in the OPD, and the graduating physicians were of necessity oriented toward inpatient services and unfamiliar with the needs of the outpatient population.[9]

Of particular concern in today's climate of cost containment initiatives are further criticisms of hospital-based ambulatory care as excessively costly per unit of service. It is argued that neighborhood-based services could be provided at lower cost. The issue of unit costs for ambulatory care provided in hospitals is quite complex. It can be argued that the hospital clinic visit consists of a whole array of services that are billed for separately when they are provided in the private sector under fee-for-service, and that in making cost comparisons, care must be taken to assure that apples are in fact being compared to apples. It can also be argued that it is the cost accounting system, not the structure of care, that is at fault in making clinic costs appear so high, and that the step-down inappropriately allocates inpatient costs to the OPD and emergency room. Additionally, when policy choices are being made, the utilization of existing capital plant must be considered as an alternative to the investment of large new sums of money for the renovation or construction of neighborhood-based facilities.

Still another set of issues has to do with convenience of access to services. A local government generally has only one public hospital. It may, as in Milwaukee, Baltimore, and St. Louis, be located quite far from the neighborhoods of some of the patients who most need its services. The inconvenience of a long trip may be exacerbated by rising costs of transportation, which may be a major deterrent to the poor in seeking preventive services and early intervention in time of illness. Given the increasing number of women who are employed, time lost from work by a family member in order to bring a child to a facility where long hours are spent in waiting is a costly consideration. This phenomenon may influence the high utilization of emergency rooms for primary care in the evening hours when many other providers are unavailable. The inconvenience of a long wait for an OPD appointment is also an influence on patient choice of emergency room or walk-in clinic in seeking care.

Closely related to convenience are other amenities which seem too often to be lacking in the public hospital OPD. The facilities are often dilapidated and crowded, as a result of the higher priority commanded by critical inpatient services in the allocation of capital resources. The physical atmosphere of a charity clinic is frequently reinforced by the attitudes of staff, both professional and support, who have been criticized as impersonal, patronizing, and unresponsive to patient needs, especially the problems of ethnic minorities.

While these conditions are certainly not limited to public hospitals, they have come to be associated with the clinic system.

The debate may revolve around the question of the appropriate mix of ambulatory care services in a given setting. Few observers would disagree that primary care should not be concentrated in the emergency room to the degree that it generally is provided there. And few realists would challenge the prediction that in major teaching institutions, the specialty clinics will continue to be an important source of ambulatory care. The legitimate training needs of new physicians, as well as the need of patients for specialized care of high clinical quality, dictate this eventuality. Even so, the provision of primary care, the ordinary "garden variety" medicine, conceivably might be moved out of both the emergency room and the specialty clinics. One approach to this strategy is the establishment of hospital-based primary care centers with some degree of organizational distance from the specialty clinics. Such clinics could even be located at an off-site satellite. Another alternative is the fostering of publicly sponsored, neighborhood-based primary care programs.

MANPOWER AND RECRUITMENT ISSUES

Public facilities are often bound by civil service requirements and personnel systems which some consider not suited to the complex technical, professional, and managerial skills required in running a modern health care facility. For example, civil service scoring systems may inappropriately weight the kinds of skills essential in technical positions in hospitals and permit insufficient flexibility in the selection of candidates. Pay ceilings provide strong disincentives to the recruitment of personnel of the level of talent and experience desirable in a well-managed health facility. St. Louis suffered under a $25,000 salary limit for all personnel, including physicians and administrators, until as recently as August, 1980. In addition, political interference and patronage have often been cited as dysfunctional elements that are nearly unavoidable in public sector operation of health facilities.

Salary levels that are not competitive with those of the voluntary hospitals are among the reasons for the difficulties of urban public hospitals in recruiting sufficient numbers of nursing personnel. Other disincentives to nurses include the antiquated physical plant and equipment and the supply shortages often encountered in public facilities. Also, many public hospitals are located in deteriorated slum neighborhoods in which travel and personal safety present problems. Public hospitals recruit many nurses directly from training programs but lose them to more attractive employers after they have had a year or two of experience. Staff turnover costs for public hospitals are high. Additional high costs are incurred for the placement of temporary agency nurses to cover unfilled staff positions.

In the past, public hospitals have, except for those institutions with strong medical school affiliations, faced protracted difficulties in recruiting sufficient highly qualified physician manpower. Public facilities typically have been forced to rely heavily on foreign medical graduates (FMGs) for both house staff and attending positions. During the late 1970s, the public hospitals in the five study cities each depended to some degree on FMGs. Cincinnati General had more than 75 foreign-trained residents and fellows as late as 1981. At Baltimore City Hospitals, pediatrics and pathology, which used to be heavily staffed by FMGs, are now staffed by Johns Hopkins Hospital, which has a policy of seeking American-trained physicians. St. Louis's Homer G. Phillips had a large proportion of foreign-trained physicians before the closure of inpatient services and continues to employ many in its outpatient services, as does the St. Louis Health Department. The level of dependence on FMGs has decreased in recent years, however, and as some service chiefs in Baltimore report, there should be enough American graduates soon to meet most hospitals' requirements.

The expansion of new physician manpower is the outcome of federal health manpower policies which paralleled the financing and service program initiatives we have described in detail. Establishment of new medical schools and the expansion of existing schools from the mid-1960s through the 1970s have swelled the annual increment to the physician pool to about 16,000. Availability of these large numbers of young physicians has eased the recruitment problems of many public hospitals, as well as those of health department and other neighborhood clinics.

ADMINISTRATION AND MANAGEMENT

In the series of ad hoc studies and general audits of the public hospitals in the five study cities, there have been litanies of complaint about incompetent, outmoded, inefficient, ineffective, and bureaucratic management. A school of thought nationwide contends that public administration of health facilities is inherently inferior to private management and therefore local government should contract with the private sector for care for the indigent. Among the specific managerial shortcomings attributed to the public hospitals are the following problems.

Public hospitals, particularly when they are operated as branches of local government, are frequently hampered by bureaucratic procurement systems that are too cumbersome and slow to respond to the hospital's needs to obtain medical supplies, pharmaceuticals, and sophisticated equipment in a timely and cost-saving manner. Other areas in which ties to the city may hamper efficient operations include services provided by the city, such as data processing, laundry services, utilities, general accounting services, and vehicle purchase, operation, and maintenance. In some cities such as Baltimore, consultant studies have determined that the public hospital pays much more to receive such services from the city than comparable hospitals pay for services in the private sector.

One overarching complaint about public hospital systems has been their seeming inability to make strategic decisions about the course an institution should pursue to remain afloat financially. The blame has most often been laid at the feet of governance. For instance, Baltimore's 1979 Kearney Report noted that the current organizational structure of BCH spread responsibility among several parties, including various agencies or departments within the city government, the Board of Commissioners for the hospital, and top level management. As a result, singular responsibility for overall management of the hospital resided with no one person or office. The Board of Commissioners, for example, perceived itself as insulated from responsibilities, noting that "decisions are often made downtown."

A 1979 position paper issued by the Milwaukee county executive's office characterized the County Hospital's recent history as follows:

Only three short years ago, the credibility of the County Medical Complex was in shambles. The backlog billing mess revealed administrative deficiencies that led to the eventual resignation of key Institutions staff and a call for shake-ups, reorganization and even the dissolution of the County's hospital.[10]

The debate became heated in 1976 with the discovery of millions of dollars (estimates vary) of unbilled charges for Medicare and Medicaid eligible patients. A senior state official commented on the extent and long-standing nature of the problem in an interview in August 1979:

All I know is that they had an uncashed check from Medicaid for over $1 million that they did not cash for a period of weeks. Even in my union days, the County Hospital had a certain number of days in which things should get processed. I think it was 60 to 90 days after the service in order to get paid. The County would not file claims until much later, until way after the expiration date. At that time, the union and the (insurance) Company went together and screamed at County Hospital. They have a management problem there.[11]

It was clear that management of the hospital required improvement. A number of changes in personnel and billing practices have since been instituted. Numerous other changes were recommended in the many studies commissioned in the past several years.

It should be noted that while there is validity in many of the managerial criticisms voiced above, there is also very little empirical evidence that public management is inherently inferior to private management. Ginzberg, Millman and Brecher quote the report of the Task Force on Public-General Hospitals of the American Public Health Association:

Given the special kinds of problems they treat and the conditions under which they function, public general hospitals are not inefficient. Studies controlling for scope of services have found no difference in costs between public and voluntary hospitals.[12]

Ginzberg, Millman and Brecher further conclude:

Criticism of public management fails to give proper consideration to the fiscal position of public hospitals. Comparisons cannot fairly be made between public and voluntary institutions provided quite different levels of funding. Public hospital critics often fail to recognize that the weaknesses of these institutions are, at least in part, related to their historical underfunding rather than exclusively to the auspices of their management.[13]

With whatever strengths and weaknesses individual public hospitals face the future, some problems appear to be endemic. The administrative and financial difficulties in which these institutions find themselves are closely intertwined. A poor financial base often precludes the employment of high-quality personnel and the implementation of effective management techniques, which in turn leads to suboptimal revenue generation and inefficient operations. Several widely prevailing conditions appear to prevent public hospitals from breaking out of this cycle.

Under the current system of entitlement programs in the United States, "good management" in the voluntary sector often means limiting the flow of uninsured patients through an institution, thus limiting the amount of bad debts. The public hospital's basic mission of providing care for those without means does not permit these sorts of administrative controls. Those public hospitals located in states with relatively generous Medicaid reimbursement policies are less vulnerable because they can use the revenue to cover some portion of the costs of uninsured patients. In the final analysis, however, successful public hospital management to a great extent entails marshaling the political capital to secure adequate local public subsidies. In the following section we will consider the financial and reimbursement difficulties facing public hospitals.

FINANCIAL MANAGEMENT AND REIMBURSEMENT ISSUES

The financial difficulties in which public hospitals find themselves spring from two distinct sets of influences. The first consists of shortcomings of financial management in the areas of accounting procedures, billing and collections, budgetary skills, internal fiscal controls, and management information systems. The second set of issues includes the effects of biased or at best disadvantageous reimbursement policies of third-party payors, increasing resistance from local taxpayers to maintaining or increasing operating subsidies or to financing needed capital improvements, and the continued necessity to provide large volumes of service to poor and unsponsored patients who cannot pay for the costs of care in a context of overall inflation and intensifying strategies of cost containment by reimbursers and private sector hospitals. Each of these sets of influences will be discussed separately.

All the public hospitals under study have in recent years been the subject of audits which revealed millions of dollars lost annually in potential revenue. These well-publicized findings invariably point to inadequate internal controls, irregular billing, faulty record-keeping, and understaffed accounting departments. A short-term response to these allegations is to attempt to deal with deficiencies directly by instituting managerial improvements through the appointment of special task forces or by purchasing management consulting services. More extreme measures involve alterations in governing structures—for example, establishing the hospital as an autonomous public authority free of civil service and other local government encumbrances—or contracting with a private firm for complete management.

In general, improvements in public hospital financial management, as measured by the generally accepted indicators of increased collections and decreased deficits, are achieved only as the result of a concentrated and intensive attack on shortcomings. When political and managerial pressure is lifted, the situation can revert to poor performance, according to William Shonick, who discussed the effect of the organizational structure of health and hospital departments on improved collections:

From the start, as far back as 1952, the combined agency in Indianapolis, as an autonomous corporation, operated with its own separately identified income; part of it was raised by an allotment of millage on the property tax bill and the rest from fees collected, which it retained. Yet the same low key attention was reported as in other places through 1971. In that year the top leadership of the Health and Hospital Corporation was changed and the new incumbents forcefully directed to pay serious attention to collections. They improved dramatically. Under this form of semi-autonomous public benefit corporation, "retaining collections" is clearly not a sufficient incentive to collect vigorously. But even if collections increase materially, will the financial position of a quasi-autonomous public hospital necessarily improve? In most cases the local government continues to supply an annual subvention to the public hospital. Will this government continue to maintain previous levels of subvention in the face of declining hospital deficits? This is highly doubtful and places the "incentive" argument in a very nebulous light. Only if the survival of the public hospital depends politically on lowering the local tax contributions can we expect improving collections to become an internalized organizational imperative, but in that case it is difficult to see how the hospital would be any better off.[14]

Shonick concludes that organizational structure had little to do with improved collections, but rather that direct action and assignment of personnel to correct the problem were the key ingredients to improvements. He goes on to note, ominously:

Furthermore, an exaggerated impression of the increased volume of collections that can be realized over the long term by such efforts has been given by reports of early experience with instituting them. The relatively large initial increases in collections were due to reducing backlogs of bills. On an ongoing basis much more modest results were subsequently attained. In any case, the improvements were transitory, the net revenue improvement after deducting the cost of the additional required collection effort is not clear, and the financial condition of the public system was nowhere substantially and permanently altered by improved collections. These efforts did not remove any of these agencies from the financial "critical list" despite occupying a very large share of administrative resources that were thereby not available to help make the merged program run. If such systems are to remain financially viable, other means of funding are required.

It was one of the ironies of these developments that the emphasis upon more intensive billing and improved collection by local health agencies after 1970 coincided with the atrophy of available sources to collect from. Federal and state programs were being cut back. Rising inflation and unemployment were increasing the pre-existing limitations on private ability to pay.[15]

Shonick's contentions find some support in the history of financial management audits, task forces, and collections improvements in the five public hospitals in our study. For example, over the decade 1965 to 1975, Baltimore City Hospitals suffered a decline in inpatient utilization and experienced high operating costs and substantial operating deficits. Following critical reports on the hospital's condition, high-level administrative changes were instituted in 1977. The new management and city administration modified areas such as accounting, record keeping, and management controls. These efforts resulted in a substantial reduction of the acute care hospital deficit (operating loss) from $8 million (of a $30 million budget) in 1977 to $3 million (of a $32 million budget) in 1978. These improvements were not sufficient to permanently deflect criticism, however, and it was subsequent to them that the long-range study by the Kearney Committee was ordered. The Kearney Report identified continued inadequate accounting practices and management information systems that constrain the hospital from recovering its costs at an optimum level. In addition, the Maryland Health Services Cost Review Commission judged the hospital's level of bad debts to be unreasonable and refused to allow the complete recovery of this money through the BCH reimbursement rates.

Similar financial management problems have been identified in other public hospitals. Billing and accounting shortcomings at Milwaukee County Medical Center were described above. San Jose and Santa Clara County have experienced problems as well. In the past decade Valley Medical Center (VMC) has negotiated these waters by flirting with managerial consultants and experimenting with funding mechanisms. After the Santa Clara Board of Supervisors voted in 1975 to maintain the hospital as a county institution, they were still left with the problem of improving its management. An internal audit prepared for a grand jury investigation of VMC shortly thereafter revealed serious problems in its billing and accounting practices. For example, it was discovered that program losses for the first six months of fiscal year 1977 had not been listed or reported for reimbursement. The audit reports of the grand jury, along with other consultant reports, indicated that the accounting system should be redesigned and automated accounting and reporting systems be used by the fiscal officer. Although the hiring of an experienced administrator and a fiscal officer was also recommended, VMC continued to operate with existing staff untrained in up-to-date hospital management techniques.

Thus, in 1977 the supervisors, discontented with the existing management structure and under lobbying pressure by several private management firms, voted to bring in an outside management company to augment the administrative structure. The original idea was to contract with a firm for two years to operate VMC. But in public debate concern was expressed over how much control the Board of Supervisors would be able to exercise over a private organization. There was also fear that a private contractor would place profits ahead of care for the poor. The result of heated public debate over the issue was the temporary engagement of a private management firm on a consulting basis only. Due to continuing confusion over the authority structure, the firm terminated its two-year contract after only nine months. Issues of public accountability carried enough weight with community groups in Santa Clara County to counterbalance the forces pressing for private management to cut losses.

It has been clear throughout the preceding discussion that although specific improvements are needed in financial management systems in public hospitals, questions of reimbursement policy have far greater implications for the continued financial viability of the public institution. The case of Valley Medical Center in San Jose serves to illustrate the impact of reimbursement policies in the last fifteen years.

In California, county hospitals operate fiscally either as a general fund of local government or as an enterprise fund. Among other things, an enterprise fund is supposed to force an institution to do a full cost accounting, spreading all costs to all parts of the operation. County institutions opting for general fund operations do not break out the full cost: usually overheads are absorbed in varying ways. Enterprise funding requires that a complete cost and revenue budget be utilized, allowing for the development of a private sector style profit and loss statement. While enterprise funding may be viewed as primarily an improved accounting system, it has also taken on a political significance. It is the perception of most county actors that the enterprise fund is intended to be somewhat independent of the rest of the county budget. There appears to be a bit more flexibility in enterprise fund budgeting, with the result that personnel and supplies may be handled more easily and rapidly than in the health department, for example.

The shift to the enterprise funding system was made in 1966, primarily as a result of the then new Medi-Cal program. It was assumed that the Title XIX program would mainstream patients, and that VMC should compete to capture part of the newly mainstreamed population. In the view of some, the enterprise fund was to have been an intermediate step between a totally county-dependent hospital and an independent institution. As costs were recovered, the amount of county funding was to have gradually decreased (and, it was hoped, ultimately ceased). During the generous years of Medi-Cal, the enterprise fund did begin to wean itself from county support, but after the Medi-Cal reform cutbacks of 1971, the trend began to be reversed. While Medi-Cal revenues represented between 40 and 50 percent of total revenues in the very early 1970s, they had declined to 34 percent by 1977. This trend has continued, and has worsened dramatically with the state and county tax cuts enacted under Proposition 13.

The limits on local governments' tax-generating capabilities are coupled with policies at the state and federal level that limit revenues and specifically cut health-related expenditures. Although local government, through its public hospital, experiences the demand for services by the disenfranchised poor patient, local government, through specific legislated restrictions or general taxpayer opposition, will have fewer resources with which to respond.

Reimbursement policies of the major third-party payors have exacerbated financial problems of public (as well as private) hospitals. The process of rate-setting frequently excludes services, ignores such critical factors as debt service and capital plant replacement, and establishes payment at only a fraction of cost. Medicaid financing particularly injures public hospitals, as its insufficient rates cause private hospitals to "dump" patients in order to avoid unfavorable reimbursement. Many third parties discriminate against the public hospital by granting lower reimbursement than a private hospital would receive or by refusing to pay at all for services their beneficiaries receive in a public facility. Recognizing these discriminatory practices, the Commission on Public-General Hospitals stated:

It is incumbent on state regulatory agencies and third-party payors to rectify such discriminatory practices. Third-party payors should establish consistent rate structures for services that reflect such items as differences in cost or in case mix between different types of hospitals but not ownership. Comparable institutions should receive payments for the same service based on comparable criteria.[16]

The most critical factor in the worsening financial plight of the public hospital is the magnitude of the population of unsponsored and inadequately insured patients. In the current period of economic slowdown, with concurrent tightening of eligibility levels and benefit packages in most states' Medicaid programs and reductions in federal contributions to the public financing program, it can be anticipated that larger numbers of patients will fall into the unsponsored or in-adequately insured categories. The public hospital is likely to edge closer to its original role as provider of last resort and to continue to require increasing subsidy of operating deficits.

Neighborhood Ambulatory Care Centers

The public hospital is not the only component of the health services system to come under scrutiny in the recent past. Local government officials have increasingly voiced concern over their appropriate role in assuring the availability of community ambulatory care services. In the context of reassessing the public hospital's role, some communities have debated discontinuing all direct personal health service delivery and providing nothing beyond the standard array of preventive public health services. Other communities are firmly committed to the public hospital but are doubtful about the extent to which local government should maintain a neighborhood-based primary care capacity. Some cities aim to establish extensive networks of clinics incorporated into a larger public system that provides a continuum of care, which in some areas competes with the private sector. In this section, the major issues involved in local policy decisions about the provision of neighborhood-based ambulatory care will be discussed.

THE MISSION OF THE CITY IN PROVIDING AMBULATORY CARE

Perhaps the most basic issue to be addressed in local health policy decisions is the question of the mission of local government in providing ambulatory care services. At the local level, the process of identifying health needs for community action can be a highly political and competitive matter. The many different interest groups involved in the local health services arena are apt to have highly divergent perceptions about the need for additional ambulatory care services or for restructuring existing services, and especially about the most appropriate means of meeting such needs once they are determined to exist.

In most cities concern about access to care for the poor stemmed originally from a perceived lack of primary care physicians located in poor neighborhoods—or at least a limited number of practitioners willing to accept poor, uninsured patients. In some cases the changing demography of certain areas of the city seems to predict future access problems as retiring physicians are not replaced. Yet although the ideal situation of the family physician in practice just around the corner may not be realized, it can be argued that in contemporary urban society, patients have reasonable access via private or mass transportation to physician resources located outside their immediate neighborhood. Indeed, the preliminary analyses by CHAS of usual source of care of residents of MHSP target neighborhoods found a high percentage (from 57.5 to 71.1 percent) reporting regular use of private physicians for care.[17] The issue of patient mobility can become quite important in the discussion whether public investment in a new neighborhood facility is required or whether emphasis should be placed instead on transportation needs of patients so that they have readier access to existing resources. Local medical societies often take the position that sufficient physician manpower already is available, and that community needs assessments draw unrealistic and narrow neighborhood boundaries. Patients in the private sector, they suggest, are quite willing to travel substantial distances to the offices of private physicians of their choice. Leaving aside the question of geographic accessibility, however, low-income patients still may not be welcome in many private physicians' offices.

A second consideration for local government is the appropriateness of establishing alternative health resources in or near the underserved community. In addition to local government services, a variety of other ambulatory care providers may be available (as described in detail in the previous chapter), and in some cities both the public hospital and voluntary hospitals may provide a large volume of ambulatory care through their outpatient clinics and emergency rooms. The city may determine that there is a need to provide services in a manner that improves upon the fragmented, episodic structure of the traditional OPD and ER. Local government must take into consideration the role of other providers when defining its mission in terms of expanded or restructured services. Each of these providers may have a specific interest in the definition of target populations for any new service to meet perceived needs of underserved groups. Voluntary hospitals in many cities, because of their concern with falling inpatient census, may be alert to the implication that expanded ambulatory care services in the public sector could divert potential inpatients from their facilities. For local private physicians and hospitals, who represent a variety of diverse interests, an expanded public health delivery system can mean many different things, depending on their roles and health market conditions within the community. An expanded public ambulatory care network may be viewed as a competitive threat or, alternatively, depending upon referral arrangements, as an opportunity to ensure a continuing flow of patients. It may also be a convenient outlet so that private institutions do not have to assume the care of patients they consider financial risks.

Given the constraints on local government budgets, and the mounting evidence that many federally supported ambulatory care programs generate workload well below the levels which had been projected and for which they are staffed, a frequent request is for a demand analysis or market study prior to a major investment of new resources. The local government policy-makers, in considering an expansion of public sector health services to meet perceived health care needs, must also consider the characteristics of the expected patient population, the health-care-seeking habits of the target clientele, and the closeness of fit between the model of new services proposed and the kind of health care desired by the target group. Patients accustomed to a private physician's office and those who frequently use an emergency room may not readily wish to change to a community clinic model. Local policy-makers must determine realistically the level of potential demand for new services in order to use limited resources most efficiently.

COORDINATION OF SERVICE DELIVERY

In view of the presence of established facilities under the auspices of health and hospital departments or community groups, a major consideration in the formulation of local health policy relates to the comprehensiveness, continuity, and quality of the existing services. After examining the current level of operations of public health clinics and hospital ambulatory care departments, analysts may have concluded that some facilities had a more limited scope of services than others; or that the continuity of care was compromised by inadequate sharing of information and lack of administrative staff to establish effective linkages with other parts of the health system; or that segments of the population who were deterred from seeking care might be accommodated through extended clinic hours, special outreach efforts, and alterations in clinic procedures and personnel. These conclusions may have led to recommendations for the restructuring of services. Quality of care, while it may not be easily defined or measured in operational terms, is nonetheless an important goal of health care reorganization. Quality may mean a number of things, including a more experienced professional staff, established medical audit procedures, or efforts to overcome sources of patient dissatisfaction, to name just a few elements.

One of the most frequent criticisms of the current health service delivery structure is the lack of coordination and referral linkages between neighborhood-based ambulatory care (whether in health department clinics or community health centers) and specialist physician services and inpatient care. Improved linkages among these services is almost invariably identified as a goal in proposals to reorganize existing services or initiate new ones. As earlier discussion has pointed out, the motivation behind this goal has its origins in two distinct and quite different considerations. The first is a legitimate concern for the quality of care available to patients. Continuity of primary care physicians and close ties for referral for specialty and inpatient services and subsequent follow-up would contribute, it is presumed, to improved quality of care for patients. This incentive may not be strong enough, however, to effect a restructuring of relationships among providers.

A more compelling incentive for coordination of care between neighborhood clinics and hospitals is, of course, the expectation that more patients will be referred to the cooperating institution for in-patient care. As we have seen, competition among hospitals for in-patients has now expanded into competition for control of new ambulatory care ventures which create strong referral relationships with the back-up hospital. Local governments which initiate ambu-latory care reorganizations to help, among other goals, bolster the census at the public hospital may find quite powerful pressures being generated by local voluntary hospitals to assure their participation in new ventures along with the public hospital. Depending upon how local hospitals define their markets and service areas, choices about where to locate public clinics may become matters of delicate nego-tiation or even open contention.

As the local government attempts to respond to articulated pres-sures for more or better health services, it must determine how to allocate its available resources (which in most cases are shrinking) to achieve the desired improvements. The county or municipality must weigh various options, assessing as well as possible the comparative costs of such choices as contracting with private providers for selected services or restructuring public services to achieve desired goals. De-spite the potential for resistance from established bureaucracies to changes in structure and role, the reorganization of traditional public health and public hospital services appears to be a logical choice for local policy-makers. In many cases, however, no single choice can be clearly made, and public and private sectors will accommodate and produce a cooperative venture where one or more voluntary hospitals provide some back-up care for public clinics. Consideration of coor-dination and referral linkages and the competition that is brought to the surface by public policy discussion inevitably leads into the issues of the cost and financing of ambulatory care services, which will be discussed in the section that follows.

COST AND FINANCING OF AMBULATORY CARE

Concerns about the cost of providing ambulatory care services to the urban poor are a major stimulant of discussion by local government officials and other interested groups, in particular about alternative models for delivery of primary care. The uniformly high cost of serv-ices provided in the emergency room and outpatient clinic, often as much as $85 to $100 a visit, has led to a widespread sentiment that ambulatory care should be moved out of the hospital setting into neighborhood clinics, which ostensibly operate at much lower costs. Naturally, the argument that services are substantially less costly in the community clinic setting is particularly attractive to local officials faced with shrinking health dollars. Opposing lines of argument—that hospital ambulatory care costs are actually the product of intricate and unjustified stepdown cost allocation procedures, or that a hospital-based visit is really a more complicated mix of services than that provided by the community clinic—are not as persuasive as the bottom line, cost-per-visit figures.

Local officials must also consider the implications of state and federal reimbursement regulations for the physical location, mix of, and accounting for services. Hospital-based, as opposed to community-based, ambulatory care may provide the opportunity for advantageous shifting of certain inpatient or ancillary costs, depending upon the individual public hospital's situation. Certain services may be even less adequately reimbursed in a free-standing neighborhood clinic than in the hospital setting.

The dilemma for local government, once it has agreed upon the need and/or demand for more or different ambulatory care services, is to determine how best to provide care efficiently and get paid appropriately for the services.

Cost. A series of elements involved in the costs of ambulatory care services must be addressed by local health policy-makers. Once a decision has been reached to expand neighborhood-based ambulatory care, an intricate negotiating process generally ensues over the clinic location and physical plant. Capital costs may vary dramatically, depending upon whether the locality chooses to use an existing public health clinic, to renovate a nonhealth-related site, or to build a new clinic facility. Availability or lack of outside funding for capital plant uses may be critical to the future of a clinic plan. If an objective of the program is to draw a new patient clientele who previously used private providers, the facility must be able to offer reasonable physical amenities. Thus, it is likely that substantial expenditure on furniture and equipment may be necessary. Renovation is likely to be much less costly than new construction. Rental of space is an option, but may be more expensive in the long run, depending upon local realty prices.

Decisions must be reached as to the degree of sophistication of diagnostic services to be provided. Managers must determine what level of laboratory and radiology services can be provided economically on-site, and must locate cost-effective means of obtaining those services that cannot be provided directly. The back-up hospital, a central public laboratory, or private vendors may present the least costly option. Pharmaceutical services must be assessed in similar terms.

The scope of physician and middle-level provider services will be a major determinant of clinic costs. Physician staffing must be carefully planned to correspond to actual workload. The range of other professional care (health education, nutrition, dentistry, mental health, etc.) and the depth of such services must be assessed in terms both of patient need and demand, and of cost and reimbursability. Similar attention must be paid to the choice of support services and the staff necessary to carry out essential tasks most efficiently. The constraints of civil service regulations, and often of seniority-dictated staff transfers when inpatient services are contracting, must be dealt with.

As examples in previous sections have illustrated, the neighborhood clinic may face the same dilemma as other public agencies about the benefits and disadvantages of the governmental procurement system for supplies. Bulk buying and public bidding procedures may reduce costs, but quality control may suffer, and materials which are needed promptly may simply not be available in a timely fashion.

The more far-reaching implications of neighborhood-based care for service costs have not yet been satisfactorily established. Assuming that the direct cost of producing identical services in the neighborhood clinic is less than that in the hospital, savings to the system should accrue. Other arguments that have been advanced are that the continuity of patient contact with a personal provider in the community clinic will result in less unnecessary duplication of diagnostic procedures than would result from the fragmented services of the OPD or ER, where the same doctor rarely sees the patient twice. A second argument, which similarly posits cost benefits for neighborhood clinics, is that by offering timely preventive and therapeutic care, which reduces the likelihood that a patient will require hospitalization, these facilities offer cost savings. It could alternatively be argued that appropriate models of ambulatory care which achieve the same ends can be introduced and operated within hospitals. This issue is for local interests to resolve.

Financing. The financing and reimbursement issues common to neighborhood ambulatory care programs were discussed in detail in earlier chapters. The major issues will simply be summarized here. The issues fall into several categories.

The first group of financing issues has to do with third-party payor coverage. Private insurers often fail to provide ambulatory care coverage at all; Medicare and Medicaid provide coverage for certain services and not for others. The benefit package is a critical element in that ambulatory services are often uncovered or highly limited services, even for those who have insurance. Second, many patients have no coverage at all. Medicaid eligibility rules differ from state to state, but as Chapter Three discussed, millions of poor patients are ineligible for Medicaid and have no other insurance. Thus, eligibility for coverage is a critical issue, particularly for the publicly operated clinic whose mandate is to serve the unsponsored patient.

The second set of financing issues is related to reimbursement restrictions. The calculation of Medicare and Medicaid rates disallows certain costs of producing health services. Further, within allowable costs, reimbursement is generally at a percentage of total cost rather than at full cost. Specific rules and practice codes in some states prohibit payment to clinics when service there is provided by less expensive paraprofessional personnel, such as nurse practitioners and physician assistants. Neighborhood clinics are not recognized as institutional providers in some states, and their services are reimbursed as though they were provided by a private physician.

The third set of financing issues is relevant to public health clinics whose programs have been transformed from traditional categorical services into direct primary care. The regulations stipulated for the administration and accounting of categorical grants are often incompatible with financial management of direct personal care service delivery. They require excessive staff for independent record-keeping, and greatly complicate billing and collections procedures for combined programs. On the other hand, since direct reimbursement for preventive services is often unavailable, categorical grant support is a necessary underpinning of a comprehensive primary care program. The issue facing local government is how to maintain existing categorical funding, while improving the structure of services, and still meet reporting requirements.

Another set of financing issues is related to billing and collections for services. Public health clinics have traditionally provided free services and have never developed financial management systems or the capability to bill and collect for services. Neighborhood health centers funded by federal grants have also been slow to develop adequate billing and collections procedures. Part of the problem is simply lack of appropriate managerial technique. A more profound issue, however, is the conviction of many health center planners and staff that poor patients should not be charged for services because they will be deterred from seeking needed care. Given that appropriate mechanisms for billing and collections can be put into place, the issue for local government is to determine policies on how much and when to bill patients and when to provide discounted and free care, while still maintaining financial viability. This decision will be affected by the willingness of the citizenry to be taxed to support health services for the poor, and upon local managers' dexterity in acquiring external sources of funding.

COMMUNITY PARTICIPATION AND GOVERNANCE ISSUES

Community groups recognize the value of expanded health resources capacity beyond the important service benefits. Health facilities often provide needed jobs and job training in economically depressed areas of the city. They are also seen, along with other efforts of neighborhood redevelopment, as a hedge against economic abandonment. In the past, the community boards that govern neighborhood health facilities have also served as a conduit for residents to gain a voice in the larger local political arena.

Community participation, as discussed in the first chapter, was mandated in the original Office of Economic Opportunity (OEO) neighborhood health center legislation: subsequently, in the community health center legislation (Section 330 of the Public Health Law), community governance of health centers was required. Community control came to be regarded as intrinsic to neighborhood-based ambulatory care. The intent of the original legislation was to create new models of health care outside the traditional institutional sponsorship and control, and to vest policy-making authority and operating responsibility in community sponsors. Over the years, medical schools, voluntary hospitals, and local government health agencies which sought to participate in the community health center program have become embroiled in fierce battles over the issue of policy and management control. Unsatisfactory performance by some community-run centers (for instance, in Cincinnati) led to criticism from the federal program monitors and to increasing involvement of institutional sponsors. Nevertheless, the legislation that required the community governing board to control all aspects of an institutionally sponsored program effectively prohibited most local governments from participation until the late 1970s, when amendments to the Section 330 regulations loosened government restrictions for public agency grantees.

In the past, new community health centers were seen by community groups as sources of new jobs for local residents. By 1980, as a result of budget strictures in most municipalities, ambulatory care programs were seen not so much as new job sources but as possible employers of personnel laid off from inpatient facilities where workload and resources were shrinking. Faced with pressure from employee groups to preserve as many jobs as possible, local officials are likely to see neighborhood ambulatory care services as a less expensive means than hospitals to provide care and avoid the anger and frustration of laid-off workers. Transfers of staff to jobs whose content is quite different from their previous duties create management and training problems for the health center administrators, as frequently there are few resources available to retrain employees in primary care skills.

The question of community support for specific services and facilities was discussed in some detail above. As there appeared in many cities to be an absence of a strong user constituency for the public hospital, it can be expected that a neighborhood clinic, a much smaller facility, may have difficulty mobilizing vocal and effective advocates. In some cities, such as San Jose, we have seen that quite powerful constituencies do exist for individual clinics, while in other areas there is little organized support. The developmental history and auspices of each clinic may suggest whether it has strong community support. Community backing may help assure high utilization as well as pressure on funding sources for continued subsidy. Local policy-makers must balance the benefits of community support with their own needs to maintain necessary authority and voter support.

LINKAGES BETWEEN HOSPITAL AND CLINICS

The coexistence in most large cities of a public hospital and a series of clinics operated by the public health department (city or county) with a generally limited degree of integration poses problems of several types. A number of patient care related issues, including fragmentation and the episodic, uncoordinated nature of care, have been discussed above. The lack of structured linkages between the public hospital and the public health clinics also has implications for the staff of the clinics. In most cases, the health department clinic personnel work in isolation from the rest of the system. Physicians generally do not have admitting privileges or staff appointments at the public hospital, and often there is suspicion and hostility between them and the hospital's medical staff, which is usually a faculty group associated with the local medical school. Health department physicians, who may be older, may be foreign medical graduates, or may have less advanced and less sophisticated training than the hospital staff, are often community physicians with dwindling practices who have difficulty qualifying for staff appointments and use health clinic sessions to supplement their income. A closer relationship with the medical faculty at the public hospital could provide them with better opportunities for continuing education and positive peer review, as well as provide to the health clinics a resource for medical audit and quality of care oversight.

Improving the linkages between public health clinics and the public hospital presents a major challenge, as the discussion of this issue in Chapter Two pointed out. Long-established differences in structure and in behavioral patterns separate the two bureaucracies. Hospital-based and clinic-based professionals, physicians, and especially nurses, have fixed perceptions about their own roles and about the style and the programs of the providers who practice in the opposite setting. Bringing community and preventive health personnel into closer cooperation with the hospital staff's diagnostic/therapeutic approach is a delicate endeavor.

Summary

In addition to having concern for segments of the city's population who are deprived of health resources and for the limitations of present publicly sponsored health services, actors in the local health arena are also aware of the nexus between health policy and other issues. For public officials the cost implications of any alteration in current practice is of key importance. Can the city embark on an expanded public system under current and anticipated fiscal constraints? How quickly and how sharply will other levels of government reduce their commitments to improved urban health services? Will private philanthropy maintain or expand its role?

From the organizational point of view, can proposed innovations in ambulatory care be used as leverage for structural changes within the local bureaucracy to create a more effective and economical operation? From the political perspective, will voters within the community support the maintenance, not to mention expansion, of services? These are issues that must be addressed at the local government level in determining the appropriate policy response to the expressed need and demand for more or better health services within the constraints of limited local resources.

References

1. Hospital Research and Educational Trust, *The Future of the Public-General Hospital: An Agenda for Transition*, Report of the Commission on Public-General Hospitals (Chicago, 1978).

2. Conservation of Human Resources, "Municipal Government and Health Care in New York City: The Scope for Reform," Report prepared for the Josiah Macy, Jr., Foundation's Task Force on Health Policy for the City of New York (Columbia University, 1980).

3. David Carley, Paper to the Milwaukee County Hospital Executive on the future of Milwaukee County Hospital, 1979 (unpublished).

4. Hospital Research and Educational Trust, *The Public-General Hospital*, p. 4.

5. Ibid., p. 2.

6. William Shonick, "Mergers of Public Health Departments with Public Hospitals in Urban Areas," Supplement to *Medical Care* 18, no. 8 (August 1980): 21.

7. Ibid., p. 22.

8. Hospital Research and Educational Trust, *The Public-General Hospital*.

9. Mutya San Agustin, "Primary Care in a Tertiary Care Center," *Annals of the New York Academy of Sciences* vol. 310, June 21, 1978, 121.

10. "Health Care Reorganization," Milwaukee County Executive Office, 1979 (unpublished paper).

11. Ann Lennarson Greer, personal communication, 1979.

12. Eli Ginzberg, Michael Millman and Charles Brecher, "The Problematic Future of Public General Hospitals," *Health and Medical Care Services Review* 2, no. 2 (Summer 1979), p. 3.

13. Ibid., p. 3.

14. Shonick, "Mergers," p. 20.

15. Ibid., p. 21.

16. Hospital Research and Educational Trust, *The Public-General Hospital*, p. 33.

17. Ronald Andersen and Gretchen Fleming, "Evaluation of Municipal Health Services Program" (University of Chicago, Center for Health Administration Studies, 1981, unpublished).

CHAPTER FIVE

Strategies for Improving Municipal Health Services in a Changing Environment

This volume began with a history of the major federal policy initiatives in health service delivery and financing for the poor and elderly that were enacted in the mid-1960s. By their scale and scope, these programs, including Medicaid, Medicare, expanded categorical health programs and community health centers, marked a significant redefinition of the role of the federal government. The categorical programs built upon a tradition of support for mothers and infants, which reached back to the early days of this century with the efforts of the Children's Bureau to protect young people from exploitative labor practices and to assure basic levels of nutrition, shelter, and health care. Medicare and Medicaid were both enacted as amendments to the Social Security Act of 1935. Medicare was an extension of the philosophy that the society, through its federal government, should provide security against the vicissitudes of ill health and inability to work of its older and disabled members, a philosophy which had been articulated through the New Deal programs implemented during the Great Depression by Franklin D. Roosevelt. Protection of the citizenry against the financial costs of illness had been sought by spokesmen for social welfare for decades. The growth of the federal role in both expenditure level and programmatic involvement in health care with the enactment of Medicare and Medicaid paralleled similar expansion in such other domestic programs as education and housing.

The community health center program typified a new mode of

federal activity that was adopted by many Great Society domestic programs. This was the direct federal-to-local program grant which bypassed state government and in some cases went directly to a private entity, bypassing local government as well.[1] This strategy was intended to circumvent perceived or expected inequitable or discriminatory distribution of resources at the state and local level. Local officials sometimes perceived that the direct involvement of federal bureaucrats in resource allocation decisions at the city and county level preempted their authority and complicated the resolution of conflict among competing local interest groups. State officials generally prefer that the state be the route through which moneys are channeled so they will have the opportunity to set priorities and apportion resources as they find appropriate. Accordingly, this new trend did not gain support among state policy-makers, and was favored by local officials only in cases in which they perceived they could gain leverage over funds or programs under which they might have received fewer benefits had the dollars flowed through state channels. Larger cities have benefited from the direct federal relationship in many states where rural interests still dominate state legislatures and bureaucracies, and urban leaders tend to favor continuation of these programs.

Early Cost Containment Efforts

The Great Society federal health initiatives brought a larger group of beneficiaries into the health care system by financing services that had previously been unavailable to many of them. The costs of providing this new range of services, particularly under Medicaid and Medicare, grew rapidly. The major factors contributing to the cost escalation were the expansion of the numbers of beneficiaries and inflation in the cost of producing medical services. The Medicare program served a growing beneficiary group due to the aging of the U.S. population, with an increasing proportion of its members over 65, and as the average life span lengthened, with many more persons in their seventies and eighties. In the late 1960s and the early 1970s, downturns in the economy left more people without work or income, the Medicaid rolls grew, and more enrollees inevitably led to higher costs. The number of Medicaid eligibles nationwide peaked in 1976, and has remained fairly constant, even declining slightly since then. Growth in program costs in recent years is attributable to increases in medical prices and, in particular, to the costs of long-term institutional care, which now account for nearly half the Medicaid program's expenditures. While Medicare cost increases are of concern, state and local governments are much more sensitive to rising Medicaid costs, for which they share responsibility with the federal government.

When Medicaid first became fully operational in 1967, total state and federal costs were $2.9 billion. During the next four years, Medicaid expenditures increased by 136 percent, reaching $6.9 billion in 1971.[2] This rapid early growth led many states to adopt cost control mechanisms soon after the program's initiation. California, for example, approved the use of prepaid health programs for Medi-Cal eligibles in 1971. This attempt was discredited following a series of abuses and scandals during the mid-1970s, when unscrupulous providers were exposed in a variety of fraudulent enrollment and billing activities under the prepayment initiative. More common cost control strategies included efforts to automate the vendor payment system, administrative changes to streamline eligibility determination and to reduce the error rate, establishment of fraud and abuse detection units, and most important, manipulation of the payment mechanisms.

Most states have attempted to control Medicaid costs by restricting reimbursement rather than by constricting eligibility standards or limiting the scope of services. Institutional providers have been reimbursed below cost for outpatient services, and physician fee schedules have been maintained at such low levels that many doctors simply decline to participate in the program, as earlier chapters discussed in detail. While maintaining or expanding the basic range of services available to beneficiaries, many state Medicaid programs have required prior authorization for services or have limited the volume of service covered during a given period. Days of hospital care, number of physician visits or home health visits, number of pairs of eyeglasses, and similar units of service have had specific limits imposed. Ten states have developed federally approved hospital rate-setting mechanisms that use principles other than Medicare's reasonable cost to determine Medicaid reimbursement levels, as Chapter Three detailed. For nearly a decade now state and local governments have been struggling with the burden of increasing health care costs, particularly under the Medicaid program, and have been pursuing a variety of administrative and reimbursement strategies to try to slow the trend.

Until recently, federal aid to states and localities kept pace with the rate of inflation, and this trend allowed programs to continue serving a fairly constant number of recipients. From 1977 to 1980, however, federal aid declined as a proportion of state and local government revenues, reversing a trend of several decades. With the advent of the Reagan administration, a firmly espoused policy of minimizing the role of federal government in the planning, administration, and financing of state and local programs has come to the fore.

Federal Policy Shifts

The conservative Republican administration of President Ronald Reagan is committed to a series of domestic policy changes that reverse trends established as early as 1935. Robert Pear wrote in *The New York Times* of the shift in social welfare policy:

The most significant change that has been evolving in social welfare programs this year is not simply the reduction in Federal financing, but a basic shift in purpose and philosophy, separating the poorest people from "the working poor" and middle-income families. . . .

Reductions in spending can always be made up by increased appropriations at a later date, but a change in eligibility rules or in the philosophy of a program is harder to reverse.

Earlier Democratic administrations believed that welfare programs should help not only the destitute, but also people who were attempting to work their way out of poverty. In contrast, the emerging Reagan philosophy is that the purpose of these programs is just to provide basic sustenance for poor people who have no other means of support. . . .

These are the basic tenets of the Reagan Administration philosophy, as articulated by the President and his senior aides: The poor, in some numbers, will always be with us. The purpose of the Federal government is not to redistribute income or to lift the poor out of poverty. Welfare and food stamp programs should not supplement the income of people who have income, however meager; they should provide assistance only as a last resort to people who are literally unable to support themselves.[3]

The Reagan administration has described those essential programs which should be maintained for the poor as the "social safety net." This rubric includes the federally sponsored health programs that have been analyzed in previous chapters. Entitlement programs for the elderly and for veterans have also been included in the "social safety net." Because of their relatively open-ended mandate, these represent a severe budgetary concern to the Reagan administration as it attempts to cut spending. But veterans' and Social Security entitlement programs have highly vocal constituencies and are politically difficult to trim. Therefore, health policy in the Reagan administration's first year concentrated on other objectives.

The shifts in federal health policy can be properly placed within the context of four major objectives of the administration: the reduction of domestic spending, particularly for social welfare; the retreat of the federal government from its central role in social welfare; the shift of responsibility from the public to the private sector; and the demise of planning and regulation with a concurrent turn to market forces. Each area will be discussed briefly.

REDUCTION OF DOMESTIC AND SOCIAL SPENDING

Probably the most visible action of the Reagan administration has been its maneuvering through Congress of budget legislation that dramatically altered federal domestic spending trends. Federal health expenditures for both entitlement and discretionary programs have been targeted for reduction from previous budget projections, with progressively greater decreases for each subsequent fiscal year. The budget reductions have been won in tough congressional battles in which health programs have presented major sticking points. Much of the health budget legislation has come about in the form of continuing resolutions.

The largest reductions in federal health spending were directed toward the Medicaid program and the categorical health programs. After a major battle over an administration proposal to cap federal Medicaid expenditures, the 97th Congress in the Omnibus Budget Reconciliation Act of 1981 enacted legislation that will reduce federal payments to each state by 3 percent in fiscal year 1982, 4 percent in fiscal year 1983, and 4.5 percent in fiscal year 1984, from the amount the state otherwise would have received under the current formula for federal financial participation. Several factors, including implementation of a hospital rate review program, a high unemployment rate, recoveries from fraud and abuse control activities, and containment of annual Medicaid cost increases below a specified ceiling, will enable a state to minimize its loss of federal revenue.

The dramatic shift from categorical health programs to block grants will be addressed below. This shift was accompanied by a 13 percent funding cut for the whole package of programs that were merged into blocks. The appropriations process and the negotiations over future budgets demonstrate a continuing administration focus on the reduction of government outlays, and further rounds of expenditure cuts are likely.

FEDERAL WITHDRAWAL FROM CENTRAL ROLE IN
SOCIAL WELFARE

The Reagan political philosophy advocates a return of authority and responsibility for domestic social programs to the states. Federal policy reflects this shift of responsibility. Enactment of the health block grant legislation marks a fundamental change in federal health policy.

After decades of commitment to a variety of single interest health programs, Congress has now combined 25 categorical programs into four health block grants. The Preventive Health block includes such disparate programs as emergency medical services, hypertension control, rodent control, home health care, school-based fluoridation, rape crisis centers, health incentive grants, and health education/risk reduction. The Maternal and Child Health block includes the former maternal and child health and crippled children's programs, sudden infant death syndrome and genetic disease research, hemophilia treatment centers, lead-based paint poisoning prevention, supplemental security income for disabled children, and adolescent pregnancy. The Alcohol, Drug Abuse, and Mental Health block combines five mental health, alcoholism, and drug abuse control and prevention programs, including community mental health centers. Finally, the Primary Care block grant, which was deferred until fiscal year 1983 to allow states time to establish administrative procedures, combines community health centers and primary care research and demonstrations.

This shift transfers to state governments a set of programs which from their inception were based on a direct relationship between federal government and community sponsors.

President Reagan has indicated that block grants are just an interim step in his plan to transfer total funding responsibility and administrative authority for social programs to the states.[4] Ultimately the states would be required to generate their own revenues for financing services now funded by federal sources. Nevertheless, with a current federal revenue shortfall, the ability of the federal government to return high-yielding revenue sources to the states is limited. For the short term, therefore, states and localities will have the responsibility for providing services with less revenue from either source.

SHIFT OF RESPONSIBILITY TO THE PRIVATE SECTOR

Another major tenet of the Reagan philosophy is the importance of returning to the private sector many of the functions that have been assumed by the federal government over the years. This theme is expressed in two streams of policy decisions: the emphasis on market forces to effect desired economies in the health care system, and a call for renewal of voluntarism in the field of social welfare and greater responsibility of family members for providing or financing care. Addressing the New York Partnership, Inc., an organization of civic and business leaders, President Reagan noted his support for market incentives and philanthropy as opposed to government action as the best way to help the poor.

> We're not going back to the glory days of big government.
> In 20 years the Federal budget increased fivefold, and the cost of welfare grew tenfold. But that didn't help many local governments, which lost effective control of their communities. It didn't help small businesses, hit by the highest interest rates in a hundred years. It didn't help the working poor and pensioners, flattened by double-digit inflation and taxation. . . .
> You in the private sector—corporations, firms, merchants, family farmers, mom-and-pop stores all over the country—you hold the key. . . . A recent Roper poll found a large majority believe that Government does not spend tax money for human services as effectively as a leading private organization like the United Way.[5]

Mr. Reagan concluded that private organizations should fill some, but not all, of the gaps left by reductions in public welfare programs. Some programs are simply wasteful, in his view.

The shift to reliance on the private sector for services for the poor presumes that contributions to charitable organizations will be sufficient to permit an increased service role. Reagan administration tax policy, however, by reducing the personal income tax, particularly for those in the highest brackets, has eliminated a primary incentive for charitable giving. New policies on tax-exempt retirement plans also deflect dollars from tax-deductible donations to charity. Administration expectations are that greater investment in savings will lead to improved economic productivity and an increase in general economic well-being for all groups, including the poor. In the meantime, citizens should make personal sacrifices to help the poor. For financially pressed voluntary hospitals, this may mean accepting additional bad debts as a public duty.

THE DEMISE OF PLANNING AND REGULATION IN FAVOR
OF MARKET FORCES

Closely related to its emphasis on private sector activity is the Reagan administration's commitment to the deregulation of industry in the belief that market forces can accomplish more efficiently the objectives of current regulations. In the health field, critics have charged for years that the regulations governing Medicare and Medicaid have driven health costs upward, as a result of the heavy administrative burdens they impose and the perverse incentives toward costlier institutional care and expensive technologies implicit in cost-based reimbursement. Earlier federal efforts to control the rising costs added regulatory layers in the form of the Professional Standards Review Organizations (PSRO) program and the health planning program. The PSRO strategy aimed to discourage overutilization by disallowing reimbursement for units of service not deemed necessary by established standards of care, while the approach of health planning was to resist the addition of redundant health facilities, equipment, and program resources to a community's health system.

The new federal policy seeks to abolish both programs as federally supported initiatives. Either state and local government or the private sector may undertake the funding of these programs, if they are considered valuable. A constituency for some PSROs may exist among Blue Cross and commercial insurance companies. Several states have highly organized and powerful state Health Planning and Development Agencies within the state health department, and may elect to take on or maintain some degree of planning and regulatory activity. The demise of PSROs and federal health planning, however, occurred before the Reagan administration could develop or even win support for its proposals to create a competitive market system for the health industry. A more intensified regulatory response to continuing health care cost escalation may be the result, since debate has already been joined over a cap on federal Medicaid expenditures. Discussion of market alternatives includes such proposals as a voucher system for Medicare beneficiaries to purchase coverage on the private market. The Reagan philosophy clearly supports deregulation, but expediency in the face of rising costs may force a retreat on this policy.

State Health Policy Shifts

State health policy is being shaped in response to the shifts in federal health policy, particularly the institution of block grants and Medicaid

cuts, described above. At least as influential, however, is the overwhelming impact that the Medicaid program has had on state budgets, regardless of federal changes. As the Reagan administration took
office, the *National Journal* reported:

There's no formal count, but state and federal officials estimate that between
half and two-thirds of the states are encountering serious difficulties in making ends meet in their Medicaid programs.

Conditions vary from state to state, but the causes are basic: health care
costs rising at a faster pace than the general rate of inflation; constraints,
formal or otherwise, on the states' ability to raise additional revenues; and a
constitutional requirement that the states balance their budgets.[6]

At the same time, a survey of the states by the Intergovernmental
Health Policy Project (IHPP), a Washington-based group of policy
analysts, found that 28 identified moderate to serious Medicaid funding problems and suggested that Medicaid cost control would dominate the states' health policy agendas for the coming year. The IHPP
identified the following reasons for the Medicaid funding problem:

1) national economic circumstances resulting in reductions in state revenue
and increases in eligibility for public assistance; 2) continued medical price
inflation; 3) a substantial growth in inpatient hospital utilization; 4) the loss
of general revenue sharing funds; and 5) state and local tax limitations.[7]

The IHPP found that until mid-1980 most changes in state Medicaid
programs increased either service benefits or eligibility. In the ensuing
months, however, administrative changes were no longer able to
effect necessary savings, and many states began to consider or institute cutbacks in services and eligibility. By late 1981, a resurvey of
the states found a variety of cutbacks affecting program benefits (copayments, limiting hospital days to as few as twelve a year, limiting
physician visits, eliminating services such as eyeglasses, drugs, and
dentistry); eligibility (14 states contracted eligibility by excluding the
unemployed, older teenagers, or some of the medically needy); reimbursement (limiting or decreasing hospital and nursing home payments and freezing or reducing physician fees); and management
("lock-in" of overutilizers to one provider, restrictions on transfer of
assets, preadmission screening, second surgical opinions, morato-
rium on construction of long-term care beds).[8] The states' response
to the provisions thus far enacted at the federal level that permit
reduction of eligibility and scope of services has been to use whatever
additional flexibility is provided to further reduce expenditures.

On October 1, 1981, the new block grants went into effect, and all
states except California, New York, and New Hampshire assumed
responsibility for the first three health blocks. New federal regulations
implementing the health block grants were issued October 1, taking
eleven pages to replace the 318 pages of regulations that had governed
the 25 old categorical programs.[9] While the Reagan administration
did not impose additional regulations, in carrying out congressional
instructions the states now found they had responsibility for inter-

preting congressional intent. The governors and state legislators had been lobbying for years for greater control over categorical moneys, and had even suggested that a small reduction, perhaps 10 percent, could be absorbed through a reduction in federally mandated administrative overhead.[10] Mr. Reagan requested a 25-percent reduction and achieved about 13 percent, which translates to close to an effective 25-percent cut when inflation is taken into account. As early as May 1981, Gov. James B. Hunt of North Carolina, chairman of the National Governors' Association's human resources committee, said that "the proposed spending cuts leave 'little doubt that block grants proposed will result in a reduction of services.' "[11]

State officials contend that state governments have the skill and adaptability to administer the programs included in block grants given sufficient transition time, but some resent being handed the responsibility for presiding over service reductions. As a series of interviews with state officials recently revealed:

In state capitals across the nation, the once positive response to President Reagan's "new federalism" plan to return authority from the Federal Government to the states has turned sour as budget cuts and the recession squeeze many state treasuries.

No state is moving to fill the gap left either by the Reagan administration's deep cuts in Federal social services administered by the states or by the reductions in Federal aid to the cities.

And even conservative supporters of the President say that about the only authority state officials have received so far is to decide which services should be cut.[12]

This survey found a number of states struggling with projected deficits by proposing new taxes. For example, Ohio has raised its sales and other taxes, most New England states have raised business, real estate, and various excise taxes, most southern and middle western states have raised taxes, and only states with energy revenues seem immune to this need. In addition, it was discovered that in a number of states, the arrival of the new block grants has precipitated a conflict between the governor and the legislature for control of disposition of block grant resources, and the squabbles are expected to intensify. As further federal budget cuts are proposed, states are making it clear that they cannot afford to assume the financial burden of taking over responsibility for those who will lose their entitlement to services.

Local Health Policy Response

At the local government level, reactions to federal funding reductions and to the Reagan administration's "new federalism" have been mixed, depending to some degree upon local political issues, partisan considerations, and intergovernmental relationships. Leaders of larger, older cities which have been heavily dependent on direct federal aid react much more negatively than, for example, officials of rural counties or smaller cities which may expect to compete more successfully for funds at the state level, where rural or suburban interests dominate the legislature. The new federalism means changes in the relationships among city, county, and state executives and legislative bodies concomitant with new responsibilities.

The *National Journal* reported on the jockeying for position among five major state and local government lobbying organizations in late 1981:[13] " 'There's no question that the Administration is firmly committed to changing the historic relationship among the players,' said Alan Beals, executive director of the National League of Cities." [14]

The U.S. Conference of Mayors, attuned to the political liability of the mayor as the most visible official to local poverty constituencies that are hurt by budget cuts, is the least sanguine about new federal policies. Conference president Mayor Helen Boosalis of Lincoln, Nebraska, believes that state governments have not been responsive to urban problems and notes that cities, given the choice, would prefer that federal aid flow directly to them, not filtered through the state.[15] Nonetheless, the five groups are attempting to form a coalition to foster federal, state and local executive and legislative consultation for the purpose of sorting out the appropriate responsibility and authority of each level of government for domestic services. A former president of the National League of Cities, Indianapolis Mayor William Hudnut, III, reflects the purview of city officials:

[Mayor Hudnut] has an additional item in mind for a summit agenda: the relationship of states and localities. In his speech to the Governors' Association, he called on the states to give the localities authority to institute a broad range of taxes and greater flexibility to determine political boundaries. He asked for an end to state mandates that are not accompanied by the money to implement them.[16]

The responses of these leaders are typical of the reactions engendered by the impact of new federal policy in two characteristic cities: Milwaukee, which is at the healthier end of the scale of urban distress, and St. Louis, which is severely afflicted by urban ills.

Milwaukee has retained its economic vitality and has made the choice over the years not to become excessively dependent upon federal funds. The local Citizens' Governmental Research Bureau estimates that of the city's net budget of $373.5 million for fiscal year 1981, 20 percent will have come from the federal government, 25 percent from local property taxes, 38 percent from the state, and 17 percent from fees and fines, etc.[17] Reductions in federal aid are not expected to be made up by the state. Milwaukee County, the level of government responsible for most direct health services and social services, adopted a budget for 1982 which raised property taxes by 40 percent while laying off employees and reducing some services from their relatively generous levels.[18]

Milwaukee Mayor Henry Maier, a strong six-term executive in a staunchly Democratic city, was severely critical of the new federal policy directions despite his city's relative health and was reluctant to raise city taxes:

"The property tax is the very leavings of the tax system," Maier said. "It is maladministered in terms of the functions for which it was designed . . . and it is absolutely overburdened. And those who say it can be stretched just do not deal with the realities of existence in the central cities."[19]

The mayor of Milwaukee believes that federal budget cuts will fall disproportionately upon the poor and elderly. The tax mechanisms available at the local level, regressive as they are, seriously aggravate this impact. Furthermore, sufficient revenues are not available at any alternative level of government to absorb the federal cuts.

St. Louis represents a city in much more difficult circumstances, having become heavily dependent upon federal assistance for basic operations. Researchers at St. Louis University's Center for Urban Programs report: "[In 1978] Federal money made up 44 percent of the city's operating expenses and Federal grants subsidized 70 percent of capital investments."[20] The city reacted early to expectations that federal funds would be dramatically cut.

The city laid off one of every seven of its employees; curtailed its street cleaning, refuse collection, park maintenance and other services; deferred capital improvements; closed libraries and health centers; and reduced the frequency of its inspections of restaurants.

Then, on October 1, when the Federal budget cuts went into effect, thousands of people here were removed from the welfare and food stamp rolls, and about 613 elderly people were removed from the free lunch program which had fed 3,419.[21]

For St. Louis, the predominance of rural interests in the state legislature has meant that as the new block grants are taken over by the state, urban problems receive less attention. The city operated the only major lead poisoning prevention program in the state, with federal funding of more than $500,000 in fiscal year 1981; the state slashed this program so severely that St. Louis received only $37,000 in federal funds for lead poisoning control for fiscal year 1982, while maternal and child health moneys initially were cut 47 percent.[22] Later they were restored partially, resulting in a net reduction of 25 percent.

Voluntary organizations in St. Louis will be hard pressed to take on any further responsibilities. A survey of voluntary agencies by the United Way of Metropolitan St. Louis found that since 40 percent of agency dollars had previously come from federal grants, most expected their revenue to decline and were already discontinuing programs.[23]

While St. Louis's mayor is much less pessimistic than Milwaukee's, the city is likely to have to retrench further in the delivery of public services. Local health clinic employees report that public clinics are seeing an increased demand for medical care from persons who previously used private physicians. They are now unemployed and uninsured and are falling back upon the public sector. Increasing demand and decreasing resources mean that mayors will be faced with harsh decisions about how to do more with less. Public health clinics and public hospitals will have to compete with other public services such as education and public safety for their share of limited resources.

Local health policy-makers must consider what strategies may enable them to make the best use of available dollars. The U.S. Conference of Mayors advised its members to act early to assess the impact of budget cuts and service reductions, to devise strategies, and to set priorities.[24] A variety of strategies will be briefly discussed.

1. *Assess Short- and Long-Term Impact of Federal Cuts.* Municipal and county governments need to document as fully as possible the fiscal and service impacts of federal budget cuts on the local scene. This is important as a mechanism for identifying the new service demands which will confront local government. It also provides the essential background for lobbying at the state capitol for the locality's appropriate share of state revenues or for needed changes in local tax authority, political boundaries, service mandates, etc.

2. *Improve Management Capabilities.* Both local health departments and public hospitals stand to benefit from implementing modern planning and management techniques and employing adequately trained professionals. Public health departments in particular will find it critical to be able to respond to the changes in the way in which categorical health programs are administered. They will need organizational flexibility, planning skills, and the ability to evaluate new program performance. Public hospitals, which may have to meet increased demands from the medically indigent as Medicaid financing declines, will require management expertise to increase productivity and cut unit costs.

3. *Improve Billing and Collections.* Many public health departments must consider implementing billing and collections procedures for services that they have provided gratis for many years. Others are reevaluating outdated fee schedules and raising charges to approximate current levels, as Cincinnati's health department has recently done. Serious efforts can be made to bill every potential payor for those services that are reimburseable. Although the collections may not cover costs, they can provide important additional revenues for health department budgets.

Public hospitals, which have frequently foregone available revenues due to sloppy billing and collections methods, are finding that automated billing systems are particularly effective in improving financial performance. Milwaukee County Hospital and New York City's municipal hospital system, which switched to computerized billing over the past several years, have greatly improved their patient revenue collections, mainly from Medicaid.

4. *Consolidate Services and Reorganize Bureaucratic Structures.* A strategy of particular appeal to health departments is the consolidation of services. Building maintenance, administrative overhead, and some direct staffing costs can often be saved if multiple sites or organizational structures are consolidated into fewer locations with more centralized control. St. Louis reduced its public health clinics from five to three sites during 1981, eliminating some staff. Cincinnati also consolidated, closing several of its smaller primary care network clinics and transferring services to the more comprehensive, higher volume centers. The consolidation strategy results in a more efficient use of limited resources, but it may present access problems for patients who have to travel to more distant, less familiar sites for care.

Consolidation offers few opportunities for the public hospital, since in most cases there is only a single public facility. St. Louis has already consolidated its two acute facilities to effect fiscal savings. Internally, public hospitals may be required to merge services to improve efficiency. Public and voluntary institutions may consolidate selected services, as Cincinnati General and Children's Hospital have done with pediatric inpatient care.

It is probable that public health departments will find it necessary to reorganize internally to respond to the changing format of public health funding. The bureaucratic structures that were shaped by administrative and reporting requirements of traditional categorical programs may no longer accommodate the new funding channels the states will develop as they redefine public health priorities. Those local health departments able to respond expeditiously to new state health policy initiatives (or even to influence the formulation of those policies) will be at a competitive advantage in securing or retaining program dollars.

As funding shrinks and costs of institutional care continue to rise, public hospitals will absorb ever higher proportions of local health resources. Public health preventive services and primary care are likely to be weak competitors relative to an acute care facility. Local policymakers may consider some bureaucratic reorganization in order to protect the delivery of preventive and primary care. It is not clear, however, whether merger or strict separation of functions would do more to protect the primary care services.

5. *Diversify Funding.* Local health agencies may seek to identify alternative sources of funding to compensate for lost federal revenues. The state is one alternative source although, as we have seen, state officials indicate either an unwillingness or an inability to replace lost funding. The private sector and voluntary and philanthropic sources are a second alternative. In general, private foundations have used their resources to support experiments and demonstrations in health

service delivery but not to subsidize basic operations. Public health departments have received no significant private funding in the past. Indications are that philanthropy will not represent a viable alternative to lost federal funding for most localities, although in some specific cases there may be significant contributions.

6. *Retrenchment.* The strategy most likely to take precedence, unfortunately, is retrenchment at the local level. In the absence of new revenues from state government or private philanthropy, local government is faced with the choice of raising taxes or cutting services. Localities are constrained in raising taxes both by state prerogatives in granting authority to levy various types of taxes and by local constituencies' general reluctance in the present economic climate to tax themselves. Also, the large, older cities hesitate to raise taxes for fear of further eroding their tax base—the middle class and the business community—and are reluctant to expand regressive property taxes that further hurt the elderly and poor. Hence, the inescapable last option for localities lies in service reduction. In St. Louis and Milwaukee, retrenchment has already led to the lay-off of public employees and the closure of health centers. Municipal leaders are nervous about continuing erosion of federal funding for health and other services. They will be expected by their constituents to provide more services with less resources. This will necessitate trade-offs and some program casualties. As John J. Gunther, executive director of the U.S. Conference of Mayors, remarked: "The states will say: 'Do you want to keep the hospital open or run a family planning center? You have to make a choice.' " [25]

Intervening Systemic Issues

Some trends are visible in the health system that are not directly related to the changes in funding and organization that have been discussed. These trends, which are the outcome of other, earlier federal health policies, may affect local health policy significantly. Among the major structural changes in the health system with implications for local health care delivery are the expanding physician supply and the growth of new health care delivery modes.

EXPANDING PHYSICIAN SUPPLY

The nation's capacity for training physicians was greatly broadened through federal and state aid to medical education during the 1960s and 1970s. New medical schools were established, and class size of existing schools was enlarged. As a result:

In the twelve years between 1978 and 1990, the best estimates suggest that the physician supply in the United States will increase by 40 percent, on a per capita basis by 30 percent, a rate of increase roughly three times faster than in the two preceding decades when the growth of the American economy was considerably greater than most experts predict it will be in the 1980s.[26]

This anticipated growth in physician manpower prompted the establishment of the Graduate Medical Education National Advisory Committee, which released its final report in 1980, concluding that by 1990 the number of physicians in the United States would exceed the number needed by 70,000; and by the year 2,000, the excess, given unchanged levels of training, would be 145,000.[27]

The implications for the health system of this dramatic increase in physician manpower are difficult to predict with certainty. It is likely, however, that physicians will be available in most parts of the country; indeed, public hospitals and clinics in inner cities already report that recruitment of physicians has been easier in recent years. Whether private practitioners will return to slum neighborhoods remains to be seen. With respect to medical care prices, it is not yet clear whether the magnitude of the manpower increase will modify the purported ability of physicians to determine the demand for their services. It is reasonable to assume that competition among physicians will intensify and probably lower physicians' relative incomes, but that overall, national health expenditures will continue to rise.

ALTERNATIVE DELIVERY MODES

A number of changes in the organization of health services delivery have been occurring in the past few years. Many of these changes are related to the atmosphere of cost containment that has prevailed among third-party payors since the mid-1970s. The physician supply increase also plays a major role in these developments. It is difficult to predict how firmly or extensively the new trends will become established, but each displays visible momentum at present.

Although it is not a new phenomenon, the prepaid health plan or health maintenance organization (HMO) concept has received considerable public policy support in recent years. Many new HMOs were begun with federal loans. Between 1970 and 1980, enrollment in HMOs tripled nationwide to a total of 9.5 million.[28] Reagan administration policy is shifting responsibility for HMO start-up and growth to the private sector. Insurers and industry have shown some interest in sponsoring or operating HMOs. In some cities, local health policymakers are considering or have already launched experiments to convert the public hospital with its patient load into an HMO (Metropolitan Hospital in New York). California's state health department has pressed for a similar strategy, a prepaid organized health system centered upon the county hospital.

A new delivery mode that has attracted considerable entrepreneurial investment is the ambulatory surgery facility, often a freestanding surgi-center. Sometimes surgi-centers are operated by hospitals which hope to preserve their share of surgical activity by responding to market demand. In many cases, however, the hospital lags in its adaptation to this new delivery mode and is frozen out by independent entrepreneurs. Freestanding maternity centers are a similar development. They generally make extensive use of midwives, and may even offer home births for uncomplicated deliveries. Both public and private third-party payors have been slow to provide coverage for these potentially less costly modes of service delivery. There may be more policy support for financing innovative modes in the future.

There is a growing body of professional and public interest in alternatives to costly, dehumanizing, institutional long-term care as well. Home health services are a primary option for the disabled or frail elderly to enable them to reside at home. Reimbursement for an appropriate mix and volume of medical, nursing, and support services has not been generally available. The high proportion of Medicaid expenditures absorbed by long-term care has stimulated a variety of demonstration programs. Although their true cost-containing potential is debatable, policy changes to encourage their implementation are under consideration.

Finally, there is the rapid growth of for-profit health enterprises, ranging from proprietary hospital chains to physician groups offering house calls, contractual emergency services in hospitals, or freestanding "emergi-centers"—health clinics that provide episodic acute care in a private office rather than emergency room setting, and which are common in California. The availability of physicians who are willing to accept salaried employment has allowed such enterprises to flourish. Many proprietary chains take over faltering community hospitals, frequently in small towns, and revitalize them by means of professional management and economies of scale. It is not clear yet whether access for the uninsured has been compromised in such communities. These developments may have varying degrees of impact on local public health policy.

Summary

Federal health policy initiatives during the first year of the Reagan presidency signal a radical break with the mounting federal influence upon health care delivery at the local level that has persisted for fifty years. Although federal revenue to the states and localities peaked in 1978 and began to decline before the current administration took office, the earlier reductions were in appropriations rather than in entitlements or entire substantive programs. The retreat from centralized federal programmatic control, the shift of responsibility to the private sector, the reduction in domestic social spending, and the demise of planning and regulation in favor of a reliance upon market forces represent a dramatic reversal in federal health policy.

The changes, while far-reaching, do not represent the total realization of Mr. Reagan's conservative Republican goals. Although the Congress substantially approved administration proposals, there were compromises and some intense battles, particularly over block grants. As the states and localities begin to respond to federal policy change, there may be additional opposition in Congress to the Reagan program. The administration will attempt to extend its new policies even further, with greater funding cuts, but it is not clear how far it will succeed in translating them into legislation. Much may depend on the congressional elections of 1982 and on public response to Reagan economic policy.

The condition of the economy will play a predominant role in public support for the president's policies in general and in the mood of Congress with respect to a further federal withdrawal in the health care arena. Concern over the rate of inflation continues to preoccupy Congress and the public, and health policy is in the spotlight because the rate of increase in medical care costs has outstripped the general inflation rate. Health care costs grew by 15.2 percent in 1980, the greatest annual increase in fifteen years, and by 15.1 percent in 1981, bringing health care expenditures to 9.8 percent of the total gross national product, according to federal statistics. Concern over limiting individuals' vulnerability to catastrophic health care costs collides with the desire to limit the nation's total health expenditures. Unemployment is of significance for health policy-makers because as unemployment increases, more workers lose health insurance benefits and may turn to the public sector for Medicaid coverage or for free care. Early in 1982 unemployment passed the 9 percent postwar peak that accompanied the 1975 recession. Increasing unemployment is coupled with a downturn in the economy, with the stagnation of productivity and real income. As a consequence, tax revenues are also stalled, giving government fewer resources with which to finance services. A further by-product of economic conditions and high interest rates is the inaccessibility of the capital markets to local government and to health care institutions, a problem which means delayed maintenance and recapitalization of plant. All these factors influence the health care system either directly or indirectly as a consequence of policy choices in the external environment.

One factor that poses a dilemma for local officials is the wave of taxpayers' revolts, first launched in California with Proposition 13, that limit local property-taxing authority. The revolt spread to other states, including Missouri and Massachusetts, both of which enacted local tax limitations in recent legislative sessions. These tax constraints have wrought havoc with local government service delivery. Initially, state budget surpluses were able to bail out localities, but the surpluses have been exhausted. The mood of taxpayers is still antagonistic to tax increases. Nonetheless, many states have enacted state, though not local, tax raises in 1981. The tax revolt may be over, but local tax increases will still be extremely difficult to enact.

Local government faces an era in which the demand for services will grow, while resources, given current constraints, will contract. Local officials are confronted with a shifting set of relationships with other levels of government. Urban government's reliance on alliances with federal elected officials and bureaucrats, and on its skills in negotiating the federal regulatory maze and capturing categorical grants, will no longer yield the program benefits of the past. Instead, ties with state legislators and bureaucrats must be developed. By establishing such linkages, cities will be able to compete more effectively for resources at the state level.

Local government will face mounting pressure on some fronts to discontinue direct health service delivery. This pressure will be contingent in part upon the size of the deficit incurred by public hospitals and health agencies in providing care to the uninsured patient. There is a strong possibility that if current economic conditions worsen and the turn in federal policy is extended further, many of the poor and of the working class will be deprived of health care coverage. This would mean that large numbers of the uninsured would revert to the local public sector for services and that bad debts in voluntary health institutions would increase.

Local health policy-makers must pursue those strategies that may effect economies in the production of public health and hospital services, such as consolidation and reorganization, managerial advances, more tenacious billing and collections, etc. Health will have growing competition for resources from public safety, education, and other services. Priorities will have to be set among the services offered: preventive services, primary care, and hospital care. Those agencies which are able to restructure their services so as to provide more care more efficiently are likely to maneuver most effectively for a greater share of limited local resources.

The Municipal Health Services Program demonstrations in the five cities that have been described in this volume illustrate strategies of local reorganization and consolidation that may provide a mechanism for efficient service delivery with sufficient local political support to survive in the changing environment. They have adapted well to change during the implementation period and show promise of continued resiliency. The utility of the diverse strategies adopted by local government will be tested by the changing health policy environment in the coming years.

References

1. Michael L. Millman, *Politics and the Expanding Physician Supply* (Montclair, New Jersey: Allanheld, Osmun, 1980), Chapter 1.

2. U.S. Department of Health and Human Services, *Social Security Bulletin Annual Statistical Supplement, 1977–79* (Social Security Administration, September 1980): 251.

3. Robert Pear, "Shift for Social Welfare: Reagan Seeking to Uproot Old Philosophy by Providing Aid Only for Truly Destitute," *New York Times,* October 28, 1981, A 22.

4. *The Blue Sheet, Policy and Research Notes* 24, no. 27 (Washington, D.C., July 8, 1981: P & R 1.

5. *The New York Times,* January 15, 1982, A 14.

6. Linda E. Demkovich, "For States Squeezed by Medicaid Costs, the Worst Crunch Is Still To Come," *National Journal* 13, no. 2 (January 10, 1981): 46.

7. Intergovernmental Health Policy Project, *State Health Notes* 16 (Washington, D.C.: George Washington University, January 1981).

8. Intergovernmental Health Policy Project, *A Fifty State Survey: Recent and Proposed Changes in State Medicaid Programs* (Washington, D.C.: George Washington University, October, 1981).

9. Rochelle L. Stanfield, "For the States, It's Time to Put up or Shut up on Federal Block Grants," *National Journal* 13, no. 4 (October 10, 1981): 1802.

10. Rochelle L. Stanfield, "Block Grants Look Fine to States; It's the Money That's the Problem," *National Journal* 13, no. 9 (May 9, 1981): 828.

11. Ibid., p. 829.

12. John Herbers, "States Growing Disillusioned About New Federalism Cuts," *New York Times,* January 3, 1981, A 1.

13. Included are the National League of Cities, the United States Conference of Mayors, the National Association of Counties, the National Conference of State Legislatures, and the National Governors' Association.

14. Rochelle L. Stanfield, "Reagan's Policies Bring Cities, States Together in a Marriage of Convenience," *National Journal* 13, no. 51–52 (December 19, 1981): 2224.

15. Ibid., p. 2227.

16. Ibid., p. 2228.

17. Linda E. Demkovich, "Milwaukee: Disaster Ahead," *National Journal* 13, no. 22 (May 30, 1981): 967.

18. Raymond E. Johnson, "'82 County Budget: More Taxes For Less," *The Milwaukee Journal,* November 11, 1981.

19. Demkovich, "Milwaukee", p. 966.

20. John Herbers, "St. Louis Struggles With Federal Cuts," *New York Times,* October 20, 1981, p. 8.

21. Ibid.

22. Ibid.

23. Ibid.

24. United States Conference of Mayors, "The Mayor's Role: Funding Retrenchment and Public Health Services," June 1981.

25. Stanfield, "Block Grants," p. 831.

26. Eli Ginzberg, Edward Brann, Dale Hiestand, and Miriam Ostow, "The Expanding Physician Supply and Health Policy: The Clouded Outlook," *Milbank Memorial Fund Quarterly/Health and Society* 59, no.4 (1981): 508.

27. Ibid., p. 511.

28. *The Blue Sheet,* Supplement, 24, No.49 (Washington, D.C., December 9, 1981): S10.

MAPS

Baltimore   Map 1

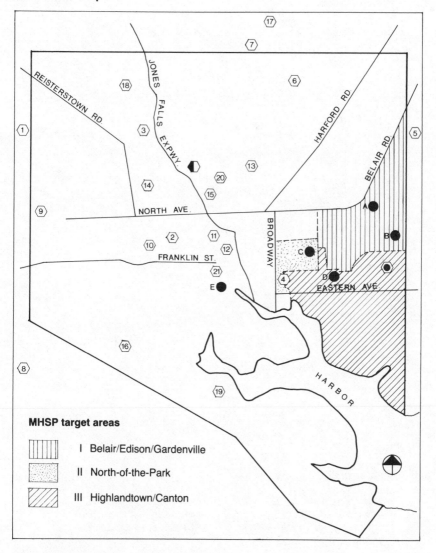

MHSP target areas

▥	I Belair/Edison/Gardenville
▦	II North-of-the-Park
▨	III Highlandtown/Canton

◉ **Public hospital:** Baltimore City Hospitals.

⬡ **Voluntary hospitals:** 1–Baltimore County General, 2–Bon Secours, 3–Children's, 4–Church, 5–Franklin Square, 6–Good Samaritan of Maryland, 7–Greater Baltimore Medical Center, 8–Howard County General, 9–James Lawrence Kernan, 10–Lutheran of Maryland, 11–Maryland General, 12–Mercy, 13–Montebello, 14–North Charles General, 15–Provident, 16–St. Agnes, 17–St. Joseph's, 18–Sinai of Baltimore, 19–South Baltimore General, 20–Union Memorial, 21–University of Maryland.

◑ **Federal hospital:** United States Public Health Service.

● **MHSP health centers:** A–Brehm's Lane, B–Hollander Ridge Clinic, C–Matilda Koval Health Center, D–Band Street Clinic, E–Washington Village Medical Center.

Cincinnati   Map 2

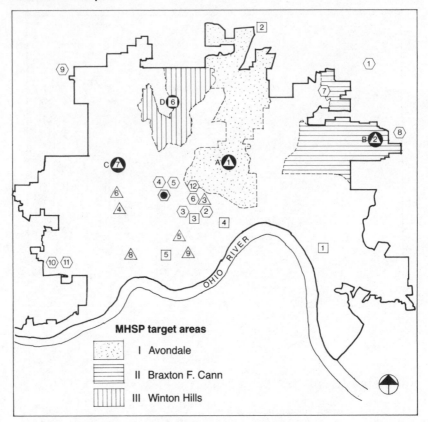

MHSP target areas

I   Avondale

II   Braxton F. Cann

III   Winton Hills

◉ **Public hospital:** Cincinnati General.

◯ **Voluntary hospitals:** 1–Bethesda North, 2–Bethesda Oak, 3–Christ, 4–Deaconess, 5–Good Samaritan, 6–Jewish, 7–Otto Epp Memorial, 8–Our Lady of Mercy, 9–Providence, 10–St. Francis, 11–St. George, 12–Shriner's Burn Center.

△ **Public health department clinics:** 1–Avondale (Catherine Booth), 2–Braxton F. Cann (Madisonville), 3–Burnet-Melish, 4–English Woods, 5–Findlay Market, 6–Millvale, 7–Muhlberg, 8–Price Hill, 9–12th Street.

☐ **Community health centers:** 1–East End, 2–Lincoln Heights, 3–Mt. Auburn, 4–Walnut Hills-Evanston, 5–West End, 6–Winton Hills.

● **MHSP health centers:** A–Avondale, B–Braxton F. Cann, C–Muhlberg, D–Winton Hills.

Milwaukee   Map 3

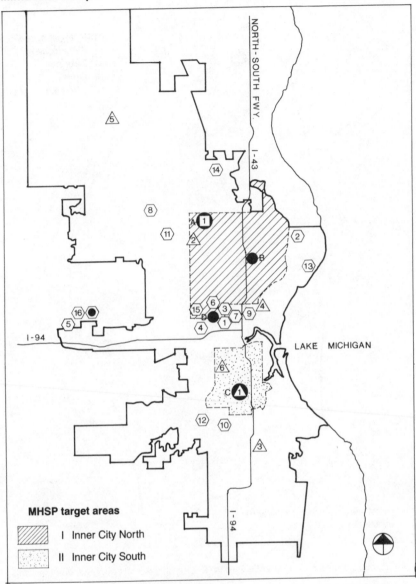

MHSP target areas

▨	I Inner City North
▧	II Inner City South

◉ **Public hospital:** Milwaukee County General.

◯ **Voluntary hospitals:** 1–Children's, 2–Columbia, 3–Deaconess, 4–Family,
5–Lakeview, 6–Lutheran, 7–Mt. Sinai, 8–Northwest General,
9–St. Anthony's, 10–St. Francis, 11–St. Joseph's, 12–St. Luke's,
13–St. Mary's, 14–St. Michael's, 15–West Side, 16–Froedtert Memorial.

△ **Public health department clinics:** 1–Johnston Municipal Health Center,
2–Keenan Health Center, 3–Lake Health Center, 4–Municipal Building,
5–Northwest Health Center, 6–South Side Health Center.

☐ **Community health centers:** 1–Capitol Drive Health Center.

● **MHSP health centers:** A–Capitol Drive–Mt. Sinai Community Health Center,
B–Isaac Coggs Health Center, C–Johnston Municipal Health Center,
D–Downtown Medical and Health Services.

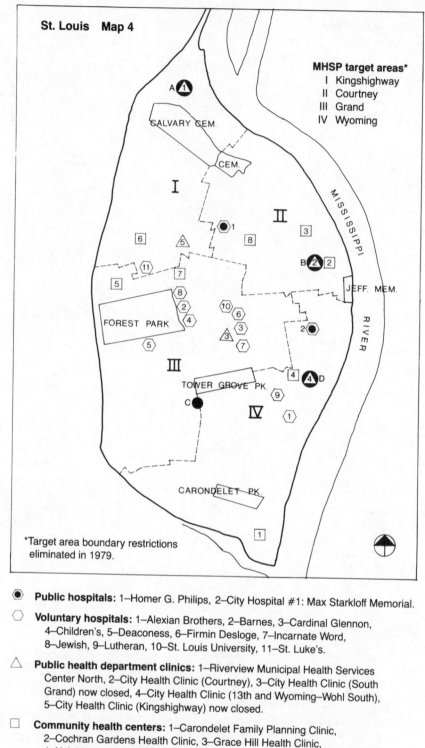

St. Louis   Map 4

MHSP target areas*
I   Kingshighway
II   Courtney
III   Grand
IV   Wyoming

CALVARY CEM.

CEM.

MISSISSIPPI

JEFF. MEM.

RIVER

FOREST PARK

TOWER GROVE PK.

CARONDELET PK.

*Target area boundary restrictions eliminated in 1979.

⊙ **Public hospitals:** 1–Homer G. Philips, 2–City Hospital #1: Max Starkloff Memorial.

◯ **Voluntary hospitals:** 1–Alexian Brothers, 2–Barnes, 3–Cardinal Glennon, 4–Children's, 5–Deaconess, 6–Firmin Desloge, 7–Incarnate Word, 8–Jewish, 9–Lutheran, 10–St. Louis University, 11–St. Luke's.

△ **Public health department clinics:** 1–Riverview Municipal Health Services Center North, 2–City Health Clinic (Courtney), 3–City Health Clinic (South Grand) now closed, 4–City Health Clinic (13th and Wyoming–Wohl South), 5–City Health Clinic (Kingshighway) now closed.

☐ **Community health centers:** 1–Carondelet Family Planning Clinic, 2–Cochran Gardens Health Clinic, 3–Grace Hill Health Clinic, 4–Neighborhood Pride Clinic—now closed, 5–People's Free Clinic, 6–St. Louis Comprehensive Clinic, 7–Sarah Union Neighborhood Health Center, 8–Yeatman Neighborhood Health Center.

● **MHSP health centers:** A–Riverview Municipal Health Services Center North, B–City Health Clinic (Courtney), C–City Health Clinic (Grand)—now closed, D–City Health Clinic (Wyoming).

San Jose   Map 5

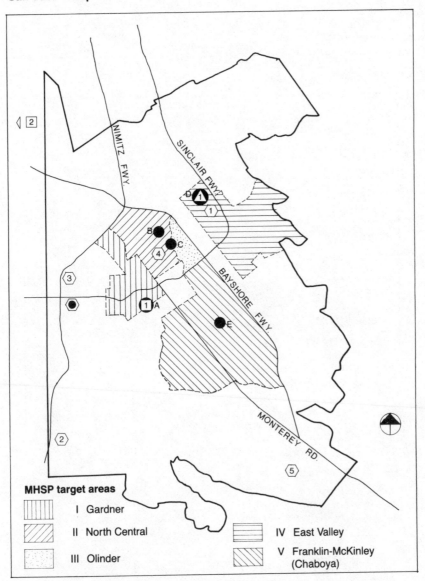

MHSP target areas

⦀	I Gardner
⫽	II North Central
⠂	III Olinder

☰	IV East Valley
⧄	V Franklin-McKinley (Chaboya)

◉ **Public hospital:** Santa Clara County Valley Medical Center.

◯ **Voluntary hospitals:** 1–Alexian Brothers, 2–Good Samaritan, 3–O'Connor, 4–San Jose, 5–Santa Theresa.

△ **Public health department clinics:** 1–East Valley Health Clinic.

☐ **Community health centers:** 1–Gardner Health Center, 2–Family Health Foundation of Alviso.

● **MHSP health centers:** A–Gardner Health Center, B–North Central Health Center, C–Olinder Health Center, D–East Valley Health Center, E–Chaboya (Franklin-McKinley) Health Center.

Baltimore Clinics   Map 6

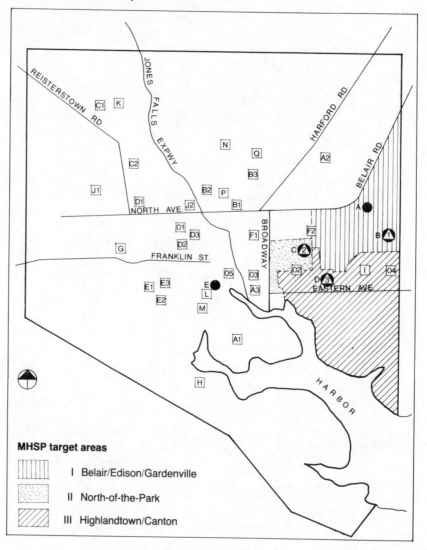

MHSP target areas

I	Belair/Edison/Gardenville
II	North-of-the-Park
III	Highlandtown/Canton

△ **Public health department clinics:** 1–Hollander Ridge Clinic, 2–Matilda Koval Health Center, 3–Bank Street Clinic.

☐ **Community health centers: A.** Mercy Primary Care Centers (through Mercy Hospital): 1–Mercy-Southern Health Center, 2–Mercy-Harbel, 3–Mercy-Little Italy • **B.** North Central Health Services, Inc.: 1–Kirk-Mund M.P.C., 2–HWR Health Center, 3–Coldstream, Homestead, Montebello Health Center • **C.** Park/West Health Services: 1–Pimlico M.P.C., 2–Lower Park Heights M.P.C. • **D.** Constant Care Community Health Center, Inc. (HMO): 1–100 Metro Plaza, Mondawmin Concourse, 2–907 Edmondson Avenue, 3–Mosher and Division Streets • **E.** West Baltimore Community Health Care Corp. (HMO): 1–1850 West Baltimore Street, 2–W.A.T.C.U. Multi-purpose Center, 3–Lexington and Stricker Streets • **F.** East Baltimore Plan (HMO): 1–1000 Eager Street, 2–Berea M.P.C. Health Center • **G.** Rosemont Doctors Center • **H.** South Baltimore Family Health Center • **I.** Chesapeake Health Plan (HMO) • **J.** The Monumental Health System (HMO): 1–Garwyn Ambulatory Center, 2–Madison Park Ambulatory Center • **K.** Sinai Primary Care Center • **L.** University Hospital Family Health Center • **M.** Washington Village Health Center • **N.** Govans M.P.C. Health Center • **O.** C & Y Program: 1–Provident/Druid C & Y Program, 2–Johns Hopkins CCC, 3–G.B.M.C. C & Y Program, 4–City Hospitals/CPPA C & Y Program, 5–University C & Y Program • **P.** Union Memorial Hospital Family Health Center • **Q.** Prepaid Health Plan of Maryland, Inc. (HMO).

● **MHSP health centers:** A–Brehm's Lane, B–Hollander Ridge Clinic, C–Matilda Koval Health Center, D–Bank Street Clinic, E–Washington Village Medical Center.

Index